Psychological Constructs and the Craft of African Fiction of Yesteryears
Six Studies

Linus T. Asong

Langaa Research & Publishing CIG
Mankon, Bamenda

Publisher:
Langaa RPCIG
Langaa Research & Publishing Common Initiative Group
P.O. Box 902 Mankon
Bamenda
North West Region
Cameroon
Langaagrp@gmail.com
www.langaa-rpcig.net

Distributed in and outside N. America by African Books Collective
orders@africanbookscollective.com
www.africanbookcollective.com

ISBN: 9956-727-66-0

© Linus T. Asong 2012

DISCLAIMER
All views expressed in this publication are those of the author and do not necessarily reflect the views of Langaa RPCIG.

Table of Contents

Acknowledgements.. vii
Foreword.. ix
Author's Preface.. xi

Chapter One: Introduction... 1

Chapter Two: Toundi (Ferdinand Oyono's
***Une Vie de boy* 1956)**.. 53
Plot Summary.. 53
State of Criticism.. 55
Toundi's Personality Structure and Claim to Anti-Heroism........... 59
The Application of psychoanalytic Theories:
Fanon and Freud... 60
Fanon... 61
Freud... 64
The Oedipus Complex Situation... 65
Toundi as Victim of Homosexual Urges.................................. 69
Toundi as Voyeur and Victim of Exhibitionism and
Sado-Masochism... 71
Oyono's Style.. 75
Notes... 78

Chapter Three: The man: (Ayi Kwei Armah's *The Beautiful*
***Ones Are Not Yet Born*, 1968)**.. 83
The Plot... 83
State of Criticism.. 85
Prescriptivist Approach... 85
Allegorist and Symbolist Approach....................................... 86
Comparatist Approach.. 87
Limitations of Critical Approaches....................................... 87

Claim to Anti-Heroism.. 88
Characterization Techniques: An Anatomy of Armah's Style.. 99
Notes.. 108

Chapter Four: Ahouna (Olympe Bhêly-Quénum's *Un Piège Sans Fin,* 1960).. 111
Plot Summary.. 111
State of Criticism.. 111
Ahouna's Personality Structure and Claims to Anti-heroism........115
Bereavement and Personality Development............................ 119
Ahouna as a Victim of Repressed Eroticism............................ 125
Jealousy as Proof of Lack of Satisfaction in Marriage.............. 129
The Murder of Kinhou..130
Characterization and Style... 132
Ahouna and Meursault... 137
Notes.. 139

Chapter Five: Samba Diallo (Cheikh Hamidou Kane's *L'aventure Ambiguë,* (1961).. 143
Plot Summary.. 143
State of Criticism.. 145
Personality Structure and claims to Anti-Heroism.................. 147
The Psychological dimensions of Samba Diallo's Victimization..... 152

Chapter Six: Obi Okonkwo (Chinua Achebe's *No Longer at Ease,* 1960)... 169
Plot Summary.. 169
State of Criticism of Character... 171
Psychological Dimension of Obi's Characterization................ 179
Achebe's Style as Foundation of Character............................. 184
Notes.. 190

Chapter Seven: Mugo (Ngugi wa Thiong'o's *A Grain of Wheat*, 1967)... 193
Plot Summary... 193
The State of Criticism and Characterization.................... 195
Character Structure and Claim to Anti-Heroism............. 197
Mugo, Guilt and the Anti-Heroic Tradition..................... 205
The Peculiarity of Anti-Heroic Guilt................................ 206
Style and Characterization Techniques............................ 207
Notes.. 217

Acknowledgements

This study would not have been possible along its present lines without the opportunity given to me by APNET which permitted me to explore libraries in South Africa, Ghana, Nigeria and Nairobi, and afforded me the time to study the manuscript material and works related to my topic. I owe a mighty debt of gratitude to several persons and organizations:

Tainie Mundondo:

Co-ordinator of APNET (African Publishers Network). For successively inviting me to four international conferences at which I delivered lectures on topics relating to my subject, and particularly for offering to distribute the published copies throughout all APNET membership countries;

Dr Caroline Kagunda:

Chief Executive and Documentalist of African Council For Communication Education (ACCE)

Henry Chakava:

Good friend and Managing-Director of East African Educational Publishers Ltd, for the initiative which eventually gave birth to this publication.

All the conference participants whose contributions spurred me on to focus attention on the issues that finally gave birth to this book, especially and most regrettably our good friend Chief Wankwo of Fourth Dimension Publishers who was brutally murdered as he arrived his hometown, Enugu in August 2006. Finally, to Professors

Stephen Arnold and Dimic I am indebted, either directly or indirectly, for many ideas and suggestions (who were on varied and frequent occasions generous in their counsel, criticisms and valuable comments through the internet) which were worked into my text and for which any precise references would be impossible. A general acknowledgement of their help can do small justice to the degree of my indebtedness

Foreword

A major stride achieved in this collection is the fact that the author has been able to draw a straight line between the art of renowned African novelists and their more established counterparts of European and American fiction. This is not just a study of African fiction, it is a dissection of the craft of fiction anywhere. Considering the extensive cross references with which he embellishes his analysis.

By using psychological constructs so extensively, something that many may have hitherto assumed to be the exclusive reserve of legends of European and American fiction, he ventures into a domain that is astoundingly new in the study of all African literature, thus sending critics of African literature back to the drawing board by providing new weapons for viewing that literature.

In the very large body of criticism that has been devoted to the craft of African fiction during the last decade or so, this very stimulating study will hold its own distinctive place for a long long while. It brings to African critical thought not only an exceptional acumen of interpretation and analysis, but something much more important to most of the previous serious literary study than mere technical dissection – a keen sense of the experience and imaginative truth that make his selected African texts living books as well as authentic record of human and moral values. Many of his perceptions are not only critically shrewd but humanly searching, alert to aesthetic quality and invention. No one interested in creative criticism of African fiction will read this book without finding its approach a challenge to his own reading of African fiction, and a stimulus to understanding the growth and enduring richness of the best of the African novel.

Attention must be drawn to the degree of balance he imparts on the work by choosing three texts in English and three in French, the two dominant colonial languages in Africa South of the Sahara. Even more interesting is the fact that although all the French texts have been translated into English, he opts to treat the three in the original language in which they were conceived and executed, a decision which keeps us as close as possible to the original idiom.

M.V. Dimic is Professor and Chair
Department of Comparative Literature,
University of Alberta,
Edmonton, Canada

Author's Preface

Although the relationship between the novel and psychology has fascinated me for over two decades during which I have read extensively in that direction mainly in the works of such legends as Henry James, Joseph Conrad, Dostoevsky D.H. Lawrence and Albert Camus, my decision to undertake this study was inspired by essays I have read concerning my own recent novels. I am talking particularly of the current Cameroon General Certificate of Education prescribed text on Cameroon Literature: *No Way to Die*, as well as its immediate sequel, *Salvation Colony*. While conceding that the psychological or psychoanalytic implications of the work are very deliberate and obvious, I have not been at ease to hear that this is the *only* novel that can lend itself to serious psychological analysis in the Cameroonian or even the African fictional landscape. And, in order to reinforce my point, I decided to reconsider some of those baobabs of African fiction (both French and English) about whom the last word is supposed to have been said. They are thus subjected to the same psychological analysis as their Western counterparts.

II

By general consent, the novel remains the most popular genre in the African as well as the Cameroonian literary landscape. Ironically it is in the domain of the novel that critics have encountered the greatest problem, and there are several reasons for this. In the first place and, at the heart of the matter, there is the reluctance on the part of the critics to explore or look for fresh analytical tools. This failing in turn results from another problem, the assumption (especially amongst African critics themselves), that the African novelist is not an artist qua artist but an agent for the castigation of social ills. All novelists are satirists, they argue, and consequently once the target of criticism is grasped, there is very little or nothing more to the book and its writers. Characters in the book are nothing but pegs on which the writer hangs his ideas. Thus as soon as the object of the satire is understood, it is thought that there is nothing more to it. And yet there is always a whole world of valuable literary or critical material beckoning to be attended to. This, I thought was wrong and needed immediate redress.

Even if it does not excuse it, it does, however, explain why the analysis of a text does not last for more than one issue in the papers, it scarcely goes beyond the socio-political and thematic considerations. And this in turn explains why our works are so quickly relegated to the past and eyes focused on new writings while the previous ones haven't yet been sufficiently attended to.

III

The most problematic of the elements of the novel appears to be characterization. As a novelist myself, I view character as paramount and so sociological, thematic considerations can only be best understood through an appreciation of the characters whose actions, motives, constitute the very substance of the book. Unfortunately, the literary character has scarcely been well understood by those so-called acknowledged legislators of the novel as a work or art. Character doesn't exist in a fictional world exactly or generally in the same way that human beings exist in the world, and the novelist is not a photographer, neither does he aim at reproducing reality exactly as it is. He creates the illusion of reality.

In a well-conceived novel a character, the protagonist, is or ought to be viewed as an *artefact*, a creation, and not a photographic representation of a human being as he exists in a society. He exists in that fictional world as part of the author's design, part of a teleological structure with its own coherent internal logic. It against this background that the writer employs various styles and rhetorical techniques to transform and to integrate the lived social elements of his work into artistic whole. To appreciate character in a novel, the data has to be a assembled, the various elements which constitute the character's *modus vivendi* the character's world view, his imagination, his likes and dislikes, his conception of himself, his relation to others around him, to space and time, his subconscious motivations and reactions in the book have got to be organized or discovered. All these usually assume a definite design, some pattern, real or apparent, which imparts to the work as a whole a deeper meaning.

Linus T. Asong

Chapter One

Introduction

Character is a very neglected dimension of the African novelist's art. In spite of the almost exclusive attention paid to plot and theme, African novels are ultimately explainable essentially in terms of the structures of the personalities of the protagonists. In each of the novels chosen here, the personality of the principal character (whom I have consciously and deliberately labelled as an Anti-hero), is the element that supplies the matrix of the story. With this in mind, I have been guided by other concerns: to define Anti-heroism, to justify the inclusion of each of the selected protagonists in the nomenclature by examining each one's mode of existence in the novel as exhaustively as possible.

Even though their Anti-Heroism does not possess a pathological basis, all the Anti-Heroes analysed in the six novels are shown to be abnormal personalities, morally and/or psychological defective individuals. In his analysis of characterization in Dos Passos's *Manhattan Transfer*, Blanche Housman Gelfant says of the disorganized characters who inhabit the book that they are:

> *Created in terms of a startling vision of human disintegration-of man rushing frenetically after false or elusive ideals, confounded by his inabilities and inner emptiness, lost in a search for an identity, self-divided and confused. And as the vision grows sharper it reveals that these are not really men at all but jigging marionettes engaged in a perpetual motion that brings them actually nowhere.*[3]

A cardinal point in my argument thus becomes a consideration of the extent to which each novelist can be said to have been motivated by the same vision in their creation of their protagonists as cited above.

Talking about disorganization, abnormal, self-divided and neurotic personalities anywhere automatically brings to mind either Sigmund Freud or Post-Freudian psychological constructs. In the African context, I have tried to show that to discuss the depiction of such personalities can be shown to be tied up to the psychological theories of Frantz Fanon - those which where chiefly embodied in *Peau noire, masques blancs*. And his study, "*Le Nègre et la psychopathologie*."[4] This, to my mind, remains the first and most authoritative account of the psychology of the black man yet written. It provides such formulations as *affective erethism* and *affective ankylosis*, which are very useful in the analysis of *Une Vie de boy*.

The general lay-out of this book is as follows: Chapter One is mainly introductory and there the theory is devised. In Chapter Two where the testing of the theory against the practice of African writing begins, I have combined both the theories of Freud and Fanon to reinforce the element of victimization which so strongly identifies Toundi as the Anti-Heroic protagonist of *Une Vie de boy*. Chapter Three deals with "the man" of Ayi Kwei Armah's *The Beautiful Ones Are Not Yet Born*, and Chapter Four deals with Ahouna of Bhêly-Quénum's *Un Piège sans Fin*. In these four chapters, despite the protestations of Bhêly-Quénum and Armah concerning European or Western influences on them, I have tried against the backdrop of the richly poetic and starkly existentialist imagery of each text, to show the extent to which existential psychological constructs may be used to identify Anti-Heroes and to provide a fresh basis for appreciating the presentation of character. To this extent, cerebration and *abulia*- unauthentic responses to the realities of the world of each of the two protagonists - have been established as hall-marks of the Anti-Heroic mould in which they are cast.

Chapter Five deals with Samba Diallo of Hamidou Kane's *L'Aventure ambiguë*, and Chapter Six with Obi Okonkwo of Chinua Achebe's *No Longer at Ease*. These characters have been thought to have several things in common: they have been viewed as cultural mulattoes, distinguished by self-division and a life situation that is beset by dilemmas. I have attempted to apply *Third Force* Psychological constructs of self-actualization and self-alienation along with Fanon's theories in order to show the extent to which the protagonist's selfhood and spontaneity have been crushed or rather incapacitated by a pathogenic environment. It has been shown that in response to the tyrannical nature of the *"shoulds"* which each environment imposes on the individual, the Anti-Heroic protagonist in Samba Diallo's case develops a socially sanctioned but personally destructive defensive strategy of compliance. In Obi's case, he develops an aggressive, openly defiant and uncompromising strategy in response to society's incursions on his private life, only to end up foundering in the quicksand of his own idealism.

In Chapter Seven, which deals with Mugo of Ngugi wa Thiong'o's *A Grain of Wheat*, guilt is established as the predominant element of his Anti-Heroic existence. The decisive affective disposition is shown to be a compulsive consciousness of guilt which makes Mugo pathologically aware of the gulf that exists between what he knows to be his true self and the reputation that he seems to command so well in his society.

Whatever the school of thought referred to, or the psychological theory employed in the explication of any given protagonist, an essential part of this project has been to show that in each text, the protagonist's emergence as an Anti-Hero was not established a priori, but that it is the direct product of the peculiar style employed by the author. Consequently, each novelist's exclusive technique has been explored, ranging from Ngugi's psycho-narration and Armah's impressionistic approach to Achebe's use of different dialects as a means of characterization. In all cases, language is shown to be capable of illuminating, intensifying and even reflecting the peculiar element of Anti-Heroism.

Notes

[1] Ever since Aristotle's declaration that "plot is the basic principle, the heart and soul, as it were, of tragedy, and characters come second," see The Poetics, trans. Gerald F. Else (Ann Arbor: University of Michigan Press, 1967), p. 28 the significance of character and characterization in literature has stimulated much controversy, speculations and theories. In this century, the debates have been centred around the theories of the American New Critics, Russian Formalists and the Structuralists. The latter have virtually taken over Aristotle's pronouncements, modifying and refining them into a distinct philosophy that appears to have permanently subordinated character to plot in any narrative. See Vladimir Propp's *Morphology of the Folktale*, trans. L.A. Wagner (Austin: University of Texas Press, 1979), p. 20. Boris Tomashevsky also considers character inferior to plot. He believes that "la présentation des personnages... est un procédé courant pour grouper et enchaîner ces derniers... Le personnage joue le rôle d'un fil conducteur destine à classer et à ordonner les motifs particuliers." "Thématique," in *Théorie de la littérature*, ed. T. Todorov (Paris: Seuil, 1965), p. 293. For the Structuralist Todorov himself, "Il n'a pas de personnage hors de l'action." (Poétique de la prose [Paris: Seuil, 1971], p. 78). According to Barthes, "la notion de personnages est secondaire, et entièrement soumise à la notion d'action" ("Introduction à l'analyse structurale des récits," in Communications, Diametrically opposed to these theories is the conception of character enunciated by Virginia Woolf, see her article, "Character in Fiction", The Criterion, vol. 2, 8 (July 1924), pp. 415-416. According to her the purpose of writing novels is to create characters. Other critics who have shared this view include W. J. Harvey, *Character and the Novel*, New York: Cornell University Press, 1965), p. 56; Charles C. Walcott, *Man's Changing Masks: Modes of characterization in fiction*, (Minneapolis: University of Minnesota Press, 1966), p. 16; William Glass, Fiction and the Figures of Life (Boston: Nonpareil Books, 1980), p. 49.

[2] *Structuralist Poetics: Structuralism, Linguistics and the Study of Literature* (London: Routledge and Kegan Paul, 1975), p. 230.

³*The American City Novel* (Norman: Oklahoma University Press, 1954), p. 162

⁴(Paris: Seuil, 1952), pp. 135-89.

⁵"Le Nègre et la psychopathologie." In this chapter Fanon contends that "on oublie trop souvent que la névrose n'est pas constitutive de la réalité humaine. Qu'on le veuille ou non," he adds, "le complex d'Oedipe n'est pas près de voir le jour chez les nègres" (p. 143). But he admits having found around three per cent incidence of that complex among the Antilleans. Besides, as Jock McCulloch points out, "the work of Anna Freud on the development of the ego and in particular her concept of ego withdrawal as a dynamic factor in neurosis provides Fanon with a useful parallel. The ego withdrawal of the neurotic in the face of voluntary social contact is obviously similar to the withdrawal and the flight of the Negro when confronted with the world of the European," *Black Soul White Artefact: Fanon's Clinical Psychology and Social Theory* (London: Cambridge University Press, 1983), p. 66.

⁶Because of their more obvious sociological implications, Fanon's other writings such as *Les Damnés de la terre*, *L'An V de la revolution* (1959) and *Pour la revolution africaine* (1964), have been treated as though they were the only texts that Fanon has ever written. It is almost as if he was never a psychiatrist, and never wrote anything else except revolutionary political tracts.

⁷*A Psychological Approach to Fiction: Studies in Thackeray, Stendhal, George Eliot, Dostoevsky, and Conrad* (Bloomington: Indiana University Press, 1974), p. 26.

⁸Ibid., p.276. The importance of bringing literature and psychology together has also been emphasized by Paris (pp. 26-27): "The psychologist and the artist often know about the same areas of experience, but they comprehend them and present their knowledge in different ways. Each enlarges our awareness and satisfies our need to master reality in a way that the other cannot. The psychologist enables us to grasp certain configurations of experience analytically, categorically, and (if we accept his conceptions of health and neurosis) normatively. The novelist enables us to grasp these

phenomena in other ways. Fiction lets us know what it is like to be a certain kind of destiny.

Through….character, novels provide us with artistic formulations of experience that are permanent, irreplaceable, and or an order quite different from the discursive formulations of systematic psychology….Taken together, psychology and fiction give us a far more complete possession of experience than either can give by itself. Psychology helps us to talk about what the novelist is talking about."

II. Survey of the Critical Landscape

> *Why is the criticism of fiction forever dealing with structure, values, point of view, social and psychological implications - all of which relate to character - without coming firmly to grips with the question of what is character exactly and how is it formulated, depicted, developed in a novel?*
>
> *(Charles Child Walcott)*[1]

When Robert Rawdon Wilson said in his article "On Character: A Reply to Martin Price," that "the problem of character in literature has been, in my opinion, the least successfully treated of all literary concepts,"[2] he was voicing not only a popular sentiment but a complaint that can be repeated with even greater emphasis with regard to the African novel. The Nigerian critic Obiajunwa echoes him when he says that:

> *The greatest challenge for the African novelist... is the question of character in so far as character lies at the centre of the structure of the traditional form of the novel, and in so as the African writer, looking for themes and settings distinctively African, becomes involved in traditional African society.*[3]

The extent, however, to which the African writer can be said to have met this challenge remains an unresolved issue. A brief excursion over the critical landscape of the last twenty years should indicate the degree to which scholars are divided on that point.

First of all, there are the Western critics who believe that the African novel is deficient in characterization. Directly opposed to this group are those critics who are convinced that the verdict of the Western critics is definitely inappropriate because it is founded on prejudice. Accordingly, critics in this category have continued to dedicate themselves to invalidating the Western claims.

There is a third group, comprising those who consciously apply themselves to the task of examining the literary character and its mode of existence in the African novel. The members of this third group may be few, and their success quite limited thus far, but their efforts are undeniably a firm indication of what it should take to establish the African novel as a more viable literary achievement.

Professor Charles R. Larson's views on the subject of characterization have come down as typical examples of the first category-the Western critics. In his rather unpopular article, "Whither the African Novel?" he said among other things that:

> the African writer...has failed to create believable characters who live outside of the situations in which they are involved...[That] when I glance over the dozens of African novels in English which have been published thus far, there are few real human beings, genuine characters who stand out in any remarkable way. Most of them are poorly drawn, flat, incidental to what the author too frequently believes is his monumental message. There are few characters who are in any sense universal, confronting the problems which all of us must confront if we are to be people at all.[4]

Many African critics found these observations and many more which featured in Larson's major work – The Emergence of African Fiction – highly provocative. They have since embarked on what their most vociferous spokesmen, Chinweizu, Jemie and Madubuike have pointedly described as "an important bush-clearing work [of] Eurocentric criticism."[5] In practical literary terms this simply means a spirited effort to refute and thereby eradicate the colonial allegations, an act which they believe should necessarily precede any profound and objective research on the form and content of the African novel.

Bush clearing has its own risks, and the possibilities of the African critic overstating his case cannot be ignored, as J.P. Karanja has demonstrated in his article in which he brands Western interpretations of character in the African novel as "Flies in Our Literary Soup."[6] Furthermore, Larson,s remarks may have been harsh, and were definitely less than justified in a good number of places in The *Emergence of African Fiction.*[7] His other lapses too, for which he has been severely pilloried by the Ghanaian novelist Ayi Kwei Armah,[8] have not done very much to acquit him of the charge of prejudice. But in all fairness to him and the European literary critics interested in the world of African letters, it must be admitted that the Ghanaian Professor W.E. Abraham had uttered virtually the same convictions about a decade earlier.

In his *Mind of African* Abraham is very convinced that "three dimensional characterization by African novelists in English and French so far [is] a failure," and that "their characters have tended to be flat and canvassy." He then goes on to explain the reasons for this shortcoming by drawing attention to the fact that "characterization, the limning of the individual in the round, was notably absent in the traditional akan literature in which the three-dimensional individual, completely subservient, and an atom, was non-existent."[9] But while Abraham justifies his claims on the irrefutable grounds of oral tradition, Larson bases his conclusions on his interpretations of the African texts. Quite often his interpretations of these texts are not perceptive enough, and so expose him to attacks from African critics who may ever have forgiven the white man for ever coming to Africa.

The nature of characterization in African oral literature has been sufficiently discussed for us to say conclusively that character in the genre is thin.[10] But it seems to me that the efforts of the researchers in the area unconsciously contradict the anger directed against the so-called "Eurocentric" critics for condemning characterization in the African novel. What I suspect they are actually doing is admitting that characterization in the African novel is weak, but that it is weak because of the influence of oral literature in which characters are very thin. This last argument seems invalidated when compared with, say, Russian literature. Characterization, I think, is not more solid in the Russian oral literature than in that of Africa. But until Socialist Realism became a literary philosophy, the great writers like Gogol, Dostoevsky and Tolstoy did not allow the oral tradition to hinder their creation of deep, fully rounded and intensely satisfying characters. What is at stake is that the individual writer's competence at his trade, his ability to manipulate the material at his disposal to produce an aesthetically refreshing group of characters. The truth of this conclusion is very well substantiated in the works of Achebe. We cannot, for example, praise his proficiency in the depiction of character in Things Fall Apart and Arrow of God as many critics have done, and then blame his lack of similar success in A Man of the People and No Longer at Ease on the influence of oral literature. If anything, the two novels in which he has achieved success are closer in spirit and tone to oral literature than those in which he has moved away from it. What seems obvious, therefore, is that when his talents were at the peak, he created solid characters, and when they flagged he did not achieve success.

If any objective judgment can be made at this point with regard to the Western and African critical standpoints, it is that strict battle lines cannot really be drawn. For, even some of the less accomplished African writers have received high praise from Western critics while some of Africa's foremost novelists have been victims of the most vitriolic and polemical assessment at the hands of their own compatriots because of characterization. A case in point is Alfred Hutchinson's review of T.M. Aluko's *One Man One Matchet*. He says:

> *The main strength of One Man One Matchet lies not so much in the magnificent characterization. There is a fascinating interplay of character and motivation. The characters are drawn with warmth and sympathy and at no point does the author try to manipulate them for his own ends.*[11]

It is quite ironical that while a writer of little reputation like Aluko received such profuse praise, Ngugi, who in the opinion of many respectable critics remains the far more accomplished craftsman, only earned scorn and condemnation from John Nagenda. In his study of Ngugi's *Weep Not Child*, Nagenda says Ngugi:

> *narrates the misfortunes in which people are caught, in a reporting, almost cataloguing manner which strangely enough for all is blood and thunder lacks any breath of real life. Part of the trouble lies in his characterization. I feel that all his characters are a continuation of his beliefs and desires and that he manipulates them at the end of a string throughout... And the result is a sterile and unmoving reproduction of many Ngugi's. And the result of this is that we feel not a flicker of spontaneous sympathy for his characters, whatever their misfortunes.*[12]

Talking about the same *Weep Not Child* which inspired Nagenda's strictures, another African critic, Alex Chudi Okeke says:

> *James Ngugi, like most proficient writers, has succeeded a great deal in his character delineation in as much as he has endowed his characters with flesh and blood so that they live before the reader. They have human feelings and reactions to situations and circumstances surrounding them.*[13]

For the reader who comes to these works with the intentions of arriving at some consistent and conclusive ideas about character and characterization in the African novel, this catalogue of claims and counter-claims must seem most obfuscating. All the critics seem to be talking mainly around the subject. They do not, as Charles Walcott has charged, come "firmly to grips with the question of what is character and how exactly it is formulated, depicted, developed in a novel."[14]

But to throw the minutes of their meetings away (if meetings they be and not clashes), would be, as the saying goes, to throw the baby out with the bath water. As Rand Bishop has phrased it, and as it will be demonstrated presently, "the place of characterization in Africa literary criticism by no means rests on this teapot tempest alone."[15] In the process of the defences or attacks of their critical positions, the criticisms have revealed certain flashes of insight which will serve as invaluable ingredients for the devising of a theory of characterization in African fiction.

We may be justified in joining Regina Amadi-Tshiwala in censuring Obiajunwa Wali for saying that "character in traditional African society does not exist,"[16] if only for the fact that we know it actually exists, and if only because as Bernard Mouralis says, "il existe enfin en milieu traditionnel des individus qui cherchent à sortir du groupe ou à romper l'équilibre par les moyens que la communauté reprouve."[17] But we cannot discount Wali's very pertinent remark that the mode of manifestation of character generates problems for the African writer "who in order to make his craft possible is forced to hammer out characters from a community where the individual does not exist in his own right but is compelled to lose his identity for the sake of social cohesion."[18]

We may also agree with Adebayo Williams that after the first reading of *Toward the Decolonization of African Literature; Vol. I: African Fiction and Poetry and Their Critics* one knows that there is "more heat than light in it," and that "the thesis that African literature suffers from a colonial malaise hangs on a theoretical redundancy...and irrational faith in the purity of the oral tradition."[19] Yet, buried somewhere in the sustained diatribe which the three critics carry out, can be found a brief sketch which a more open-minded critic can develop into a ready-made chart to which one can always turn for some more obvious techniques of characterization in the Western novel such as can be found in popular handbooks on creative writing. There the authors say:

> *Techniques of characterization in Western literature include explicit description and direct exposition, whether by means of an initial block of detailed portraiture, or by piecemeal presentation throughout the work; presentation of the character in action, with little explicit commentary by the author; reports of what the character says and does, of what others say of him, and what the author in his own voice, says of him; and presentation of the character through the workings of his mind, whether directly as in the stream of consciousness, or through reports by the author, done without authorial comment.*[20]

It remains a matter of regret that the awareness of these techniques on the part of these critics has not been applied to the interpretation of character in any one novel, for if carefully elaborated on, the formula can be very validly applied to the study of the African novel too.

It would be inaccurate, however, to conclude that discussion of character and characterization in the African novel is restricted to these sporadic insights and incidental comments gleaned from arguments designed to pay off old scores. Rand Bishop expressed an important truth when he pointed out that "the manifestation of it [character] is more often to be found in practical criticism- in reviews."²¹ But to this it must be added that within the last decade or so a few critics like Eustace Palmer, Sunday Anozie, Emmanuel Obiechina and Bernard Mouralis, have tried to focus critical attention on the subject of characterization.²² And in the sections of their works where they discuss character we find some of those rare occasions on which the fortunes of the characters, their modes of existence in the literary text, are examined for reasons other than the refutation of controversial claims.

No single text can sufficiently illustrate all the varieties of approaches manifested in the efforts of these critics. Yet, I would venture to quote at some length a passage by Obiechina which to a large extent exemplifies the general spirit as well as the strengths and weaknesses of this tendency:

> *In* The Beautiful Ones Are Not Yet Born *there is a similar polarization of characters [he had been talking about Gabriel Okara's* The Voice]. *There are the idealists who had hoped for much from political freedom but who have since reaped disillusionment. They include the Man, the Naked Man, Mannan [sic] and Koffi Billy. Then there are the beneficiaries of the corrupt status quo Koomson and his wife Estella and there is the Man's wife Oyo and her mother who would benefit if they could. They are represented rather in terms of the moral attitudes they live by than by their overt personality traits. There is of course, greater particularization here than in* The Voice. *We know for instance that the Man has a domestic life, that his wife thinks him weak for his moral scruples and that his mother-in-law hates him, that he is intelligent and would have gone to the university but for his prematurely taking up family responsibility, and that he is a railway clerk. We know also that he lives in the working-class quarter of Accra and struggles incessantly to live within his income and not enrich himself corruptly. All these details are there but they do not enhance our understanding of "the man," the inner springs of his life, the intricacies of his personal relations and the tensions that necessarily arise from them. We are most aware of him as a moral watcher, a sensitive observer of the slightest nuances of the general decay and social corruption and not as an active social agent. Koomson is the opposite of the Man, morally insensitive, active in pursuit of easy gain and achievement all at all costs, and grown fat with the spoils of office. And yet he*

never really moves out from the general backcloth of corruption to assume full autonomy. He remains to the end a figure from a morality tale, an impersonation of certain specific ideas of corruption without becoming fully autonomous as a person. The crucial fact is that these characters are morally defined and therefore best seen in their moral attitudes rather than in the revelation of their psychological development. In fact they undergo no growth at all because they are lacking in psychological depth. As soon as the moral attitudes are established, it becomes easy to follow the characters through the windings and turnings of the tale.[23]

After going through exchanges in which the subject of characterization has only occasioned blamed and counter-accusations, the virtues of a passage like Obiechina's should not be too difficult to detect. In the first place, he does not just talk about and around characters, their roundness or flatness. He examines the characters and some of the means by which they are given expression in the book. Beginning with the general aspects of the writer's technique he progresses toward the more particular ones: the first line distinguishes two broad categories into which the characters fall—"the idealists and " the beneficiaries"-a polarization which draws attention to the writer's use of contrast as a technique of characterization.

He then lowers his analytical lens on to the protagonist, "the man," and his more fortunate friend, Koomson. The man is then presented to us against the background of the emotional attitude of his family members: "his wife thinks him weak," and "his mother-in-law hates him"; "he was intelligent and would have gone to the university had he not prematurely taken up family responsibility." We are told what he does: "he is a railway clerk"; where he lives: "in the working-class quarters of Accra"; and his moral disposition vis-à-vis the atmosphere of corruption" "he struggles incessantly to live within his income," and yet is determined "not to enrich himself corruptly."

The critic draws attention to what he considers "the crucial fact"- the perspective from which to judge the characters. "These characters," he says, "are morally defined and therefore best seen in their moral attitudes rather than in the revelation of their psychological development." And we also learn that the technique employed by the writer does not make for "growth" in the characters.

Obiechina's passage certainly does not say everything about characterization in *The Beautiful Ones Are Not Yet Born*. But, given his consciousness of what character entails, it can be said with a certain degree of confidence that it will be hard to find what one might call an adequate analysis of characterization in The Beautiful Ones Are Not Yet Born which does not incorporate or elaborate on the essential points highlighted in this passage.

Nevertheless, subjected to a closer scrutiny, the passage reveals some significant limitations. The first drawback concerns the scope of the subject: it is so brief that the extent to which the critic can reasonably delve into crucial aspects of the topic is very limited. Although the section from which the extract is taken is entitled "Characterization," it is only a single element in a study which Obiechina himself declares:

> *has deliberately concentrated on the cultural and environmental background of the West African novel, on the general theme of the traditional culture, the contact with Western culture and their expression in the West African novel as a useful preparation for a fuller appreciation of the themes of politics and the problems of adjustment to modern social change with which the novels deal.*[24]

As a consequence of this wider purpose Obiechina has not allowed himself enough time and space to analyse the characters in detail.

The contributions of both Palmer and Anozie suffer too from the same limitations of the extent to which attention is paid to the subject of characterization. In Palmer's estimation, or at least as manifested in his analysis, characterization as an aspect of the writer's technique should be the very last thing to be considered. "Criticism of African fiction," he points out: "should take into account both the relevance of the work to the human condition: the sociological, if one prefers that term" and [only after this], the novelist's artistry." And in the schema which he draws up, character is relegated to the lowest rung: "And artistry," according to him:

> should include [1] coherence of plot, and structure, [2] language (making suitable allowances for any necessary and deliberate modifications the writer may have made in order to accommodate his insights), [3] setting, [4] presentation of character....[25]

Bernard Mouralis's book too is, strictly speaking not a study of character in the same way as we could consider W.J. Harvey's *Character and the Novel*. Mouralis summarises the content and direction of the book when he says that in it:

> *nous étudierons successivement, en nous fondant essentiellement sur le roman négro-africain d'expression française, le tableau qui nous trace de la collectivité, de l'individu et les problèmes qui en résultent pour le romancier*[26]

Even in Anozie's *Sociologie du roman africain*, character study is only a means to an end which the author defines among other things as:

> "*la recherché méthodologie, ayant pour le but l'éventuelle mise au point d'une théorie d'ensemble du roman africain, c'est-à-dire la possibilité de littérature dans son évolution constante.*[27]

Technically speaking, Obiechina's is unmistakably what D.B. Bromley calls "the language of personality description."[28] Obiechina uses such key terms as "moral attitudes," "personality traits," "the inner springs of his life," "the intricacies of his personal relations and tensions which necessarily arise from them." But what we have here is a description of character not much different from how we would characterize a class-mate or member of the family in real life. He does not probe into the organization of those "inner springs" and the "intricacies of his personal relations and the tensions which arise from them." Such a procedure would have removed the characters from the realm of real life into that of fiction to which they truly belong.

I do not mean to suggest that description itself as a critical technique is totally out of the question in character study. Robert Rawdon Wilson himself, who has exhibited such a profound aversion for description, has had to admit that "ultimately one will build up the character through the detail of description."[29] The point of my argument is that description should be a means to achieving a higher and ultimately literary purpose, and not stand as a terminus ad quem. The higher purpose in this respect should be to comprehend the intrinsic nature of the literary character and to make this available to the reader in unmistakable terms. The attainment of this higher purpose is possible mainly within the purview of a major theoretical conception of character. The neglect or the omission of such a theoretical conception has been pointed out by Wilson as the most serious deficiency of a work as epoch-making as Auerbach's Mimesis, which deals principally with characters.[30]

The Need for a Theory

In "Critical Bearings in Africa," Regina Amadi-Tshiwala asserts that a "systematic approach to criticism would lie in the redefinition of literature in modern African society and a close examination of the African individual."[31] The "African individual" in this respect does not refer to the African as a socio-historical entity, for such a quest would lie within the domain of sociologists, historians and anthropologists. She means the literary character, the African as he emerges from the pages of the novels. It is not reading too much meaning into her statement to say, then, that she may unwittingly have been advocating some kind of theory of character. For, in the African critical context some kind of working aesthetic system is an urgent necessity. I do not mean an ideological or cultural banner that masquerades as an aesthetic, but an aesthetic that reflects the literary rather than the socio-political contents of a work, a literary aesthetic that would broaden taste, deepen insight into character studies and rescue them from the dead-end of extra-literary conventions of interpretations that currently engulf them.[32]

The relationship and confusion between literature and life (to which Cervantes gave such an exquisite dramatization in *Don Quixote*), may be as old as Plato's *Republic*,[33] but that confusion is just as applicable to the present situation. Without necessarily championing the cause of strict contextualism in the tradition of the American New Critics, it needs to be indicated that many of the problems which plague the examination of character in African novels emanate from an inability on the part of the critics to focus attention on the information afforded by the fictive text. The position taken by the critics on Sociological as opposed to Artistic criticism has been too rigid to be productive. The sociological critics, for example, assume a stance which is reflected in Austin J. Sheldon's argument that:

"some understanding of the culture depicted in the African works is needed, based upon sources other than those details furnished in the piece of writing. Without such knowledge the reader will likely misconstrue much of the action, motivations and other meanings of the work.[34]

The basis for such an assumption is that art does not exist in a vacuum, and that the novel is the work not only of a particular individual but of that individual fixed in time and space and answering to a community of which he is an important part. True as this may be, it must not be forgotten that the work is first of all literature, and that to take such an approach is to be guilty of misconstruing many of the actions and motivations. An obvious example of the dangers they run into appears in Sheldon's criticism of Achebe for making Okonkwo the hero of Things Fall Apart when he would not stand as a faithful representative of traditional Ibo life.

Anthony Astrachan takes the opposite extreme of the artistic critics:

If a novel gives me a society and an individual with manners, good or bad, that is enough. I may not be able to provide more profound insights into Nigerian novels as I learn more about the world out of which they were written, but I can still make valid criticisms of the novels—of the world within the novel—without knowing too much about Nigeria or Africa. All I have to do is read the book.[35]

While I would insist on much more concentration on the text than the sociological critics are apt to do, I would not advocate a reading reminiscent of Cleanth Brook's philosophy in The Well-Wrought Urn which cuts the work off completely from the writer, the reader, other works in the genre and the literary history or tradition with which it can be usefully identified. Mine is a kind of moderate contextualism akin to that of the Russian Formalists like Tynnianov and Jakobson who in The Latest Russian Poetry (1919), insisted that examination of a work of art has got to take into consideration the background of the reigning literary tradition, the background of the practical language of the time and the movement of the literary tradition.

The knowledge which the African critics have acquired or the experience which they have undergone in real life are being allowed to intrude unduly, so much so that a real explication of character seems almost impossible. Solomon Tyasere has described the situation confronting the critics as a case of failure "to recognize the dialectical distinction between lived reality and art."[36] The verdict which Joseph Okpaku passed on the main characters in his study of Chinua Achebe's *A Man of the People* illustrates this shortcoming very well. He said:

> *Odili's inability to live up to his masculine responsibility by failing to go to Elsie's aid when she calls to him at the height of Nanga's barbarous and unbridled passions.....is very unconvincing. No Nigerian, especially one bold enough to spit in the Chief's face the next morning, and considering his great sensual will at that crucial moment, would have failed to attempt to rescue his girlfriend from an amoral brute whose intentions he has suspected all evening.*[37]

It is an incontestable fact of literary creativity that the writer often gets his models from real life, that Odili can very easily be identified with one of the hundreds of high-handed, idealistic young graduates in modern Nigeria. But, as Henry James said in his discussion of

Hawthorne:

> ...there is no strictness in the representation by the novelists of persons who have struck them in life, and there can in nature be none. From the moment the imagination takes a hand in the game, the inevitable tendency is to divergence, to following what may be called new scents. The original gives hints, but the writer does what he likes with them, and imports new elements into the picture.[38]

Thus, the novel in this context is, above everything else, the product of a creative mind which, as S.T. Coleridge once said in relation to poetry, "dissolves [reality], diffuses, dissipates in order to recreate."[39] The novel is the product of that imagination which shapes elements of human personality into a unique entity which expresses its own reality. It is not, as Martin Price insists, "analogous with society."[40] Rather, it is closer to what W.J. Harvey might have called "a structure of artificially formed contexts."[41]

While it is true as Chinua Achebe once said that the writer may "want to tell a story that is valuable in terms of the ideas it conveys,"[42] it is even more true, as Solomon Iyasere has also observed, that the writer invariably "employs various styles and rhetorical techniques to transform and to integrate the lived social elements of his work into an artistic and coherent whole."[43] Therefore, whether we are dealing with the meticulously delineated concrete situations of the world of Things Fall Apart and Arrow of God or the conceptual abstractions and metaphysical contingencies of The Voice and La Plaie, the literary character is built into or grows from the narrative structure. It is not for nothing that R.S Crane has described literary characters as "narrative constructs."[44]

The upshot of this argument is that the literary character does not exist in his fictional world exactly or generally in the same way that human beings exists in this world. He does not, as Price would have us believe, "exist within the novel as persons in society.[45] He is an artefact. This theory of the artificiality of the literary character remains unfalsified even when the character, Achebe's Okonkwo of Things Fall Apart, is made to represent the very incarnation of the complexity and destiny of traditional Ibo society in the wake of its confrontation with Western civilization. It is not altered even when, as W.J. Harvey has posited as characteristic of great novels, the literary character overflows the strict necessities of form, consequent upon "a surplus margin of gratuitous life, a sheer excess of material, a fecundity of detail and invention, a delighted submerges in experience for its own sake."[46]

Francoise Rossum-Guyon came closest to what might be called the critical truth about the literary character's mode of being when in her study of Michel Butor's La Modification she declared that "le personage Romanesque n'est rien d'autre, rien de moins non plus, qu'un ensemble de mots, une convention, un artifice littéraire"[47] [my emphasis]. In a further elaboration of this point Bernard J. Paris has said that literary characters:

> *do not belong to the real world in which people can be understood as the products of their psychological histories, they belong to a fictional world in which everything they are and do is part of the author's design, part of a teleological structure whose logic is determined by formal and thematic considerations.*[48]

Depending on the subject of the inquiry, such an approach to character could be very well the most appropriate, if only because it offers a greater possibility of fruitful research than the more prevalent socio-cultural criticism.[49]

From this standpoint, granted that Odili, "the Man," or any other major literary character is, or ought to be viewed is an artefact and not as a full-blooded Nigerian or Ghanaian who just happens to inhabit the pages of a book rather than the streets of Lagos or Accra, then our study of such characters has got to be guided by the same principle of artificiality. Not to look at things in this light is to miss, in Seymour Chatman's words, "an absolutely fundamental literary experience,"[50] from which alone a true and fuller assessment of character in the novel is possible. "The writer's act of creation and the reader's of re-creation are parallel,"[51] says Norman Holland in his Psychoanalysis and Shakespeare. Stephen Pepper puts it even more pointedly: "the critic recreates in the process of judgment what the artist creates."[52]

Because interpretation is itself an art, any theory of character has to involve or evolve principles, skills and/or techniques which should be deliberately acquired and then applied in the elucidation of the modes of characterization in any given novel. And since a theory, as Calvin Hall has said, "is a means of organizing and integrating all that is known concerning a related set of events,"[53] or in Harvey's words, "a device for seeing certain things with precision and intensity,"[54] the critic's responsibilities need not be taken lightly. The critic should not, in fact, cannot afford as Samuel Johnson recommended of his artist, to be content to "remark general properties and large appearance." He would have to "number the hairs of the head, or describe the different shades in the colouring of the iris…and must not neglect the minuter discrinations"[55] [my emphasis]. But even more than that, "the critic's job of work" (to borrow R.P. Blackmur's expression),[56] should be, as Price said, "to recover the inevitable artifice in the novelist's conception of character."[57] This is precisely what Walcott meant when he insisted on the exploration of the "what and how of characterization."[58] And Iyasere was also thinking along similar lines, though in a different context, when he advocated "going beyond demonstrating what is there to showing how it works and to what effect"[59]

When regarded in this more comprehensive light, the investigation of character portrayal techniques has to be given particular attention. It cannot be really fruitfully undertaken merely as an incidental subject in contexts dedicated essentially to the examination of plot mechanics, socio-cultural implications, theme and the like, which have usually been given pride of place in the discussion of African novels. "Characters, like theme, like plot, like all content and technique," Wilson has pointed out, "are there to be analysed. Their natures, their attitudes and construction…are open to intelligent discussion."[60]

"Theorists," said Calvin Hall, "are free to exercise a choice, to pick a particular option to represent the events in which they are interested."[61] To treat all protagonists as heroes, the way we find in criticism of African fiction now, has not led to any "intelligent discussion." The critic has to device or find some more effective and possibly particularized means. Such titles as "Character and the Novel," "Characterization in ....," which we find very frequently in the studies on the subject, are rather broad, although Harvey and Walcott have been able to encompass much in their books on the subject. When Wilson laments the "lack of theoretical significance in studies of character," at the present time,[62] his disappointment is justified. But one has the odd feeling that he has not quite identified the source of the "lack" in ascribing it to the fact that "each new writer on the problem of character (few as they are) appears to write in solidarity independence, like a primitive philosopher viewing the universe in such a way that 'tradition' with respect to character, is clearly impossible."[63] For the studies to fall "into the pattern of a cumulative, self-nourishing tradition,"[64] which he would like to see, they would need to be much more typologically inclined. Other than that, even though Wilson is confident that "the dossier that might in time, support a generally acceptable theory of character has begun to come into existence,"[65] productive studies on characterization will take a much longer time to arrive than he anticipates. There exists, for example, in the spectrum of the label of "protagonist" on which studies on the subject generally dwell, a whole range of types— positive heroes, picaresque heroes, anti-heroes and the like—each of which can with such profit be isolated, defined and analysed in terms of any given conception of character. In this study I intend to give logical consistency to my aesthetic stance on character by focusing on the Anti-Hero.

Notes

[1] Man's Changing Mask….., op. cit., p.5.

[2] Critical Inquiry 2, no. 1 (Autumn 1975), p. 191. But it would be safe to say that the subject is now receiving very much attention. Following the publication of W.J. Harvey's Character and the Novel and Charles Walcott's Man's Changing Masks: Modes of characterization in fiction, a series of individual articles have appeared in the last ten years which have put the subject in a better perspective. Martin Price and Rawdon Wilson have been engaged in a very enlightening disagreement on character and characterization which has run through several issues of the Critical Inquiry: Martin Price's "People and the Book: Character in E.M. Forster's A Passage to India, Critical Inquiry, 1, no. 3 (March 1975), pp. 605-622; Rawdon Wilson, "On Character: A Reply to Martin Price," Critical Inquiry, vol. 2 (1975), pp. 191-198; Martin Price's "The Logic of Intensity: More on Characters" Critical Inquiry 2, no. 2 (Winter 1975), pp. 369-379; New Literary History, vol. 5, no. 2 (Winter 1974) also carries several articles under the title "Changing Views of Character."

[3] "The Individual and the Novel," Transition vol. 4, no. 18 (1965), p. 33.

[4] Paper delivered at the African Studies Association meeting in Los Angeles, 1968. It was subsequently published in CLA JOURNAL, XIII, no. 2 (December 1969), pp. 142-147.

[5] Chinwizu, Onwuchekwa Jemie and Ihechukwu Maduibuike, Toward the Decolonization of African Literature; Vol. I: African Fiction and Poetry and Their Critics (Washington D.C.: Howard University Press, 1983)l p. 7.

[6] BUSARA vol. 8, no. 1 (1976), pp. 33-38. In his particularly ingenious argument Karanja completely reverses all previously accepted interpretations of Characterization in Things Fall Apart. The crux of his debate is that the hero of the book is not Okonkwo but Okika because the former has been acclaimed by Western critics "so much because he fits into their stereotypes of Africans," p. 35.

His grievances are understandable, but unfortunately the case he presents for making Okika the hero is built more on sentiment than on evidence deducible from the text.

[7] The Emergence of African Fiction (Bloomington: Indiana University Press, 1972). His controversial views on character and characterization which are scattered all over this text—pp. 17-18, 33, 38, 110-111, 147-166,--have often been allowed to overshadow some positive aspects which Ebele Obumsela has pointed out in her review of the book in Research in African Literature vol. 4, 2 (1973

[8] "Larsony: Fiction as Criticism of Fiction," First World, 1, no. 2 (1977), pp. 50-55. In this intensely polemical article Armah contributed the word Larsony to the lexicon of African literary discourse. "It would only be a fitting tribute to this bold, resourceful and enterprising Western critic of African literature," says Armah, "if on his name became synonymous with the style of scholarly criticism of which he is such an inimitably brilliant exponent, that style which consists of the judicious distortion of African truths to fit Western prejudices, the art of using fiction as criticism of fiction. I suggest we call it "Larsony" (p. 55). Proving the historical inaccuracies of the evidence with which Larson backs some of his claims is no proof of the absence of Western influences in Armah's works. These are very obvious. A good example is the "myth of Plato's Cave," in The Beautiful Ones Are Not Yet Born which is such a central symbol in the novel. It is clearly Western in origin, and has no equivalent in African Mythology. Or if it has, Armah has not indicated that he is aware of any such equivalence.

[9] Willie E. Abraham, The Mind of Africa (London: Weidenfeld & Nicolson, 1962), pp. 96-97

[10] See in addition to Professor Abraham's comments, D.S. Izevbaye's "The State of Criticism in African Literature," African Literature Today, no. 7 (1975), pp.4-5; Nancy Schmidt's Nigerian Fiction and the African Oral Tradition, "JNALA, no. 5 (Spring 1968), pp. 10-19; Emmanuel Obiechina's "Characterization," in his Culture, Tradition and Society in the Western African Novel (London: Cambridge University Press, 1975), pp. 82-121, and also the section on "Oral Tradition," pp. 25-41.

[11] "Quality and Less," The New African, IV, 5 (July 1965), p. 114.

[12] Makerere Journal, no. 10 (November 1964), p. 70.

[13] "Ngugi Recounts the Ills of Colonialism," The Record (Nsukka, October 15, 1966), p.4.

[14] Man's Changing Masks: Modes of characterization in fiction, op. cit., p.5.

[15] "On Identifying A Standard of African Literary Criticism: Characterization in the Novel," JNALA, no. 10 (1971), p.9. I am particularly indebted to Bishop in this article which I find sufficiently informative by virtue of the range of variety of opinions he incorporates in the work. What is somewhat disheartening is the degree to which he uses Larson as the frame of reference even after he has proved that Larson's arguments are fallacious. He does not himself examine characterization in any particular text, but I am reluctant to hold that against him because the nature of the work implies that it was purposefully meant to be a survey, and a very brief one at that.

[16] "The Individual and the Novel in Africa," Transition, vol. 4, no. 8 (1965), p. 32.

[17] "L'individu dans le roman africain," in his Collectivité dans le roman négro-africaine d'expression française (Abidjan: Université d'Abidjan, 1969), p. 66. In her article "Critical Bearings in Africa, "Présence Africaine no. 115 (1980), Amadi-Tshiwala has insisted, contrary to what Wali says, that character does exist.

[18] "The Individual and the Novel," p. 32.

[19] "The Crisis of Confidence in the Criticism of African Literature, "Présence Africaine, no. 123 (1982), pp. 92-93.

[20] Toward the Decolonisation of African Literature; vol. I: Africaine Fiction and Poetry and Their Critics, p. 118.

[21] "On Identifying a Standard of African Literary Criticism: Characterization in the Novel," JNALA vol. III (1971), p. 9.

[22] Although Palmer has been very prolific in the sphere of criticism of the African novel and has published in numerous magazines both in Africa and abroad, his most important works in which characterization is given a good amount of space are An Introduction to the African Novel, op. cit., and The Growth of the

African Novel (London: Heinemann, 1979); Anozie's Sociologie du roman africain (Paris: Aubier-Montagne, 1970), contains several chapters dealing with the delineation of characters in various aspects of different African novels; Emmanuel Obiechina's Culture, Tradition and Society in the West African Novel contains a whole chapter of thirty nine pages – 82-121 – devoted to "Characterization"; Mouralis's Individu et collectivité, op. cit., is essentially a study of the nature of characterization in French African novels. To this list of full-length studies can be added Larson's The Emergence of African Fiction already referred to, along with particular chapters in books, essays and reviews such as: Thomas Melone's "Des héros inefficacies," in his Mongo Beti: l'homme et le destin (Paris: Présence Africaine, 1971), pp. 67-92' Abiola Irele's "Chinua Achebe: the Tragic Conflict in His Novels," in Introduction to African Literature: An Anthology of Critical Writing (London: Longman,1979), pp. 177-188; several essays in Standpoints on African Literature; A Critical Anthology ed. Chris L. Wanjala (Nairobi: East African Literature Bureau, 1973).

[23] Culture, Tradition and Society in the West African Novel, pp. 106-107.

[24] Ibid., p. 265. In terms of geographical distribution, the title of the text may be quite misleading because it is not actually a comprehensive survey of West Africa novels as such. The weight of his emphasis clearly lies with Nigerian novels and their relationship to Nigerian society, even though he allocates some space to Ayi Kwei Armah's The Beautiful Ones Are Not Yet Born. Novels from such a rich area as Senegal or Guinea are not treated, although the critic makes a few mentions of Camara Laye in the index.

[25] The Growth of the African Novel, p. 9.

[26] L'Individu et collectivité, p. 6.

[27] p. 8

[28] Personality Description in Ordinary Language (London: John Wiley & Sons, 1977), p. 227.

[29] "On Character: A Reply to Martin Price, "Critical Inquiry, vol. 2 (1975), p. 193. Wilson's impression of Auerbach's Mimesis is extremely low indeed. His main contention is that Auerbach has

merely enumerated details. He is disappointed that in "a book which is so largely about character, there is no examination of the concept of character itself," p. 192. But the fact that Auerbach does not examine the concept of character should not detract from it the foundation it lays for any deeper study of the concept in the novels which he examines. Wilson raises a similar charge against Martin Price's study on Forster.

[30] "On Character...," p. 192

[31] Présence Africaine, no. 115 (1980), p. 152.

[32] I stress the "literariness" of the proposed aesthetic system to distinguish it from a doctrine like "The African Aesthetic" which is essentially a culture-bound phenomenon. Levis Nkosi has rightly pointed out that "it simply seeks to apply to some African works...those criteria which are based on an exclusivist notion of African culture," in Tasks and Masks: Themes and Styles of African Culture," in Tasks and Longman, 1981), Preface.

[33] Although Don Quixote (1605) was written chiefly to debunk the romance of chivalry, it is the blurring of the boundary between literature and life in the protagonist's mind that determines the main action of the book. Also, the distinction between art and reality constitutes one of the main themes in Chapter Ten of Plato's The Republic. His thesis is that reality exists only in the realm of the ideal, that whatever we see is only reflection of the ideal, and so when an artist paints a picture it is twice removed from reality because it is only the imitation of an imitation. See The Great Critics: An Anthology of Literary Criticism, eds. J.H. Smith and E.W. Parks (New York: Norton, 1967), pp. 597-99.

[34] See "Criteria for the study of African Literature," in Literature East and West vol. XII, no. (March 1968), p. 10.

Anthony Astrachan takes the opposite extreme of the artistic critics. "If a novel gives me a society and an individual with manners, good or bad, that is enough. I may not be able to provide more profound insights into Nigerian novels as I learn more about.

[35] See "Does it Take One to Know One?" Nigeria Magazine, 77 (June 1963), p. 133. reigning literary tradition, the background of the

practical language of the time and the movement of the literary tradition.

[36] "The Liberation of African Literature: A Re-evaluation of the Socio-cultural Approach," Présence Africaine, no. 90 (1974), p. 218.

[37] "A Novel for the people," JNALA, no. 2 (Fall 1966), p. 77. Ben Obumselu falls into the same error when he uses outside information to pass judgement on Ayi Kwei Armah's work. He say, for instance, that "the desire of the hero of The Beautiful Ones to get away from everybody and be alone is out of character for any ordinary African clerk," in "Marx, Politics and the African Novel," Twentieth Century Studies no. 10 (December 1973), p. 114. Oladele Taiwo also singles out Achebe's No Longer at Ease for particular praise as a work which attains excellence mainly on the strength of Introduction to West African Literature (London: Nelson, 1967), p. 59.

[38] Theory of Fiction: Henry James, ed. James E. Miller (London: University of Nebraska, 1972), p. 204.

[39] "Biographia Literaria," The Great Critics op. cit., p. 525.

[40] "The Other Self: Thoughts on Character," in Imagined Worlds: Essays on Some English Novels and Novelists in Honour of John Butt, eds. Maynard Mack and Ian Gregor (London: Methuen & Co., 1968), p. 288.

[41] Character and the Novel, p. 31.

[42] Towards African Literature Independence: A Dialogue with Contemporary African Writers, ed. Phanuel A. Egejuru (Westport, Conn.: Greenwood Press, 1980), p. 18.

[43] "The Liberation of African Literature…," p. 218.

[44] The Languages of Criticism and the Structure of Poetry (Toronto: University of Toronto Press, 1953), p. 16.

[45] "The Other Self…," p. 290.

[46] Character and the Novel, p.59.

[47] Critique du roman: essays sur "La Modification" de Michel Butor (Paris: Gallimard, 1970), p. 140/

[48] Solomon Iyasere defines this as "an approach which demands that its practitioners know the social realities behind the work, even beyond what the author furnishes," in "The Liberation of African Literature…," p. 217.

⁴⁹ Story and Discourse: Narrative Structure in Fiction and Film (Ithaca: Cornel University Press, 1978), p. 138.

⁵⁰ (New York: McGraw-Hill, 1964), p. 18.

⁵¹ The Basis of Criticism in the Arts (Cambridge Mass.: Harvard Univ. Press, 1946), p. 78.

⁵² Theories of Personality, eds, Calvin S. Hall and Gardner Lindzey (New York: John Wiley, 1978), p. 11.

⁵³ Character and the Novel, p. 193.

⁵⁴ The History of Rasselas, Prince of Abyssinia (London: J. M. Dent, 1926), p. 36.

⁵⁵ "A Critics Job of Work," in The Double Agent (New York: Arrow, 1935).

⁵⁶ "The Other Self…," pp. 292-293.

⁵⁷ Man's Changing Masks: Modes of characterization in fiction, p. 3.

⁵⁸ "African Critics on African Literature: A Study in Misplaced Hostility," in African Literature Today, no. 7 (1975), p. 27.

⁵⁹ "On Character…," p. 197.

⁶⁰ Theories of Personality, p. 10.

⁶¹ "On Character…," p. 192.

⁶² Ibid.

⁶³ Ibid., p. 191.

⁶⁴ Ibid.

III. The Anti-Hero as Anti-Thesis of the Hero

> ...*all beliefs eventually tend to their opposites, not necessarily the exact opposites. There is a kind of Hegelian drive in ideas to become anti-ideas and these to become anti-theses.*
> *(M. W. Bloomfield: "The Problem of the Hero.")* [1]

The label Anti-Hero designates a deviation from the norm of Hero, be it the Epic, Tragic or Romantic Hero. Thus, not inappropriately, Claude Aziza, Claude Oliviéri and Robert Sctrick [sic] have described him in their Dictionnaire des types et caractères littéraires as the "contre-portrait du héros epic ou tragique."[2] In The Hero in French Romantic Literature, George Ross Ridge says of him that "he is by definition the other side of the coin -the anti-thesis of the romantic hero..., a protagonist who is antipodal to the romantic hero in every respect."[3]

Victor Brombert asserts quite pertinently in his The Hero In Literature that such a figure "cannot be studied without relating him to the traditional hero."[4] Inevitably, therefore, the concept of the traditional hero becomes the yardstick by which the Anti-Hero may be measured and discussed either implicitly or explicitly.

The African critical scene in the novel. Such discussions of heroes and heroism in the novel. Such discussions generally occur not only in the context of the examination of character but also as separate studies. Charles E. Nnolim, in his Achebe's "Things Fall Apart: An Igbo National Epic,"[5] Ernest Emenyonu in The Rise of the Igbo Novel[6] and Jean-Pierre Makouta-Mboutou in his Introduction à la literature noire,[7] for instance, have devoted extensive portions of these works to explorations of the activities of heroes. In these studies, however, with the possible exception of Charles Nnolim's, the impact of their inquiries has been greatly mitigated by the fact that not enough attention has been paid to well-defined parameters such as the specific contexts in which particular terms are to be understood.

Connoisseurs of literary criticism in general and Morton Bloomfield in particular insist, in fact, "on doing what any critic or scholar must do – be[ing] clear about his subject."[8] By this they mean simply making clear what one is talking about from the beginning when one uses an illusive term in analysis. Joseph Campbell's dictum that the hero has "a thousand faces,"[9] may smack too much of the hyperbole, but it is an adequate indication of the multiplicity of forms which he may take. The tripartite definition often found in dictionaries—that the hero is a man of distinguished courage or ability, admired for his brave deeds; that he is a man who is regarded as having heroic qualities, and that he is the principal male actor in a story[10]—may be valuable for a librarian or a book-seller anxious to classify books on the shelves for easy access by readers and customers respectively. But as a reasoned source of knowledge of the full implications and ramifications of the concept, it falls far short. The word "hero" as Morton Bloomfield has tried to prove, subsumes numerous species such as "the epic hero, the romantic hero, the dramatic hero, the tragic hero, the ironic hero and even the comic and anti-hero."[11] Each of these species is capable of being broken down: the tragic into Sophoclean, Aristotelian and Shakespearean; the epic into Greek, Roman sub-species has its own peculiar identifying characteristics.

If a study is ever to find its way into "the consolidating systems of theorists," as G.E. von Grunebaum would say,[12] it then becomes rhetorically imperative for the critic using the term "hero" to make unmistakably clear from the start the sense in which he means the term to be understood. This preliminary requirement is generally fulfilled in studies on the hero in Western literature, or at least in the very good ones. Harold Lubin, for example, opens his Heroes and Anti-Heroes with a range of definitions with which the essays he has assembled are to be identified, and then proceeds to preface each essay with what he has himself described as an "introduction [which] places the readings in a particular framework and a larger perspective and raises key problems about the kinds of heroes presented in the reading selections.[14]

When we turn to the African scene we find that these rhetorical imperatives have not always been adhered to. In fact, a peculiar aura of opprobrium seems to surround the very idea of definition or what Grunebaum considers "the gratifying pedantry of classification."[15] Consequently, even in the very best studies such as Emenyonu's, a knowledge of what heroism actually means is not explicitly stated, and can be arrived at only by inference and deductions. The various comparisons he draws between Okonkwo of Things Fall Apart, his prototypical hero and other heroes such as Omenuko of Pita Nwana's Omenuko[16], and Madume of Elechi Amadi's The Concubine[17], do not grow from any established or assumed concept of heroism. Enlightening as the comparisons may be, they are not a conscious and methodical attempt to explain any given concept of heroism in terms of Achebe, Nwana or Amad. Even when he describes Okonkwo as a hero and his death as tragic, one detects a certain nervousness, an inexplicable reluctance to call him a tragic hero, a label which would have given the discussion some rallying point, and an opportunity to profit from what obtains in Western literature with which, as Abiola Irele's essay indicates, Okonkwo inevitably needs to be compared.[18]

The difficulties posed by the failure on the part of the critics to declare a definite stance or provide a preliminary definition stand out quite clearly when one reads the chapter entitled "History as 'hero' of the African Novel," in Lewis Nkosi's Tasks and Masks: Themes and Styles of African Literature. There, Nkosi places the word "hero" within quotes, which indicates that he is not using the term in the regular sense. But because he had not previously established any particular sense in which he means the word to be understood, his arguments are left floating. As a result, when he says in reference to Ngugi wa Thiong'o's *A Grain of Wheat* that "with the possible exception of Kihika, this novel has no heroes,"[19] the declaration fails to have the intended effect.

In spite of this shortcoming, it is a relief, to know that not all the works mentioned are of this nature. Charles Nnolim's article on Achebe and the Chapter "Différent types des héros et leur rôles,"[20] in Makouta-Mboukou's book approximate in spirit if not in final result, a preliminary typological hypothesis. Charles Nnolim begins his study with a fairly well-defined sense of direction:

> If we are still in agreement that narrative of the epic is a complex synthesis of the cultural, religious, and national experiences of a particular nation or civilization, and that in the national character which emerges from an epic there must be something of estimable fundamental human value behind it all – perhaps heroism, perhaps nobility, and worth suffering defeat for—then *Things Fall Apart* could be read as an Igbo Epic, and Okonkwo, the Igbo Epic Hero.

In the second paragraph he says:

> *In its tragic dimensions Things Fall Apart seems to be modelled on that celebrated Anglo-Saxon Epic, Beowulf, although it at the same time shares certain basic affinities with other classical epics like Homer's Odyssey and Virgil's Aeneid.*[21]

He then goes on to demonstrate the differences between the Greek and Roman epic heroes. Thus, by the time we have read about a third of the paper, we already know who an epic hero is and why the critic thinks Okonkwo should be considered as such.

If there are any weaknesses in the study, they are to be found only in the fact that it is far too brief. And within this limited scope Nnolim would seem to assert his judgment in cases where it would have been better to be more tentative. He is, for example, over-anxious to prove that Okonkwo is in fact an epic hero in the strict tradition of Homer and Virgil, with the result that the idea of dimension of action which is so vital in the definition of an epic hero virtually disappears. One comes away with the impression that Things Fall Apart is not a novel at all, but an epic, which is definitely not what he wanted to say.

Makouta-Mboukou, after distinguishing between categories of heroes in African literature, does not follow up the exercise with discussions which might put his categories into proper perspective.

Of "le héros violent" which according to his classifications is the equivalent of the traditional hero, he says very little.

Yet, once these lapses are ignored or forgiven, the substance of a good number of the studies on character in African literature can be seen to be of immense value in attempting a character sketch of a hero in the African novel. In particular, Ernest Emenyonu has executed an analysis sufficiently elaborate to permit us, with the benefit of research available in Western literature, to establish some working, paradigmatic structure of the traditional African hero. From his examination of Okonkwo, four main elements emerge as characteristic of the hero: his stature, his status, his achievements and his temper.

The first identifying trait he explores is the hero's bulk, his awe-inspiring physique. What strikes him first in Okonkwo is Achebe's emphasis on stature:

> *he was tall and huge, and his bushy eyebrows and wide nose gave him a severe look. He breathed heavily, and it was said that, when he slept, his wives children in their out-houses could hear him breathe. When he walked, his heels hardly touched the ground and he seemed to walk on springs, as if he was going to pounce on somebody. And he did pounce on people quite often.*[22]

He sees Amadi's Madume from the same standpoint when he quotes from the text:

> *There was one thing which Madume had and that was bulk. He was tall and axe-headed and the old men said he had the best pair of calves in the village. His presence during inter-village negotiations always lent a little extra strength to his village Omakachi.*[23]

Although there is no room in Emenyonu's analysis to point this out, these physical characteristics fit in properly with what Western scholarship has long established as a distinguishing characteristic of the hero. Hercules, Ajax, Achiles and Hector, the heroes par excellence in Greek mythology and literature, were all men of great bulk. In his essay on "The Moses of Michaelangelo,"[24] Sigmund

Freud described the hero in similar terms – with great emphasis on his great frame and impressive beard, his noble brow and piercing, inscrutable glance.

The second characteristic trait is the hero's status. Ever since Aristotle's recommendation that the hero should be "a man of great reputation and prosperity, like Oedipus and Thyestes and conspicuous people of such families as theirs,"[25] birth and status have become paramount accompaniments of the hero's very existence. C.M. Bowra says of the hero that he is often "recognized from the start as an extraordinary being whose physical development and characteristics are not those of other men, [and that]… there is about him something foreordained, and omens of glory accompany his birth."[26] Status is crucial in Emenyonu's analysis. But as he is bent on proving, and consistent with the Igbo social organization, the hero is made, not born. Nobility of birth is not a necessary precondition for heroism in these African heroes. I stress these points because they will be conspicuous by their absence in the world of the Anti-Heroes.

Both Omenuko and Okonkwo are depicted as product of very humble beginning. In particular, as Emenyonu points out, "Okonkwo starts life with a terrible disadvantage, his father Unoka, in his day was a carefree and unambitious man." Okonkwo, we are shown:

> *begins life with nothing, but soon gets over the rough beginnings to attain a position of distinction in his clan by sheer hard work, and by assiduously cultivating the energetic and aggressive qualities which tend to be most admired in Umuofia.*[27]

What distinguishes this type of hero then, and what will be found lacking in say, Ferdinand Oyono's Toundi, is the drive to beat all odds, to rise from obscurity to eminence, the striving according to popular expectations to overcome the handicaps of a lowly birth. "The shame and ugly reputation which Unoka had brought to his lineage," says Emenyonu," Was seen by his son Okonkwo as imposing on him an urgent responsibility to restore a name and dignity to the family both for the sake of his own ego and the security of posterity.[29]

Closely allied to this second element and almost inseparable from it is the third: fulfilment, success, achievement. Success and achievement are only measured in terms of the values of the particular society at the particular time. "The hero," says C.M. Bowra, "possesses those gifts of body and character which bring success in action and are admired for that reason."[30] And while Victor Brombert stresses that "the question of the hero cannot be isolated from the total experience of man,"[31] Harold Lubin puts it even more pithily when he says "the hero has been defined as he who takes the risks that we are not prepared to take for the things we believe in."[32]

In Emenyonu's study, Okonkwo's heroism is best appreciated against the backdrop of society's expectations. The people of Umuofia, as he points out:

> *Admire a man of wealth, a man who has a big compound with wives, many children, numerous farms and yam barns. Warriors should bring home heads from battle, and surpass their opponents in wrestling matches. A man must work hard and distinguish himself if he is to be reckoned with in his community, or if he aspires to be a leader of his people.*[33]

Against these values Okonkwo can be said to have acquitted himself with distinction. For when the book opens he is already very "well known throughout the nine villages and even beyond." His fame, we are told, "rested on solid personal achievement," because "as a young man of eighteen he had brought honour to his village by throwing Amalinze the Cat, a great wrestler who for seven years was unbeaten, from Umuofia to Mbaino."[34] In addition, he is said to have taken three out of four ozo titles in the land. Okonkwo's claim to heroism is therefore indisputable.

But mere physical prowess is not enough, nor is it all that makes a man a hero. Emenyonu's analysis of Omenuko proves that honesty does not and should not be regarded as the best policy when heroism is concerned. When he describes Omenuko as "intelligent and resourceful, but…also cunning and capricious,"[36] memories of

Odysseus, that intractable genius of Homer's Illiad and Odyssey come to life. Omenuko is portrayed as a man with an overpowering tendency to use to his personal advantage anyone who comes his way. For example, he is not above selling his apprentices into slavery to make up for his lost goods. This singular act of indiscretion turns out to be the root cause of the main conflicts in the novel.

The fourth identifying trait in the make-up of the hero is his temperament. Emenyonu does not see, or if he does, he fails to emphasize it as a heroic element. He describes Okonkwo as:

> *More presumptuous and less tactful [than Omenuko], ... strong-willed, inflexible to a fault, and a clog in the wheels of change and progress. He is dogmatically committed to his personal beliefs, and so intolerant that he alienates himself from both the world of the old and that of the new. It is his wrong judgment as much as the pressures of the new order that destroy him in the end.*[36]

But the emphasis he places on these qualities is so weighted as to make them look like elements which only serve to tarnish or diminish Okonkwo's heroic statue rather than enhance it.

Although idiosyncrasies of the sort exhibited by Okonkwo have scarcely been admired, let alone encouraged by any one society at any given time, Okonkwo is not a literary freak, without precedents in that respect. Students of Sophoclean drama will have no problem understanding and identifying him as a typical hero because on the score of his temper alone the line between him and any Sophoclean hero or heroine is a straight one, be it Antigone, Ajax or Oedipus. It is difficult in a study of this scope to treat satisfactorily all the issues raised by the comparison. But a few lines from Bernard M.W. Knox's The Heroic Temper should justify the force of the analogy. The verdict he passes on the Sophoclean hero states that such a character is:

> *Immovable once his decision is taken, deaf to appeals and persuasion, to reproof and threat, unterrified by physical violence, even by the ultimate violence of death itself, more stubborn as his isolation increases until he has*

no one to speak to but the unfeeling landscape, bitter at the disrespect and mockery the world levels at what he regards as failure, the hero prays for revenge and curses his enemies as he welcomes the death that is the predictable end of intransigence.[37]

It is reasonable to believe that this would do as an apt epitaph for Okonkwo as well as for Antigone or Ajax.

Although Emenyonu does not make any attempt to remark or to emphasize it, a brief examination of the portrayal of the hero in the recent novels in which such a character is prominently portrayed would indicate that he is becoming less and less awesome, less representative of the ideals of his society. His virtues, physical and military prowess, receive the most emphasis in those novels set in earlier times, as we drift into modern times, his heroism receives a systematic impairment until what is left of him becomes only an assemblage of unheroic or Anti-heroic tendencies. In *Things Fall Apart*, set around the turn of the century and in *Omenuko,* set between 1915 and 1930, it is possible to talk of a hero in all or most of the generally accepted senses of the word. Even then, Okonkwo is depicted as more heroic, strictly speaking, and more daring, more uncompromising, yet more representative of the values of his society. On the other hand, Omenuko, with only a decade and a half separating him and Okonkwo, cannot be described in the same terms. He is not as strong, not as dogmatically committed to his personal beliefs as Okonkwo. In Emenyonu's words, "Omenuko is not a fanatic of the old religion and so does not burn churches or strike down human beings because the oracle has so ordered"[38]. In other words he is not cast in the heroic mould. It is true that the skill of the artist has an effect on the way his hero is portrayed. But even when the skill is not at the very best, as in Pita Nwana's case, it is not impossible for the writer to emphasize heroic qualities wherever they exist.

In *The Concubine*, a novel set in a more recent era, what used to be a crucial aspect of the personality in *Things Fall Apart*, is reduced, as Emenyonu himself puts it, to "snapshots of characters testing their strength" their strength."[39] This explains why the protagonist of *No*

Longer at Ease resembles his ancestors only in name. The hero at this point has been reduced to his opposite - an Anti-Hero.

The Anti-Hero Defined

The term "Anti-Hero" has been described by Claude Aziza and others as:

> "*néologisme...rendu commode pour designer certaine figures qui tiennent le devant de la scène ou du récit, malgré un statut médiocre, ou plutôt en fonction même de ce statut...*"[40]

And while Harold Lubin's view that the Anti-Hero is a post-World War I creation has been widely supported by such critics as Orrin E. Klapp in *Heroes, Villains and Fools*...[41] and Esther Jackson in "The Emergence of the Anti-Hero in Contemporary Drama,"[42] there is sufficient evidence to the effect that the label has been used to describe a particular literary type from the days of Hesiod and Petronius through Cervantes to Dostoevsky, Thackeray and Stendhal.

Notwithstanding this long ancestry, however, and unlike the hero proper, "the anti-hero," as Sean O'Faolin has observed," is a much less neat and tidy concept."[43] Devoid of any real characterological basis, he poses practically the same types of problems of definition as those which Charles I. Glicksberg has detected as characteristic of the portrayal of man in twentieth-century literature. Such problems, Glicksberg says, arise not just from the fact he "is seen as so infinitely complex that no single perspective can do him justice, but because there is in him no inner and enduring truth of self to be grasped, no presiding pattern of unity.[44]

In this *Dictionary of Literary Terms*, J.A. Cudden equates the Anti-Hero with the "non-hero" and says "the anti-hero is the man who is given the vocation of failure."[45] Karl Beckson and Arthur Gantz who consider the narrator of Dostoevsky's *Notes From Underground*, and Meursault of Albert Camus' *L'Etranger* as the prototypical Anti-Heroes, define the Anti-Hero as:

> *A type of hero lacking the traditional heroic qualities (such as courage, idealism, and fortitude)...frequently a pathetic, comic, or even antisocial figure, [who] finds commitment to ideals difficult or impossible because of his sense of helplessness in a world over which he has no control, ... or whose values he suspects.*[46]

Numerous other definitions of the Anti-Hero exist, and some relevant ones will be encountered during our treatment of particular protagonists. But by far the most elaborate definition of the character seems to me to have been provided by Edward F. Abood. In his book *Underground Man*, a name which Dostoevsky gave to his protagonist who was the first to declare himself an Anti-Hero, Abood says that such a character:

> *is generally a rebel against the prevailing norms of the society he lives in and the great forces that perpetuate them: government, the military, business, labor, the mass media, the classroom, the pulpit – institutional powers of any sort. He may even extend his indictment to include not only society, but nature, Being or God as well. His antipathy may become active revolt, or it may turn in upon itself, reducing him to despair and a longing for death. But whatever action he takes (if he is capable of action), it is always essentially personal; even when he joins a group, his commitment is subjective, and he is thus ultimately isolated. Moreover, his characteristic attitude is negation; if he does develop a positive philosophy of his own, it begins with, and is conditioned by a denial of other codes of conduct, particularly the values by which the majority of his contemporaries live. Consequently he lives in a constant state of tension and anxiety, aggravated by what is perhaps his most distinguishing quality - a keen, often morbid, sensibility.*[47]

In the opinion of Esther Jackson, "the anti-hero is not only a divided and incoherent man; he is guilty." But this guilt, she insists, must be distinguished from the guilt or tragic flaw of the Aristotelian tragic hero. The Anti-Hero's guilt is "a schism, a division which has developed from conscious and wilful action, the appearance of profound error – sin."[48]

Even in this motley collection of definitions it is possible to discern certain recurrent epithets, motifs, attitudes or emotions which stand out: his life is generally empty, desolate and barren; in terms of receptivity towards and stimulation by the world, he is generally bored, dull and mired down in apathy; as far as human respectability is concerned, he is generally scorned, slighted and held in contempt; in terms of personal freedom, he generally has little or none, is often checked and hindered, trapped or even smothered by numerous demands and constraints. On the scale of sociability, he is consistently withdrawn, detached from vivacious society into solitary confinement or general isolation. In terms of personal moral judgment he is devoid of any self-approving sentiments, is obsessed with the feeling of unfulfillment and is constantly tormented by guilt and self-loathing. He seldom attains any measures of elation, since depression and gloom dominate his days and nights. As for confidence, he has none because he is forever sensitive to the fact that both his performance and capabilities are too limited to be productive of anything but failure.

It is totally unrealistic to imagine that any one Anti-Hero is capable of embodying all these traits. But generally, any character deserving of the label of Anti-Hero reveals a good range of them in his make-up. To this extent, if one were to use this arbitrary profile as a background against which to test the nature of character in African novels just before and since independence, one would have no choice but to conclude that Nadine Gordimer was obviously mistaken when she declared that:

While Europe's - Britain's specifically – hero of our time was the anti-hero, the angry young man, Africans were concerned with the country boy coming to town – very much the hero, and eager instead of angry.[49]

It is of course possible that Gordimer's expression "hero of our time" was actually meant to refer to the 1950's and not as Henry Gifford uses the expression in his book *The Hero of Our Time* (1950) to refer to an extended period of over fifty years in which a definite and recurrent theme is discernible in Russian literature. If that is the case, then she would be partly correct. But there is no indication of the sense in which she means the term to be interpreted, and so the claim is open to doubt.

The Anti-Hero does in fact exist in African fiction, and, as it will be seen in my analysis of Oyono's *Une Vie de boy*, it is not impossible for a "country boy coming to town ... and eager instead of angry," to become and Anti-Hero. Even before this study, Pierre Makouta-Mboukou had demonstrated a more conscious awareness of the realities of the situation when he not only asserted but followed up with ample evidence to show that:

> *le héros négro-africaine n'est pas toujours le combattant violent que l'on represent prêt à cracher sur le visage du colonisateur, ou à sauter dans les rangs de l'ennemi, le coutelas à la main, et à sabre de tous côté ... il en est ... le héros lâche, qui ne fait que constater et qui ne propose aucune solution, ou qui se dérobe devant ses responsabilités de négre.*[50]

Despite the fact that Makouta-Mboukou does not use the term Anti-Hero in his very valuable study, there is not the slightest doubt that Samba Diallo of Cheikh Hamidou Kane's *L'Adventure ambiguë* and Ferdinand Oyono's Toundi of *Une Vie de boy*, whom he describes as samples of "le héros lâche," are every inch Anti-Heroes in the tradition illustrated by the foregoing definitions.

But, apart from cases like this and many more occasions in which characters are described in a language which brings together many of the essential attributes of the Anti-Hero as he exists in Western literature, quite a few African critics have gone so far as to apply the label itself to discussions of character. A case in point is Emmanuel Obiechina. In the chapter of his *Culture, Tradition and Society in the West African Novel* entitled "Characterization" (to which references has already been made), he discusses generalized and particularized methods of character portrayal and concludes that the former is more characteristic of the West African novel. Such characters he says, "are deployed as fixed traits rather than explored for their psychological complexities." This leads him to argue that "the approach yields stock characters morally defined, like the trickster, the villain, the sage, or soothsayer, the picaresque hero and the <u>anti-hero</u>"⁵¹ [my emphasis]. Unfortunately, however, he does not explain what the Anti-Hero means. But this omission is hardly surprising because it is a characteristic of his study that no time is wasted on defining literary concepts.

In his article "Novels of Disillusion," Arthur R. Ravenscroft also describes Odili of Chinua Achebe's *A Man of the People* as "anti-hero who is no better than the corrupt politician, Chief Nanga." Again, as in the case of Obiechina, we are not told what the term stands for. But it would seem from the context that Ravenscroft equates it with treachery and vanity, for prior to that he describes Odili as "pseudo-innocent, self-decieving."⁵²

With Eustace Palmer there is far less doubt that he knows the full implications of the term, even if he is not quite ready to dwell at any length on them. In his discussion of Ngugi's *Petals of Blood* and his *The Growth of the African Novel* he says "Munira is an anti-hero," by which he means "an ultra-sensitive young man whose life is a failure." This is as close a definition of Anti-Heroism as any we have met in the analyses of Western critics. And not only does he define the term so neatly and precisely, he gives us a brief account of the character's life to back up his claim: Munira is not only insecure, but "his sense of insecurity degenerates into an inferiority complex, a conviction of irretrievable mediocrity." He goes on to add that:

> *During his student days at Siriana he had been involved in a strike resulting in his expulsion, but where the other leaders, like Chui, were able to reorganize their lives by sheer determination and resilience, Munira, lacking the capacity to engage in the world of adult endeavour and experience, can only drift from one failure to another. He is a passive spectator hovering on the fringes of important actions, withdrawing from involvement, like Mugo.*⁵³

Although this is all that Palmer says to illustrate the concept of the Anti-hero, it has the merit of drawing attention to the fact that it is possible to apply the concept to the study of character in the African novel. It is this last observation that makes my own study all the more necessary because it is centred on an issue which has hitherto been taken for granted and/or treated offhandedly.

Recapitulation and Rationale for Approach Selected

If this introductory section has served any purpose so far, it has been mainly to indicate that the greatest problem facing critic of the African novel has been his failure or reluctance to devise or adopt a sound critical perspective and to employ the proper analytical tools for the examination of character. Because the critic, for whatever reason, has been unable to do this, it has been almost impossible either to appreciate the achievements of the writers in that respect, or, if appreciated, to judge them rightly. Toundi, Obi Okonkwo, Mugo, "the Man," Samba Diallo and Ahouna, all these are great creations in their own right, capable, as it will be observed in the second part of the project, of being subjected to the same in-depth psychological and even philosophical analysis as any Anti-Heroic protagonist of Western literature.

What Bernard J. Paris once said with regards to devising a new method of studying characters in realistic fiction can also be said of the situation that confronts studies in characterization in the African novel, namely that:

> *the great characters have been there all along, of course, and have been appreciated by many readers. But without the conceptual system offered by an appropriate psychological theory, we have not been able to see them clearly and talk about them in detail.*[54]

To appreciate character in a novel, whether African or European, the data has to be assembled, the various elements which constitute the character's *modus vivendi* in the book have got to be organized. And in the words of Ernst Prelinger and Carl N. Zimet, "for any systematic organization of data leading to the assessment of a literary character, a theory of some kind is necessary."[55]

The field of African literacy criticism does not seem to me to have furnished so far, a study that provides a comprehensive system of character analysis within the frame-work of a coherent theory, not even in the much-used and/or much-abused sociological approaches. A psychological investigation of those literary characters we classify and identify as Anti-Heroes, would go a long way to satisfy that critical need. Their behaviour patterns which constitute the main strands of the stories of their lives, need to be identified. We need to understand their psychological motivations, the inner workings of their minds, if we are ever to reach a full appreciation of their modes of existence in the texts.

But these Anti-Heroes, as Mary Doyle Springer once said of all literary characters, "cannot have sprung full-blown from the head of Zeus. They are not born but made."[56] Obi Okonkwo, Ahouna, Mugo and the others, are *artefacts*. This means that they are, as Springer would have said, "constructs designed for the job with all the imagination, intuition, and practical rhetorical skill their authors can summon up."[57] There is in the being of each of them, therefore, a deliberate patterning, a conscious (and sometimes even an unconscious) selection of details which suggest unconscious motives to the reflective reader, and which should provide the critic with some formal design of ethical and psychological basis by virtue of which the characters can be examined.

The character's world view, his imagination, his likes and dislikes, his conception of himself, his relation to others around him, to space and time, his subconscious motivations and reactions, all these usually assume a definite design, some pattern, real or apparent, which imparts to the work as a whole a deeper meaning. It may not be immediately obvious to the undiscerning eye, but with the right preparation and the right analytical tools, the critic should be able to discover or establish such a pattern.

Organistic strategies will play a major role in this analysis. "Organicism," says Stephen Pepper, "is the world hypothesis that stresses the internal relatedness or coherence of things," in the sense that "it is impressed with the manner in which observations at first apparently unconnected turn out to be closely related, and with the fact that as knowledge progresses it becomes systematized."[58] The context of each Anti-Hero will be examined as detailly as possible in order to identify those traits which in their particular configuration form his personality structure. As Erich Fromm once said, "a person acts in accordance with the demands springing from his character structure."[59]

Each of the six novels we will examine will be seen as constituting a patterned sequence of behavioural actions and events in which each protagonist gets caught up in circumstances not necessarily of his own making, but nevertheless beyond his control, and from which he emerges either as victim or failure or both.

Notes

[1] Morton W. Bloomfield, "The Problem of the Hero in the Late Medieval Period," in *Concepts of the Hero in the Middle Ages and the Renaissance,* eds. Norman T. Burns and Christopher J. Regan (Albany: State University of New York, 1975), p. 41.

[2] Claude Aziza and Claude Oliviero, *Dictionnaire des types et caractère littéraires* (Paris: Fernand Nathan, 1978), p. 16.

[3] (Athens: The University of Georgia Press, 1969), p. 82.

[4] *The Hero in Literature* (Greenwich Conn.: Fawcett Publications, 1969), p. 13.

[5] *Modern Black Literature,* ed. S. Okechukwu Mezu (Buffalo, N.Y.: Black Academy Press, 1971), pp. 55-60.

[6] (Ibadan: Oxford University Press, 1978), pp. 111-154, 157-161. 164-181.

[7] (Yaounde: Editions CLE, 1970), pp. 80-104. Other studies on the subject include: S.P. Kartuzou, "African Novelists and Their Heroes," *SIMBA,* vol. 2, no. 4 (1960), pp. 32-36; Judith Illsley Gleason, "The Heroic Legacy," in her *This Africa: Novels by West Africans in English and French* (Evanston: Northwestern University Press, 1965), pp. 41-68; Julie Hetherington, "The Concept of the Individual as Hero in Modern African Literature," in *Journal of African and Asian Studies,* 1. 3 (1973), pp. 18-22; Roger Chemain, "Le héros et la ville," in his *La Ville dans le roman africain* (Paris: Editions L'Harmattan, 1981), pp.218-271.

[8] "The Problem of the Hero ...," p. 27.
[9] *The Hero with a Thousand Faces* (New York: Meridian Books, 1956).
[10] *Random House Dictionary,* ed. Jess Stein (New York: Balantine Books, 1978), p. 421.
[11] "The Problems of the Hero ...," p. 29
[12] In his review of Isidore Okpewo's *The Epic in Africa* [Research in African Literature, vol. 11, no. 4 (Winter 1980), pp. 552-559], Kunene brings out an interesting but delicately argued distinction between the hero in Western epic like Hector or Odysseus. He says "here we are dealing with the most persistent and outstanding ethical objectives of the African epic – namely, to present the hero as operating within the social law. The hero himself must be punished if he violates the requirements of reasonable revenge. This situation differs from that in the *Odyssey,* for instance, where the anger of the epic hero is all-consuming. Aristotle is describing the Western epic when he says that on the hero depends destiny of the community. This statement is by no means a universal law, but Aristotle's own assessment of the qualities of the Greek tragedy. This claim for the hero or central figure is exactly the opposite of the African heroic conception in which the community remains all-powerful" p.556.
[23] "The Hero in Medieval Arabic Prose," in *Concepts of the Hero in the Middle Ages...,"* p. 86.
[14] *Heroes and Anti-Heroes: A Reader in Depth* (San Francisco Calf.: Chandler Publishing Company, 1968),
[15] G.E. von Brunebaum, "The Hero in Medieval Arabic Prose," p.86.
[16] (London: Longman, 1933; repr. 1963).
[17] (London: Heinemann, 1963).
[18] In his essay, "Chinua Achebe: the Tragic Conflict in His Novels," Irele talks of an Oedipus touch to the relationship of Nwoye, Okonkwo's son, to his father. But he does not make any further mention of the possibilities for comparison which we find in the characterization of Okonkwo.
[19] *Tasks and Masks: Themes and Styles of African Literature,* p. 40.
[20] *Introduction à la littérature noire,* p. 84.
[21] "Achebe's Things Fall Apart...," p.55.

[22] *Things Fall Apart* (London: Heinemann, 1958), pp.3-4.
[23] *The Concubine,* p.6.
[24] *Collected Papers* vol. IV, trans. Joan Riviere (New York: Basic Books, 1959), p. 257.
[25] Aristotle, *The Poetics,* p. 33.
[26] "The Hero," in *The Hero in Literature,* p. 24.
[27] *The Rise of the Igbo Novel,* p.114.
[28] Ibid., p. 113.
[29] Ibid.
[30] "The Hero," p. 23.
[31] *The Hero in Literature,* p. 11.
[32] *Heroes and Anti-Heroes* p.5.
[33] *The Rise of the Igbo Novel,* pp.112-113/
[34] *Things Fall Apart,* p.1
[35] *The Rise of the Igbo Novel,* p. 38.
[36] bid., p. 158.
[37] *The Heroic Temper: Studies in Sophoclean Tragedy* (Berkeley: University of California Press, 1964),
[38] *The Rise of the Igbo Novel,* p. 159.
[39] Ibid., p. 165.
[40] *Dictionnaire des types,...* p. 17.
[41] In the chapter "Mockery of the hero," in his *Heroes, Villains and Fools: The Changing American Character (*Englecliffs, N.J.: Prentice-Hall, 1962), p. 157, Klapp says "a significant thing about the age in which we live is its anti-heroism – its tired, apathetic, cool, and beat rejection of lofty goals." His description of man in contemporary literature is also very enlightening for the concept of the Anti-Hero. He says: "In modern literature we find an inadequate hero whose shortcomings are, on the whole, comic rather than tragic or pathetic … The common theme is an adequacy to meet the grand part, which may be freely admitted by the hero…"Harold Lubin considers the Anti-Hero as a reflection of the bitter aftertaste of the War. He associates his birth with "the collapse of the nineteenth century dream of progress, and perfectibility of man"; p. 310. A.C. Ward places the birth of the

Anti-Hero at later date. He says "it was after World War II that the anti-hero became a predominant character," in his *Longman Companion to Twentieth Century Literature* (London: Longman, 1975), p. 24.

⁴²Esther Jackson affirms that the development of the anti-hero grows out of new demands, demands related to the dilemma of man in the twentieth century.

J.D.P. Bolton has pointed out in the chapter entitled "The Birth of the Anti-Hero" in his *Glory, Jest and Riddle* that the Anti-Hero was born of the "tension between the old aristocrats whose claims to *arête* were based birth, and the new timocrats, men of no family but measuring their worth by the standards of material wealth" in the early days of the Greek city states (London: Duckworth, 1973), p. 21.

In his article, "The Use of Language as a Means of Characterization in Petronius," Frank Frost Abbott describes the protagonist as "the anti-hero Encolpius," *Classical Philosophy* 2 (1907), p. 44. But Cervante's Don Quixote is generally taken to be the true beginning of the concept. Frank Wadleigh Chandler considers the concept as synonymous with that of the picaro. He therefore looks at his book *Romances of Roguery* (New York: Burt Franklin, 1961) as a study of the Anti-Hero. As far as he is concerned, "the spirit of the story of the anti-hero was necessarily satirical and corrective." Jest and farce and comedy were to him inseparable from the nature of the Anti-Hero, pp. 16-17. Although Harold Lubin supports this interpretation when he says "Comic and satiric forms of the anti-hero can be found throughout the history of Western Literature (p. 311), the twentieth century. Oyono's Toundi is a rarity among Anti-Heroes these days.

⁴³*The Vanishing Hero: Studies in Novelists of the Twenties* (London: Eyre & Spottiswoode, 1956), p. 17.

⁴⁴*The Self in Modern Literature* (Pennsylvania: The Penn. State univ. Press, 1963), p. xii.

⁴⁵(London: Andre Deutsch, 1977), p. 46.

⁴⁶*Literary Terms: A Dictionary* (New York: Farrar, Straus and Gibroux, 1960), p. 15.

⁴⁷*Underground Man* (San Francisco: Chandler & Sharp, 1973), pp. 1-2.

⁴⁸ "The Emergence of the Anti-Hero in Contemporary Drama," *Central States Speech Journal,* 12 (1960-61), pp. 96-97.
⁴⁹*The Black Interpreters* (Johannesburg: Raven Press, 1973), p. 9.
⁵⁰*Introduction à la littérature noire,* pp. 84-85.
⁵¹*Culture, Tradition and Society in the West African Novel,* p. 107.
⁵²*Readings* in *Commonwealth Literature,* ed. William Walsh (Oxford: Clarendon
Press, 1973), p. 200.
⁵³(London: Heinemann, 1979), p. 295.
⁵⁴*A Psychological Approach to Fiction...,* p. 275.
⁵⁵*Ego Psychological Approach to Character Assessment,* p. 4.
⁵⁶*A Rhetoric of Character: Some Women of Henry James* (Chicago: University of Chicago Press, 1978), p. 5.
⁵⁷Ibid., pp. 5-6.
⁵⁸*The Basis of Criticism in the Arts,* op. cit., p. 74.
⁵⁹*Escape From Freedom* (New York: Harcourt Brace, 1941), p. 283.

Chapter Two

Toundi (Ferdinand Oyono's *Une Vie De Boy,* 1956)

Plot Summary

A diary supposedly translated from Ewondo into French, Ferdinand Oyono's *Une Vie de boy* tells the sad tale of the adventures and systematic physical and psychological victimization of Toundi-Joseph Ondoa, a most submissive and ingenuous village boy who abandons his home in the village for a life of permanent servitude among white French colonialists and missionaries.

Told on a double narrative level reminiscent of Abbé Prévost's *Manon Lescaut* (1731), the novel opens with a flashback depicting the painful end of the protagonist. When the story effectively begins, Toundi has just missed being beaten by his father because of his involvement in a village brawl with other children over lumps of sugar that had been thrown to them by le Pére Gilbert, a white father in whose residence Toundi takes refuge for the night.

Returning under cover of darkness the same evening that he escapes, Toundi is shocked by a sight he watches through an opening on the wall: he sees his father and uncle devouring food out of his beloved mother's pot. For some reason he is seized with such sudden bitterness against his father that he contemplates killing him. He decides to go and live the rest of his life with Le Pére Gilbert in Dangan Mission, inwardly resolving never to return to the village, even after his parents die.

Le Pére Gilbert, on the other hand, very enthusiastically receives Toundi and (though to Toundi's delight) he physically and consistently abuses him, he spares no pains in educating him. The very idea of keeping a diary is the direct result of the education Toundi undergoes under the care of Le Pére Gilbert. As fate would have it, Toundi's education is not pursued to its logical end: Le Pére

Gilbert dies accidentally and with him goes every promise which his intimate relationship with the priest had held out.

Since the thought of returning to his home village does not occur to him, Toundi's wish to continue to serve the white men is granted when he finds work as a steward in the household of Robert Decazy, the Commandant du cercle. With him Toundi maintains a relatively happy, though degrading black-servant and white-master relationship until the arrival of the Commandant's wife, Suzy.

This beautiful, enticing and most frivolous woman who suddenly becomes the paramour of the Prison Superintendent, engages the services of Toundi as a letter carrier between her and her lover. For some reason, Toundi seems not to hate the errands, dangerous as they are, should his master discover that he is an accomplice to his cuckoldry. Along with the other servants in the house who have not been unaware of their mistress's sexual promiscuity, Toundi enjoys very many privileges. But just as it happened in the case of Le Pére Gilbert, Toundi's luck is but a mere spell, the lull before an oncoming storm. Ignorant of the extent to which Toundi likes the punishments customarily doled out to him, and even the sheer act of running dangerous errands, Madame Decazy becomes extremely suspicious of her messenger and servant. Before the commandant himself discovers his wife's infidelity, the woman's love and tolerance towards Toundi has already turned to hostility.

Curiously enough, though he quarrels with Suzy, the two reconcile almost immediately, a reconciliation which spells doom for Toundi whose involvement in the misdeeds of Suzy cannot long remain a secret. But while this becomes obvious to all the other servants in the house, Toundi characteristically refuses to see the danger. Or if he sees it, he refuses to be frightened by it. He ignores warnings by the more perceptive servants to flee for his life, and very naively continues, for no apparent reason, to pledge his wholehearted support for and trust in the protection and friendship of the Commandant.

It therefore does not come as a surprise to anybody else but Toundi when he is suddenly arrested on a trumped-up charge of complicity in theft. Belatedly, Toundi begins to see an urgent need to protect himself from his masters. He escapes from the prison into which he had been thrown. But the damage has already been done and eh soon dies in the Spanish Guinea from the inhuman beatings he had received in the prison.

State of Criticism

Few critics are more aware of the difficulties confronting the appreciation of *Une Vie de boy* than Eustace Palmer. In his *The Growth of the African Novel* he draws attention to two studies on Oyono's novels – Jeanette Kamara's review which suggests that Oyono's chief aim in the novels is to entertain, and which claims that any other information included in the story is merely to enrich a basically funny book[1], and Mukotani Rugyendo's rejoinder which asserts that Oyono's main purpose has always been to expose the evils of the colonial situation in pre-independence Africa.[2] Palmer says of both studies that they "constitute overstatements of the respective cases."[3] He blames Rugyendo for not paying enough attention to the novel's technique. A more reliable approach, he argues, would be for the critic to understand that Oyono's humour and other aspects of the style are inextricably woven into his political and social concerns which are the crux of the novel. In conclusion he says that "where Beti and Kane are largely concerned with the cultural implications of French imperialism, Oyono is preoccupied with the social and political ... [and that the] work is almost entirely devoted to a presentation of the ruthlessness of the French administration in those territories over which they had sway."[4]

One thing which emerges with particular clarity from these comments is the degree to which Oyono's art as a creator of characters is totally subordinated to the socio-historical content of the novel, even by those who are aware of the importance of technique. At least one critic has drawn attention to the inadequacy of exclusively socio-historical interpretations of the work. In his article, "Jungian Archetypes and the Main Characters in Oyono's *Une Vie de boy*," Charles Nnolim steps out of the beaten path to say that:

> *Many critics rightly see Oyono's* Une Vie de boy *as a work that makes a great satiric thrust at colonial injustices in Africa ...But the danger lies in critics reading* Une Vie de boy *solely as a satire. Satire can be a potent weapon in the hands of the novelist, but when satire becomes the end rather than the means (as it is in Swift's* Gulliver's Travels *or Voltaire's* Candide*) it ceases to be a novel and becomes what Northrop Frye calls an anatomy.*[5]

Nnolim makes reference to Jung's identification of the human psych as comprising the three structural components of Shadow, Persona and Anima. And his division of the characters in *Une Vie de boy* is quite ingenious. But he fails to relate these three components to the central consciousness, Toundi. Had he attempted to show that the Anima and Persona are but projections of the protagonist's consciousness, or could be regarded as such, a rallying point for the disparate elements in the novel would have been established a whole decade ago. But as the article stands, it merely indicates that he is conscious of the possibility of identifying Jungian archetypes in the novel. According to Charles Nnolim, and rightly so, the novel is not an anatomy – what C.H. Holman defines as a prose work organized around ideas and dealing with intellectual themes and attitudes[6] – but a work of art. Nnolim's arguments are brief, and he seems reluctant to pursue any detailed analysis using his knowledge of Jung's concepts of *Shadow, Persona* and *Anima.* But the article suggests directions in which psychological constructs can be quite profitably used to redeem the work from the oblivion into which it has long been condemned.

What makes the psychological approach a matter of pressing necessity now is the fact that it offers clues, if not answers, to the most thorny problems of interpretation, especially of Oyono's portrayal of the protagonist. The case seems almost closed now on the point that Oyono is very poor in character portrayal, and that his protagonist in *Une Vie de boy* is psychologically deficient. The opinions of Dorothy Blair and Eustace Palmer on the "unsuccessful" depiction of Toundi epitomize the general tendency. Blair cannot understand why Toundi, who prides himself in having learnt so much about the white man's ways, would fail to apply his common sense to forestall the traps which are laid in his way, and into which he fails headlong. She cannot understand why Toudi's judgment of white community which has been so sharp and satirically accurate does not put him on his guard against the dangers which threaten his position. She asks why, in spite of the opportunities open to him to escape and save his skin, Toundi vows to stay on, retaining "an unjustified faith in his employers who are only waiting for some pretext to get rid of the witness to their shame, making him their innocent scapegoat."[7] She considers these to be inexcusable failings on the part of the novelist, and which she says, rob the novel of any psychological subtlety.

Eustace Palmer is equally confused. He writes:

> *One of the novel's puzzles is why Toundi chooses to stay, even though he must be aware of the storm clouds gathering around him. Kalisa, the new chambermaid, warns him of his danger in even clearer terms than the cook who urges him to leave ...*[8]

Then later on he says:

> *One could have expected him to try to prove his innocence, as he could quite easily have done, but he makes no real attempt at this. Is this a flaw in the novel, or is it due to a realization by both Toundi and his creator that defence would be useless? Or must we trace it again to that resolute spirit of defiance?*[9]

What these two critics stop short of saying is that Oyono is very weak in character portrayal. I think they are even too kind in posing only so few unanswered questions regarding Toundi's mode of existence in the novel. More specifically, anybody anxious to grasp the total essence of Toundi's life would want to have more facts explained. Why, for instance, would the same person who is capable of telling his father boldly: "je n'ai rien fait, père, pour être battu" (p 19), and "je ne veux plus être battu et c'est tout" (p. 21), be so enamoured of an institution like the Mission in Dangan where cruelty is the order of the day? Why, for instance, would Toundi who boasts "j'aime caresser les jeune filles blanches sous les mentons" (p. 25), fail to take advantage of the opportunity offered him by fate to ease his sexual instincts realistically by sleeping with the very obliging and unscrupulous Sophie?

The answers to these and many more questions regarding Toundi's behaviour in the story take us right into his inner life, a life which other critics do not think he has. What Blair and Palmer do not immediately see is that very much craft has gone into producing the type of personality which we find in Toundi. Oyono, it has to be admitted, is a very skilful craftsman, and the novel can be shown to be very rich in psychological sophistication. In fact, it is a measure of Oyono's subtle, deep and indirect approach to character that his achievement has not been immediately obvious to the majority of critics.

To say with Palmer that "the triumph of the method is the brilliant penetration into the growing boy's mind and the fascination with which we watch his development as his eyes are gradually opened... to the realities of imperialism,"[10] gives only one side of the psychology of the character, it does not touch the heart of the problem. A deeper appreciation lies in a psychoanalytic interpretation of his character. Such a method, which should begin with the establishment of a personality structure for Toundi, would undoubtedly help us discover a measure of psychological consistency in his behaviour.

By correlating the predominant affects of his character as they are revealed at crucial stages in the development of the story, and by reinforcing these with some of the symbols associated with them, a system can be established. Within such a system many apparently unrelated elements in the novel can be seen to constitute a pattern. In particular, a hitherto neglected aspect such as the conflict within Toundi's family circle can be seen as providing the psychological cause of the main-spring for the seemingly inexplicable questions about Toundi's behaviour throughout the rest of the book.

Toundi's Personality Structure and Claim to Anti-Heroism

There are several aspects in which Toundi could be regarded as a typical Anti-Hero and not as a Hero, as critics have consistently described him. First of all, his status as a houseboy rules out most possibilities of heroic actions in his life. But even more than that is the fact that he is portrayed as an out-and-out victim, a man caught in a life situation which may be considered one of the strongest elements in the definition of the Anti-Hero: not only is he spat on, kicked about and trampled on, or as he himself puts it, "bousculé, renversé, piétiné,"[11] but is dedicated to services which are neither rewarded nor reciprocated, and is eventually tortured and driven to die as miserably as he had lived.

To this extent *Une Vie de boy* can be said to constitute a paradigm for what Edward Strauch calls "plot as victimization." Such a plot, he says, "usually relates the fate of a victim, a sufferer, a scapegoat or a sacrificer."[12] Toundi is condemned to a lifetime of victimization very early in the novel. Prior to his quarrel with his father, he admits that "nous étions une bande de jeune païebs à suivre le missionnaire qui allait de case en pour solliciter des adhésions à la religion nouvelle" (p. 18). He further states that:

> *Il nous lançait se petits cubes sucrés…C'était un véritable bataille pour s'approprier l'un de ces délicieux morceau blancs que nous gagnions au prix de genour écorchés (p. 18).*

But despite the fact that several other children were involved, it is Toundi alone who bears the brunt. His father accuses him: "c'est toi, Toundi, la cause de toute cette histoire!" (p. 19). The man then goes on to beat up Toundi. This unfortunate tendency to suffer for others is repeated over and over again in the course of the story: when Mr. Decazy discovers that his wife has been flirting with M. Moreau, he shies away from confronting the adulterer and transfers his own cowardice to Toundi whom he accuses in a manner which makes the letter carrying a much more serious offence than the infidelity. When Sophie escapes with the Agricultural Engineer's money, the man does not blame himself for getting involved in relationships with women of dubious repute, but accuses Toundi of being Sophie's lover and accomplice, and makes him suffer for a crime he did not commit.

Along with these misfortunes and trumped-up charges, go certain acts of denigration perpetrated both by Toundi himself and his masters. Central to his personality is the cynical impotence and unquestioning manner with which he reacts to his dehumanising environment. In an interview on his depiction of the protagonist of *Invisible Man* (1952), Ralph Waldo Ellison said "the major flaw in the hero's character [war] his unquestioning willingness to do what [was] required of him by others as a way to success."[13] Oyono's Toundi suffers from the same flaw, a flaw which places him squarely in the tradition of the Invisible Man, whose appearance on the literary scene has been described by William J. Schafer as "the birth of the Anti-Hero."[14] With a power of endurance which can be compared only to the patience of the biblical patriarch, Job, Toundi is content to look on himself as nothing but "la chose qui obéit" (p. 36). And rather than aspire to greater things, he is perfectly satisfied with being a dog because "le chien du et le roi des chiens" (p. 33).

The Application of Psychoanalytic Theories: Fanon and Freud

Toundi's mode of existence as an Anti-Hero in *Une Vie de boy* can be apprehended at various levels of abstraction. In this chapter I chapter I have chosen to focus on two main psychological theories which provide us with some insight into what I presume to be the subconscious patterns underlying Oyono's creation of the protagonist as a victim and as a failure. There is first Frantz Fanon's "éréthisme affectif" and his "ankylose affective."[15] These, growing out of the colonial situation, and virtually comprehensible mainly in terms of it, focus on those factors of the white/black relationship which completely undermine the self-confidence of a black man like Toundi, thereby robbing him of that psychological readiness which is a natural and necessary prerequisite for positive action. Secondly, there is Sigmund Freud's theory which views (*inter alia*) an inability to surmount the Oedipus Complex, to break with the father while at the same time identifying with his masculine role, as a central ingredient in the make-up of the weakling or Anti-Hero.[16]

Fanon

Although generally overlooked, many of the psychological undercurrents in the relationship between Toundi and his family, and between Toundi and his white masters can be quite profitably understood when examined against the backdrop of Fanon's theories of "éréthisme affectif" and "ankylose affective." He coined the term éréthisme affectif" in order to describe and explain (as far as his grievances against white domination of the black race could carry him), the consuming feeling of inferiority which impels the black man to draw toward the white woman and the black woman toward the white man. He tells us in his *Peau noire, masques blancs* that:

> *C'est parce que la négresse se sent inférieure qu'elle aspire à se faire admettre dans le monde blanc. Elle s'aider, dans cette tentative d'un phénomène que nous appellerons éréthisme affectif (p. 68)*

Frantz Fanon talks specifically of the black woman. But one does not distort his meaning by extending the phenomenon to include male individuals like Toundi who completely submit themselves, even more passionately to the power of the white man than the black women in the book.

One of the most puzzling questions in the interpretation of the character of Toundi as already suggested, remains the precise reasons for his neurotic or even masochistic submission to white authority. Fanon's theory provides us with part of the explanation: it is a feeling of inferiority that drives the black man to give up his freedom. But "éréthisme affectif," Fanon is at pains to point out, is not a natural disposition of the black world. It occurs only upon contact with the white world. Fanon regards it as an acquired product of a peculiar social experience and conditioning emanating from the oppressive presence of the white man. To this extent he also coined the term "ankylose affective" to describe the perennial attitude of superiority which makes a white man like Le Pére Gilbert or the Commandant Decazy look on a black man like Toundi as a culturally as well as a biologically inferior species, just one step above animals.

Fanon sees the confrontation between the black and white worlds as a kind of neurotic enslavement on both sides. He says with regard to his findings that:

> *Quel soit le domain par nous considéré une chose nous a frappé: le nègre esclave de son infériorité, le blanc esclave de sa supériorité, se comporte tous deux selon une ligne d'orientation névrotique (p. 68, PNMB).*

In each encounter the black man's behaviour assumes the form of an obsessive neurosis. He says:

> *Aussi avons-nous été amenés à envisager leur aliénation en référence aux descriptions psychanalytiques. Le nègre dans son comportement s'apparente à un type névrotique obsessionnel ou si l'on préfère, il se place en pleine névrose situationnelle (p. 68, PNMB).*

It is only in the context of an obsessional neurosis that the black man's behaviour (and Toundi's most particularly) can be understood.

Applying these theories specifically to *Une Vie de boy*, Toundi's behaviour can be seen to follow very closely Fanon's claim that "Il ya chez l'homme de couleur tentative de fuir son individualité, de néantiser son être-là" (p. 68, PNMB). The first and most decisive step towards Toundi's loss of individuality is to found in his flight from his village, his abandonment of the family.[17] The arrival of the white men instils a sudden spirit of rebelliousness in him. All filial obligations of respect and fear are instantly abandoned. When he runs into the arms of Le Père Gilbert, he brags: "avec le Père Gilbert, je ne craignais rien. Son regard semblait fasciner mon père qui baissa la tête et s'éloigna tout penaud" (p. 23). When he leaves his village (symbolically on a motor cycle, a white man's invention which will not only kill his idol, Gilbert, but turn his dreams into a nightmare), Toundi does so shaking the dust off his feet, bubbling with the hope that the first step had been taken up the scale of human value: "j'étais heureux… Je ne suis jamais retourné au village" (p. 24). Fanon also made another point in his study which puts Toundi's conduct here in proper perspective. He said: "L'individu [like Toundi] qui monte vers la société – la Blanche, la civilisée- tend à rejeter la famille – la Noire, la sauvage – sur le plan de l'imaginaire, en rapport avec les *Erlebnis* infantiles" (p. 141, PNMB):

> *"Éréthisme affectif" reaches its apogee when Toundi throws his own humanity to the winds and announces he is but "la chose qui obéit" (p. 36). This point is given symbolic amplification when later in the story Oyono makes the cook tell the apparently emancipated Toundi:*

> *tu ne connaîtras jamais ton métier de boy. Un de ces quatre matins, tu seras cause d'un malheur. Quand comprendras-tu donc que, pour le blanc, tu ne vis que par tes services et non par autre chose! Moi, je suis cuisinier. Le blanc ne me voit que grâce à son estomac … (p. 131).*

Early in the story, however, before Toundi is consumed with neurotic pride, he boasts with unctuous self-satisfaction and a sense of achievement that he, "le chien du roi est le roi des chiens" (p. 33).

Fanon points out the inevitability of doom which a black man, like Toundi, introduces into his life when he warns that from the moment that the man abandons his family, he is forever condemned to a life of suffering. To desert one's family, says Fanon, is to inferiorise oneself and to expose oneself to dangers which one is not psychologically capable of coping with. Consequently, "le nègre infériorisé va de l'insécurité humiliante à l'auto-accusation ressentie jusqu'au désespoir." (p. 68, PNMB). From this standpoint, Toundi's portrayal in the book can be said to offer a classic paradigm for Anti-Heroism because the more vigorously he pursues the fulfilment of the desires of his white masters, the more irrevocably he dooms himself.

Although he speaks quite complimentarily of Le Père Gilbert, that "il me présente à tous les blancs qui viennent à la mission comme son chef-d'oeuvre" (p. 26), his status as a human being with a pride to defend has only fallen. In fact, he tells us in the same breath what being a masterpiece entails: "un boy qui sait lire, servir la messe, dresser le couvert, balayer sa chamber, faire son lit ..."[11] (p. 26). Toundi is not the type of character to detect contradictions, and although these services conflict with his original intentions of living *like* the white men, he is not discouraged. One is reminded here of Fanon's observation that "L'Européen en general, le français en particulier, non content d'ignorer le nègre de leurs colonies, méconnaissent celui qu'ils ont formé à leur image" (p. 72 PNMB). Toundi takes no money, and, characteristically, does not complain because "de temps en temps, le prêtre me fait cadeau d'une vieille chemise ou d'un vieux pantalon" (p. 26). The whites tolerate him because he fits into their stereotype of the good nigger, not because, as he deceives himself into thinking, he has the potential to "vivre come eux" (p. 24).

It thus becomes easy for us to see some logic in the conduct of the whites and in Toundi's response to it. Both forms of behaviour fall into a definite psychological pattern, a psychological plot, as it were, which determines character and therefore provides some answers to the problems of apparent improbabilities.

Freud

Fanon's theories provide us with psychological explanations why Toundi deserts his family and why he throws himself into the arms of the white man with such abandon. But because Fanon's motives for devising the theories were not the same as those of Oyono when he wrote the novel, the theories do not quite tell us convincingly or even conclusively, why he should be so ready to risk his life to serve people from whom he gets only disgrace. They do not explain the complex nature of Toundi's sexual inclinations. Freud's theories provide explanations which fill in these missing links.[18] The effectiveness of these theories can be best appreciated in the context of a character design. By character design here I simply mean the shifting constellations into which the cast of characters can be divided and out of the inner workings of which crystallizes the affective environment of the work.

The Oedipus Complex Situation

The first constellation is the triangle consisting of Toundi, his father and mother. The material from which this first group is constructed is provided by the tensions within the family: there is an obvious hostility between Toundi and his father and in which his mother sides with him. The incident which brings this to the fore is the fight in which Toundi gets involved in an effort to secure the sweets thrown to him and his playmates. As a result of this apparently slight event Toundi receives a beating out of all proportion to the severity of the offence, and which is explainable only in the light of some hidden or long-standing grievance between him and his father. When he returns at night and watches his parents at table, he is seized by a murderous instinct: "pout la première fois de ma vie, je pensai à tue mon père" (p. 22). As was said in the case of his father dishing out a severe punishment for a misdemeanour, Toundi's killer-instinct can never be sufficiently explained merely on the evidence afforded by the table scene. The expression of that murderous urge is only a final outburst of a smouldering hatred. When this is considered against the fact he discloses that "Ma mère vint me voit pendant la nuit. Elle pleurait. Nous pleurâmes ensemble" (p. 23), we have in hand a classic example of a situation that is amenable to explanation in psychoanalytic terms.

The human instincts and emotions that necessitate such a rift within a family circle have been very well formulated and explained by Sigmund Freud who in *The Ego and the Id* describes the child's plight as the Oedipus Complex. There he says:

> *At a very early age the little boy develops an object-cathexis for his mother, which originally related to the mother's breast and is the prototype of an object-choice on the ... model; the boy deals with his father by identifying himself with him. For a time these two relationships proceed side by side, until the boy's sexual wishes in regard to his mother become more intense and his father is perceived as an obstacle to them; from this the Oedipus complex originates. His identification with his father then takes on a hostile colouring*

and changes into a wish to get rid of his father in order to take his place with his mother.[19]

The relationship between Toundi and his parents can therefore be said to illustrate Freud's concept of Oedipus Complex which he saw as the nucleus of neurosis.[20] Whether or not the son develops into a strong, self-assertive and rationalizing personality who leads a normal and healthy sexual life, or turns into a wantonly submissive individual who leads a depraved sexual life, would depend on the manner in which the Oedipus Complex situation is resolved. A normal resolution, one in which an intensification of the boy's identification with his father results or follows the dissolution of the Oedipus Complex, produces a consolidation of the masculinity in the boy's character.[21] At the same time an affectionate relationship with the mother is retained. On the other hand, an Oedipus Complex that is not resolved in the normal way produces a severely defective personality.

Freud distinguished three major systems as constituting the structure of the human personality. A knowledge of these systems, however simplified, is crucial to an interpretation of a situation like the one Toundi presents us with. These systems are the Id, the Ego and Super-ego. The interacting effects of these three are responsible for the formation of a particular behaviour pattern that governs the life of a character both in literature and in life.

The *Id* generally refers to that unconscious part of the mind which provides a storehouse for the basic instinctive urges and drives of personality, those drives which demand immediate satisfaction or gratification, irrespective of rational considerations.[22] The *Ego* refers to the largely conscious part of the mind, concerned with perception, rational thought and conduct and adjustment to reality, and which is in a sense oriented to the self-preservation of the person.[23] The *Super-ego* is that part of the mind described by Anna Freud as an "inner court of judgment," because it represents an internal incorporation of the authority of parents and parent-figures, constituting the source of inner moral dictates and prohibitions as well as standards and ideals established internally. Sometimes it is treated as being synonymous with conscience.[24]

The relationship between these three systems and the Oedipus Complex was stressed by Freud when he said:

> *The broad general outcome of the sexual phase dominated by the Oedipus Complex may, therefore be taken to be the forming of a precipitate in the ego, consisting of these two identifications in some way united with each other. This identification of the ego retains its special position; it confronts the other contents of the ego as an ego ideal or super-ego.*[25]

What this finally means is that an Oedipus Complex that has not been resolved in the normal or healthy manner is bound to lead to a deficient Ego-personality and an even more deficient super-ego-personality.

All the evidence presented by Oyono points to the fact that Toundi's Oedipus Complex was never allowed to develop in a normal way. Between his contemplation of his father's death —"pour la première fois de ma vie, je pensai à tuer mon père" (p. 22) – and the later announcement that "Mes parents sont morts. Je ne suis jamais retourné au village" (p 25), we are not given the slightest inkling of the fact that there had been any reconciliation between father and son. From this point Toundi's behaviour becomes highly predictable.

Psychoanalysing Dostoevsky in 1927 drew conclusions from certain facts which are almost exactly paralleled in Toundi's case.[26] He proved as we have tried to do with Toundi's predicament, that Dostovesky was born with an unusual intensity of emotional life, a predisposition to bisexuality and a vicious impulse to kill his father which he never actually got rid of. In consequence, says Freud, Dostoevsky's ego, the developing rational self, became extremely passive with respect to the incorporated influence of his father, the conscience or the Super-ego. From this too he established that Dostoevsky was bound to develop a great need for punishment, humiliation and misery. He says "Dostoevsky's condemnation as a political prisoner was unjust and he must have known it, but he accepted the undeserved punishment ... as a substitute for the punishment he deserved for his sins against his real father. Instead of punishing himself he got himself punished by his father's deputy."[27] Here, he says, is the psychological justification of the punishments inflicted by society. It cannot be forgotten that Toundi is a literary character and Dostoevsky a historical figure. But in his application of the Oedipus Complex concept it made no difference to him whether the character to be examined was human or literary. What mattered were the steps through which the life of the individual had passed and the extent to which these steps make it possible for him to apply the defensive and structural models.

From the analogy drawn between Toundi's fate and what Freud saw in Dostoevsky as a specimen for analysis, we catch a glimpse of why Toundi would describe punishment dealt out to him with such a resigned acceptance, and even make a joke of it:

> Le Commandant me décocha un coup de pied dans les tibias qui m'envoya rouler sous la table. Le Commandant a un coup de pied plus brûlant que celui du regretté Père Gilbert (p. 38).

His departure to live with Father Gilbert makes very much sense when viewed against the fact that his conflict with his father had deprived him of the one opportunity within his family to secure an Ego-Ideal. The Ego-Ideal is the expression for the totality of ideals, norms, standards of conduct, and levels of aspiration set up as a mental image by which a person measures the value of his Ego and behaviour.[28] Since the animosity between Toundi and his father had ruled out the possibilities of finding one within the family, a vacuum had been created in Toundi's life which needed to be filled.

On a second level, Toundi's conflict with his father over the possession of his mother is presented in a language so loaded with sexual implications and symbolism that we cannot say it is a mere coincidence. Rather, the rhetoric must be regarded as a symptom of, if not a prelude to the disoriented sexuality that will dominate Toundi's life. We do not find here the type of erotic relationship between mother and son that we find in, say, D.H. Lawrence's *Sons and Lovers*. But the nocturnal visits and the tears the woman and her son shed together are tremendously suggestive of an unhealthy relationship even if only at the unconscious level. The entire scene which makes him want to kill his father is framed in a language that could be taken as the depiction of the rape of the woman by a man and his brother: "Ma mere se leva et leur apporta la marmite je vis la main de mon père et celle de mon oncle y plonger. Puis j'entendis ma mere pleurer" (p. 22).

Marmite is obviously a pot, but it could without any danger of overstretching the point, refer as well to a woman's genitals. The hands of the man and his brother *plunge* into the pot in manner which is also highly suggestive of violent, hungry intercourse. At this point Toundi notices his mother weep. And why not? In his fantasy his mother is being raped by his father and his uncle. Hence he says "je pensai à tuer mon père" (p. 22)

There is, in addition the gluttony motif, the constant accusation levelled against him: "ta gourmandise nous perdra" (p. 19), "si tu n'avais pas le sang des gourmands..." (p. 20). Gluttony is an excess which can be made to mean more than meets the eye. What it suggests here is that Toundi had a predisposition toward compulsiveness in eating, an urge which in psychoanalysis is equivalent to an excess of libido on the psychic energy behind the sexual drive.[29] All these seemingly outrageous and unconnected elements begin to fall into a definite pattern as the story progresses.

Toundi as Victim of Homosexual Urges

Toundi's flight to live with Father Gilbert provides us with a second constellation of characters in the book, with the various personalities he encounters in Mission Catholique Saint-Pierre de Dangan. What he says about Father Gilbert is a logical outgrowth of the motif of a quest for a father-figure a role which Gilbert fulfils both as a secular care-taker as well as a temporal father. Toundi tells us:

> *Je dois ce que je suis devenu au Père Gilbert. Je l'aime beaucoup, mon bienfaiteur. C'est un homme qai qui, losque j'étais petit, me considérait*

comme un petit animal familier. Il aimait tirer mes oreilles et, pendant ma longue éducation il s'est beaucoup amuse de mes émerveillements (my emphasis; pp. 25-26).

No matter how innocent and naïve Toundi may be, his description of the relationship with Le Père Gilbert is full of unhealthy sexual implications and innuendos. The acts of pulling the ears and fondling, for example, have definite erotic significance.

Toundi does not disapprove of this type of petting. And the main reason is that he comes to Father Gilbert's house with a scarred sexual life. In his *Collected Papers* Freud has said that a prime cause of homosexuality lies in the fact that the son remains too strongly fixated to the mother from childhood, and too hostile towards the father.[31] Freud also stated that what saved Dostoevsky from an overt homosexual life with the males who dominated his future life was the fact that he was able to sublimate his homosexual urges into writings in which repressed homosexuality is very prevalent.[32] But Toundi would not be that lucky, for his literary talents would be limited to only one work-a recording with very little modification of the self-torturing events of his painful life. He leaves his father's village with a very strong deviance disposition towards homosexuality or a propensity towards deviance from sexual norms. This explains why he is so much in love with Father Gilbert, of whom Toundi says with obvious suggestions of homosexuality that "il me présente à tous les blancs qui viennent à la Mission comme son chef-d'oeuvre" (p. 26). The very idea of "chef-d'oeuvre can be understood in several ways. One obvious one is that Father Gilbert had made of him an ideal object for the satisfaction of his paedophiliac urges, paedophilia here referring, as George W, Kisker has said, to a sexual deviation in which the love object is a child characterized both by naiveté and a lack of sophistacation.[33]

Very gleefully, Toundi acknowledges that Father Gilbert had made a pet of him. And when he says that the man was responsible for "ce que je suis devenu" (p. 250, we are not to believe that it can only refer to his ability to read and write. From being an object for petting he himself had also acquired the skills of petting and fondling which he practiced whenever the occasion presented itself: "J'aime caresser les jeunes filles blanches sous le menton avec la patène que je leur présente lorsque le prêtre leur introduit l'hostie dans la bouche" (p. 25).

What is significant in the construction or reconstruction of Toundi's character structure is the fact that none of these activities in which he is involved actually provides a realistic outlet for the repressed urges. Neither the caressing of the young girls nor his subjection to Father Gilbert's petting offers any releases for his pent-up appetites which must have been striving for fulfilment ever since he fled his home village.

Toundi as Voyeur and Victim of Exhibitionism and Sado-Masochism

The death of Father Gilbert gives Toundi another chance to continue his quest for a father figure or the very elusive Ego-Ideal. His departure for the Commandant's residence is designed to meet that psychological need, a need which is trebly met in the Commandant who is not only a white man and a military leader, but also Toundi's employer. His arrival at the Commandant's offers an opportunity for a more elaborate and complicated character constellation which involves The Commandant himself, his wife, the Agricultural Engineer, Monsieur Moreau and his lover Sophie, and Kalisia the new chambermaid. This may sound like a very high society, but it is one with terribly low morals. It is a society in which sexuality and sexual intercourse constitute the most common diversions.

In Father Gilbert's parish, Toundi could give vent to his desires only by caressing young girls during communion. But he is being brought to share the same house with women who could make any part of their bodies available to him just for the asking. But because the experience of his youth include the unresolved Oedipus Complex, he is incapable of getting realistically involved with either the commandant's wife or Sophie. Accordingly, he exists in this morally depraved circle as a voyeur. Voyeurism, as defined by psychologists is "a sexual deviation... [in which] the patient receives his erotic satisfaction from *watching*. The observation of sexually arousing situations becomes a substitute for participation in such activities."[34]

In distinguishing the long-term effects of an abnormally resolved Oedipus Complex, Freud said:

> *there is the inclination towards a narcissistic object-choice, which lies in every way nearer and is easier to put into effect than the move towards the other sex. Behind this factor there lies concealed another quite exceptional strength, or perhaps it coincides with it; the high value set upon the organ and the inability to tolerate its absence in a love object. Depreciation of women, and aversion from them, even horror of them, are generally derived from the early discovery that women have no penis.*[35]

Herein lies one explanation which critics have sought for over twenty-five years for Toundi's enigmatic behaviour towards women. Toundi's relationship with Kalisia is designed to emphasize his frigidity. Kalisia who can be said to have come in as an accusing consciousness to haunt and even fire Toundi up into behaving like a sexually potent man, tells him: "Tu es pourtant un homme" (p. 144).

Although she is new in the precinct, she is convinced that Toundi had every opportunity to sleep with his mistress. "Là-bas, du côté de la mer" she insists, "les boys couchant avec leurs patronnes, c'est courant" (p. 144). It was hardly because, as Kalisia says, "ici vous avez peur des blancs" (p. 144). In point of fact, the reverse was true, for Madame Decazy feared him to the extent that she addressed him "Monsieur Toundi" (p. 153). If he had refused to sleep with Sophie because as he was to say belatedly during his torture, "ce n'est pas mon genre de femme" (p. 161), what reason did he have for not sleeping with Kalisia? She was not only young and beautiful but was capable of assembling all the wiles that would arouse any normal man. She pointed out rather suggestively that "des petites hanches comme les tiennes sont souvent le nid des grands boas" (p. 143), while pinching Toundi's buttocks. Not only this, for as he tells us, "elle m'empoigna les parties et poussa un petit cri rauque" (p. 143).

Then follows the teasing accusations: "tu vois, j'en suis certaine. C'est toi l'homme de Madame!" (p. 144).

But Toundi is no normal person. In his view, she has lost her mind: "Si tu es folle, moi je ne suis pas fou" (p. 144), he tells her. He seems quite satisfied to play peeping-Tom: "je revins furtivement regarder la fenêtre du salon d'où filtrait la lumière. M. Moreau embrassait Madame sur la bouche" (p. 101). These activities constitute the highlights of his sexual experiences.

It is only in the context of his voyeurism that his obsession with the nature of the Commandant's penis can have any meaningful significance in his character structure.

The entire scene in which the penis is discovered to be uncircumcised, coupled with the changed emotional attitudes that follow, comes as close as possible to what psychologists have described as psychic masturbation. In the words of Frank S. Caprio in *Variations in Sexual Behaviour,* "in psychic masturbation a person may be sexually stimulated while looking at obscene pictures. Sexual thoughts resulting in fantasies of various kinds are capable of causing sufficient sexual excitement to bring about an orgasm."[36] His description of the way the commandant approached him is a mixture of coyness and regret at a missed opportunity to be seduced: "il s'avança vers moi et arracha le flacon des mes mains. Je quittai la sale de bains à reculons pendant que le Commandant esquissait un geste vague et haussait les épaules" (p. 45). But later on we find that in that split second that he confronted the Commandant's penis some psychic consummation had taken place. And the behaviour that follows is well high an orgasmic relief: "Cette découverte m'a beaucoup soulagé. Cela a tué quelques chose en moi" (p. 46). What else could this thing be that has been killed in him if not a sex urge? And thereafter he will behave towards his master like a man would, who has finally slept with a woman who hitherto proved to be unattainable! He tells us with a peculiar feeling of conquest that "je sens que le Commandant ne me fait plus peur... Je restai impassible sous ce regard qui m'affolait auparavant" (p. 46). According to George Kisker, voyeurism is always associated with another type of sexual deviation, exhibitionism. In this type of behaviour, the individual "obtains sexual relief by showing or exhibiting, his body to other people."[37] The Commandant here represents the exhibitionist *par excellence,* to which Toundi plays the voyeur.

After having fitted the seemingly isolated bits and pieces of Toundi's sexual life into a growing pattern, we need to know why he would be reluctant to seize the opportunity to escape the torture which he knows full well awaits him. This too can be explained as the next logical step in the degeneration in sexual activity. Psychoanalysts have referred to Sado-Masochism as the last step in the decline in sexual behaviour in human beings. Masochism, to be sure, has been defined as a tendency of an aggressive character, directed inwards against the self, so that the self-experience either physical or mental pain, accompanied with some gratification of sensuality from the suffering.

If we agree with Sigmund Freud in his analysis that the masochistic tendency such as he detected in his analysis of Dostoevsky is a direct result of the undissolved Oedipus Complex, then the last third of *Une Vie de boy* where Toundi submits to all sorts of tortures can be seen as growing quite naturally from the past. The novel would then be seen to reveal a character structure that leaves very few loose ends, one in which every act of behaviour on the part of the protagonist grows from a definite psychological basis, and from which the death emerges as a logical conclusion. In considering Toundi as an Anti-Hero it has therefore been possible and necessary to show that he was a victim not only of colonial injustice but more especially, of his own emotions. One can safely say that in his creation of his protagonist, Ferdinand Oyono, perhaps only subconsciously, may have been aware of those psychological frames which define a weak personality, and that in Toundi he had produced a character who meets the definition of the Anti-Hero in both the socio-physical and the psychological senses.

Oyono's Style

Samuel Holt Monk once said of Swift's *Gulliver's Travels* that "the surface of the book is comic, but at its centre is tragedy *transformed through style and tone into icy irony*" (my emphasis)38. The same statement can be made about Oyono's *Une Vie de boy*, and it is my intention here to explore the peculiarities of Oyono's style and the bearing it has on the portrait of the Anti-Hero that emerges in Toundi.

The first and most conspicuous aspect of Oyono's style in the novel is the degree of objectivity he has achieved. The story is told in a very rigorous first-person point of view in which, as James Joyce's Stephen Dedalus would have said, Oyono "finally refines himself out of existence."[39] Much of what we know- I say *much* and not *all* because the implications of many of the things which baffle Toundi are generally accessible to us – is basically what Toundi sees and knows. We know for instance that the small bags which he discovers are contraceptives and not just accoutrements for a certain part of the body. Objective narration provides the writer with an excellent opportunity for making ironical statements about reality. But it also reinforces our impression of Toundi as an Anti-Hero. In this regard, the character that comes closest to mind in Western literature is Lemuel Gulliver, the protagonist of *Gulliver's Travels* whom Paul Russell appropriately describes as a character who, like Toundi, "generally suffers rather than acts ... the archetypal victim."[40]

There is a cardinal rhetorical principle which goes as far back as Aristotle's *Poetics* and which demands that "a person of a given character should speak or act in a given way, by the rule either of necessity or probability; just as this event should follow that by necessary or probably sequence."[41] Ferdinand Oyono appears to have been very sensitively aware of this principle in his creation of Toundi. Once he establishes from the very first chapter that Toundi is a simpleton transported from the village like a fish out of water, and without any prior apprenticeship or orientation or learning, to work as a servant amidst Europeans, Oyono dedicates his best efforts to keep him at that naïve level. Naïveté, which has generally been considered as a major element in the characterisation of some Anti-Heroes, particularly in the comic tradition,[41] becomes for Oyono a framing device. This is first noticeable in the nature of his language. He communicates in a plain, unliterary, unadorned language that is commensurate with his unsophisticated, extremely limited, moral, psychological and geographical background. The images and symbols of his language, self-denigrating though they are, and therefore Anti-Heroic in tendency, refer to homely things –to chickens and dogs: "il nous lançait ses petits cubes comme on jette du grain aux poules" (p. 18).

So long as naiveté remains the core of Oyono's meaning in his depiction of Toundi, certain crucial aspects of the latter's mode of existence as an Anti-Hero are definable though mainly by their absence. This is especially obvious when he is compared to such a prototypal Anti-Hero as Roquentin of Sartre's *La Nausée*. The first thing to consider here has to do with the profundity of Toundi's mind. There is not in *Une Vie de boy* that compelling need to depict the inner crisis which had made it so necessary, at least in part, for Sartre to choose the diary form as his medium of communication.[43] We do not know Oyono's reasons for choosing the form. But at least we know why Toundi decides to keep a journal because he tells us that: "maintenant que le Révérend Père Gilbert m'a dit que je sais lire et écrire couramment, je vais pouvoir tenir comme lui un journal" (p. 2). He goes on to say that "je ne sais quel plaisir cache cette manière de blanc, mais essayons toujours" (p. 2).

From the very onset, therefore, Toundi is not driven by any inner compulsion to understand either people or things, or himself. His purpose, which may no doubt be quite different from that of Père Gilbert, is simply to record memories. Thus, although the narrative frame does not allow him more than ordinary access to the mental states of the people about him, neither Toundi's conception of the idea of the diary nor his execution of it raises any expectations of speculations on the human condition, or any particularly profound or penetrating study either of people, objects or phenomena.

In the case of Roquentin, the idea of a diary is dictated by the historian's urge to record facts as accurately as possible, in order to interpret them and thereby achieve self-understanding. He tells us that "le mieux serait d'écrire les événements au jour le jour. Tenir un journal pour y voir clair. Ne pas laisser échapper les nuances, les petits faits, mêmes s'ils n'ont l'air de rien, et surtout les classer."[44] Where Roquentin seeks to explain phenomena in terms of existential contingencies, to pierce through the hypocrisy that masks reality and convey to us what he has apprehended, Toundi is awed and even amused by the realization of change in his conception of his world. When, for example he discovers the Commandant is uncircumcised, a fact which shatters his whole perception of the white man, it only occasions light humour and even neurotic pride. He says nothing about appearance and reality. Unimaginative and unanalytical in extremes, he thinks the fault must be his: "Non, c'est impossible…j'ai mal vu" (p. 45).

The contrast between Toundi's shallowness and Roquentin's perspectives-an example of the unstable and even contradictory nature of the Anti-Hero- is not to suggest that Oyono is an inferior creator of character. In fact, it takes a great amount of talent and a hardening of a writer's aesthetic sensibilities to produce a character who is so consistently dull, naïve and yet endlessly entertaining.

Hence, it becomes not only possible but also very easy for us to declare that contrary to popularly held views about the book, *Une Vie de boy* is rich enough to be subjected to various layers of interpretation, and that if Toundi has hitherto been regarded an artistic failure, it is simply because his mode of existence in the novel has not been analysed in terms of all or many of the psychological constructs suggested by the text. It has also to be stressed that there is every indication that Oyono throughout the novel conceives of him as an Anti-Hero for whom naiveté, reinforced by an imperfectly guided sexual urge is the main identifying characteristic. And in the exhibition of this major characteristic, he can be said to have assembled some of the best and the most effective elements of his art as a novelist of character.

Notes

[1] *"The Old and the Medal,"* a review, ALT no. 3 (1969), pp. 50-52.

[2] *The Growth of the African Novel,* op. cit., p. 160.

[3] Ibid.

[4] Ibid., p. 161.

[5] *ALT* no. 7 (1975), p. 122.

[6] *A Handbook to Literature* (Indianapolis: The Odyssey Press, 1975), p. 24. Holman briefly but concisely traces the history of the term from Aristotle to Northrop Frye.

[7] *African Literature in French: A History of Creative Writing in French from West and Equatorial Africa* (London: Cambridge Univ. Press), p. 224.

[8] *The Growth of the African Novel,* p. 178.

[9] Ibid.

[10] Ibid., p. 172.

[11] Ferdinand Oyono, *Une Vie de boy* (Paris: René Julliad, 1956), p. 44. All further references are to this edition, with page numbers following each citation.

[12] *A Philosophy of Literary Criticism. A Method of Literary Analysis* (New York: Exposition Press, 1974), p. 204. "Plot as victimization" is listed as the fifth and last of five categories into which his principle of "Plot as Reaction or Defeat" is divided. The other four categories include "Plot as Revolt," "plot as Treachery," Plot as Vengeance." The entire realm of Plot as Defeat is especially important because it reflects the basic tenets of Anti-Heroic fiction which will no doubt figure again and again in the course of the project.

[13] "The Art of Fiction: An Interview," in *The Merrill Studies in Invisible Man,* ed. Ronald Gottesman (Columbus, Ohio: Charles E. Merrill, 1971), p. 45.

[14] "Ralph Ellison and the Birth of the Anti-Hero," in *The Merrill Studies in Invisible Man,* op. cit., p. 89.

[15] These theories, however, do not receive any particularly unified expression in Fanon's works, not even in *Peau noire, masque blancs* (henceforth abbreviated PNMB after each citation). They are

scattered all over and are discussed in the context of different topics. But on every occasion, the implications of the terms are unmistakable. Since they are not presented in any order, my intention here is to select the most significant pronouncements on the issue of Black/White relationships and show the extent to which Toundi's depiction in the novel bears them out.

[16] Davied Riesman has given us a most valuable source of information on understanding Freud's concept of Heroism and Anti-Heroism in his article "The Themes of Heroism and Weakness in the Structure of Freud's Thought," in *Selected Essays from Individualism Reconsidered* (New York: Doubleday, Anchor Books, 1954), pp. 246-275.

[17] The importance of the family on the behaviour of the individual is very well stressed in the chapter "LE Negre et la psychopatologie" where, quoting Marcus, Fanon says: "la projectée dans le comportement" (p. 141).

[18] Fanon himself stresses the importance of applying Freudian concepts to the analysis of psychological or pathological dimensions of the depiction of a character like Toundi. He says in "Le Negre et la psychopathologie" that "Les écoles psychanalytiques ont étudié les réactions névrotiques qui prennent naissance dans certains milieux, dans certains secteurs de civilisation. On devrait, pour obéir à une exigence dialectique, se demander dans quelle mesure les conclusions de Freud ou d'Adler peuvent être utilisées dans une tentative d'explication de la vision du monde de l'homme de couleur (p. 135, PNMB).

He further stresses that psychoanalysis sets as its main task, the understanding of given patterns – within the specific groups represented by the family. Quoting J. Lacan's "Le Complexe, facteur concret de la psychologie," to strengthen his argument, he states that: "quand il s'agit d'une névrose vécue par un adulte, la tâche d'analyste est de retrouver, dans la nouvelle structure psychique, une analogie avec tels éléments infantiles, une répétition, une copie de conflits écoles au sein de la constellation familiale. Dans tous les cas, on s'attache à considérer la famille 'comme objet et circonstance psychiques' (p. 135, PNMB).

[19] Trans. Joan Riviere (London: The Hogarth Press, 1962), pp. 21-22.
[20] Ibid., p. 23. The term "neurosis is used to refer to any disturbance of personality, with symptoms of anxiety or suffering.
[21] Ibid., p. 22.
[22] I consciously chose a definition of this nature provided by J.G. Starke, in the glossary of his *The Validity of Psychoanalysis* (Sydney: Angus and Robertson, 1973) because it is simple, and yet retains the essential aspects of the term.
[23] Ibid., p. 140.
[24] Ibid., p. 145.
[25] *Sigmud Freud: The Ego and the Id*, p. 24.
[26] "Dostoesvky and Parricide (1928)," in his *Collected Papers* vol. V, ed. James Strachey (New York: Basic Books, 1960), pp. 222-242.
[27] Ibid., p. 233.
[28] J.G. Starke, *The Validity of Psychoanalysis,* p. 140.
[29] *New Introductory Lectures on Psychoanalysis,* trans. W.J.H. Sprott (new York: Norton, 1933), p. 115.
[30] George W. Kisker, *The Disorganized Personality* (New York: McGraw-Hill, 1972), 224-228.
[31] *Sigmund Freud: Collected Papers* vol., p. 233.
[32] Ibid.
[33] George W. Kisker, *The Disorganized Personality,* p. 230.
[34] Ibid., pp. 220-221.
[35] *Freud: Collected Papers* vol. V., pp. 240-241.
[36] *Varitions in Sexual Behaviour: A Psychodynamic Study of Deviations in Various Expressions of Sexual Behaviour* (London: John Calder, 1975), p. 11.
[37] George W. Kisker, *The Disorganized Personality,* p. 218.
[38] "The Pride of Lemuel Gulliver," in *Gulliver's Travels:* An Annotated Text with Critical Essays, ed. R.A. Greenberg (New York: Norton, 1961), p. 282.
[39] James Joyce, *A Portrait of the Artist as a Young Man* (New York: Viking Press, 1968), p. 215. There Joyce has Dadelus say: "The artist, like a God of creation, remains invisible, refined or beyond or above his handiwork, invisible, refined out of existence, indifferent, paring his fingernails." These words seem to have

come down to readers of Joyce as though they were his original thoughts. Actually, Malarme and Arthur Symons had used it before Joyce.

[40] "The Frailty of Lemuel Gulliver" in *Jonathan Swift: Gulliver's Travels,* ed. Robert Greenberg (New York: Norton, 1976), p. 378.

[41]*The Great Critics: An Anthology of Literary Criticism* eds. Smith, James Harry and Edd Winfield Parks (New York: Norton, 1951), p. 44.

[42]Harold Lubin, *Heroes and Anti-Heroes,* p. 311. There Lubin asserts that "The anti-hero takes many forms. Sometimes he is a mockery of the old hero forms, a poor slob fumbling his way through life exposing the incongruity of the heroic stance in a non-heroic world."

[43]In an extremely valuable study, *Jean-Paul Sartre's Existentialism In "Nausea"* (Calcutta: A Writer's Workshop Publication, 1978), Ashok Kumar Malhotra points out that there were three reasons why Sartre chose the diary form: 1) he was compelled by the nature of Roquentin's struggle (inner crisis); 2) the kind of subject-matter treated in the novel; and 3) Sartre's intention to experiment with an innovative literary method. I have just reduced to almost a meaningless skeleton the substance of a very well-defended case.

[44]Jean-Paul Sartre, *La Nausée* (Paris: Gallimard, 1938), p. 11.

Chapter Three

"The Man" (Ayi Kwei Armah's *The Beautiful Ones Are Not Yet Born*, 1968)

> *The anti-hero is a character who is nameless, crawling somewhere in the mud, pre-occupied with his body and its needs but also reaching out for human contact, vaguely remembering the past. He suffers the unremitting torment of existence, too overwhelmed by inner and outer confusion to say no to life...His quivering consciousness, all that remains of him, that is still restlessly alive dissolves the last outlines of reality.*
>
> *(Charles I. Glicksberg: "A Trinity of the Absurd")* [1]

The Plot

The Beautiful Ones Are Not Yet Born tells the brooding tale of the futile efforts being made by "the Man" (henceforth simply: the man, without emphasis) the anonymous protagonist, to survive in a Ghana reeking with putrefaction, filth and excreta, a world irreparably consumed with greed and endemic corruption. When the story begins, the man is on his way to his colourless and ill-paid job as in a telegraph operator. He is drooling profusely in his sleep in a municipal bus, which itself, is in the last stages of dilapidation.

When the dishonest conductor who had been deeply engrossed in his cheat discovers the man sleeping and messing up his bus, he rains obscene insults on the man and compels him to clean the seat. The man obeys without a word of protest and departs while the conductor continues to insult and spit at him. The man journeys through the squalid, garbage-ridden neighbourhood, and after narrowly missing death at the wheels of a taxi whose driver heaps more insults on him, he arrives his office at the decaying Railway Administration Block.

After a characteristically boring day in the office where he has unaccountably refused to accept bribe from a desperate timber merchant, the man meets Koomson. Koomson who was once his classmate is now a Minister, and his very success in life is a standing reminder to the man as well as an accusation for his own abject failure to make life comfortable for himself and his family.

Back home he narrates the adventures of the day to his forever-reprimanding wife, Oyo. Not surprisingly, Oyo rebukes him, but she does it so mercilessly and with such vivid logic that the man leaves the house. Braving the darkness outside he pays his friend, Teacher a visit. He goes there hoping that Teacher's isolation from society places him in the best position to give useful advice on how to survive in a world as corrupt as theirs.

The man turns out to be wrong, and returns from Teacher's house worse off than he went. Teacher has nothing but blame and rebuke for him for going against the current of society's commitments. This reproach leads the man to retrace, to his heart's bitterness and frustration, his past as well as his country's--those promises of youth which time has failed to fulfil.

Party man Koomson decides to pay the man's family a visit, and the man has to live through days of intense emotional torture as it prepares to receive the Minister: to satisfy his wife's vanity he finds that he has to stretch his purse far beyond his means in order to welcome the guest. When Koomson finally comes, his "chubby profile" and debonair comportment which contrast sharply with the man's sullenness only serve to alienate the man further from his wife and mother-in-law. Koomson, the heart and soul of the party, caps the evening's fun with an irresistible offer—that the man's family and his enter into a join boat deal. The man does not refuse, although he knows better than his wife and mother-in-law that Koomson is only exploiting their naiveté. Oyo and her mother fall for it.

Koomson's visit is soon followed by a return visit from the man's family, during which the deal is ratified, giving them, at least on paper, partial possession of the rights of Koomson's boat.

The boat which the man had never actually approved of, brings some fish, but the returns fall far short of the hopes which the initial idea had fanned in Oyo and her mother. Then, suddenly, Koomson is overtaken by events: a military coup topples the regime in which he is Minister and he has to flee for his life. From the Luxury and splendour of his lodge in the ministerial quarters Koomson descends into the man's shabby home and actually has to carry his already stinking body through the filth of the latrine hole—the man crawling sheepishly behind him—before swimming to safety across the border.

The end of Koomson's government is only the beginning of another wave of corruption. Only a few hours after the coup that ousts the corrupt regime, the man again watches a bus driver secure the release of his bus at the road block, using the same old tricks in bribing a willing policeman on duty. Thus, quite aptly, the misspelled lettering on the bus as it drives away sums up the terrible message of the book: "The Beautiful Ones are not yet born."

State of Criticism

Compared to thematic studies, symbol-hunting and the quest for sociological implications of the novel, character study in *The Beautiful Ones Are Not Yet Born* has received very little attention. A brief examination of discussions that have some bearing on character and characterization in the novel reveals at least three different, though not necessarily contrary approaches: Prescriptivist; Symbolist or Allegorist; and the Comparatist.[2]

Prescriptivist Approach

In this category we find criticism which involves blame or accusations levelled against Armah: about what he has failed to do with his characters, about what is found wrong with the characters, and about what he ought to have done in the novel. A critic whose remarks best exemplify this trend is Ben Obumselu. In his article "Marx, Politics and the African Novel," he says:

> *The desire of the hero of The Beautiful Ones to get away from everybody and be alone is out of character for an ordinary African clerk; it is intelligible only as an expression of the author's emotions...*

The rejection of the "familiar warmth" is common to all Armah's positive characters. And yet the interlocking African system of family obligations which is spurned is so integral a part of African life that to turn away from it can indicate the most complete alienation from the social system. Here again we are dealing with attitudes which are out of character but have entered the novel because they express the author's private experience.[3]

Later on he says that:

> *It is a flaw in Armah's design for The Beautiful Ones to make a middle aged clerk who has never left his tribe his presiding consciousness. Given an option between public sanitation and a little more money to help his parents and relatives an African in that position would not have hesitated in making his choice. His worries would have been school fees, the cost of food, rivalries and promotion in the office, not toilets and the menace of his shadow rising to meet him (p. 40). Armah chooses a working class hero in order to enable him to express the exploitation of the African proletariat. But what he expresses is the aesthetic discomfort of an American tourist.*[4]

Allegorist and Symbolist Approach

Critics in this category include those who like Eldred Jones stress the fact that the protagonist of Armah's novel is nothing more than a symbol representing something else. In his review of the book Jones says: "in his anonymity he represents the millions of victims of political organization in Africa."[5] Eustace Palmer too says the man's "anonymity represents everyman, the ordinary Ghanaian citizen."[6] Shatto Arthur Gakwandi describes the protagonist as an allegorical character. He says "the early part of the story has a haunting power which derives from its allegorical character. The people have no names and places remain unspecified. The man becomes the Everyman of folk literature."7

Comparatist Approach

The comparatists, or appropriately, the allusionists are those critics who seek to establish or allude to affinities between the man and the protagonists of European and American novels. Charles Larson points out that:

> *Armah's novels fall into the mainstream of current Western tradition and his protagonists are not very different from a whole line of Western anti-heroes: Julian Scorel, Huckleberry Finn, Stephen Dedalus, or Ralph Ellison's Invisible Man.*[8]

To Lewis Nkosi, *"The Beautiful Ones* is a 'modernist' novel at the extremist reach of consciousness."[9] His idea of modernism includes among other things, what, quoting Alan Swingewood he describes as "isolated man pitted against other men, against society, sometimes engaged in a hopeless quest for his identity or in self-conscious exploration of the act of writing." He goes on the conclude that "the nameless hero of Armah's novel is indeed such an individual."[10]

Limitations of Critical Approaches

Enlightening as these critical observations have been, they betray serious shortcomings which cannot be ignored if a really comprehensive view of characterization in the novel is to be attained. The Prescriptivist standpoint seems to me to pose the greatest impediment to the reader's appreciation of characterization in the novel.

In terms of realities of contemporary Ghana, Obumselu's strictures could be considered valid. *The Beautiful Ones Are Not Yet Born,* however, is not and was never meant as a realistic account of what obtains in Ghana today, or at the time of writing the novel. It is not, and was never meant to be mistaken for a sociological or historical tract. It is a work of art, and, whatever the man's complex and remote derivation from the inner mind of Ayi Kwei Armah, the man must be understood as an *artefact*, not a historical figure. Rather than in terms of what we know to be true either of Armah personally or of contemporary Ghana, the man should be analysed or understood in terms of the literary type and tradition to which he belongs and also in terms of the special literary techniques employed by Armah. Even such an accomplished artist as Chinua Achebe has used extra-ordinary standards to assess Armah. In his article "Africa and her Writers," in *Morning Yet on Creation Day*,[11] he praises *The Beautiful Are Not Yet Born* as a powerful first novel, but upbraids Armah for falsifying the realities of Africa in order to serve foreign artistic gods. He speaks as though his own novels are care histories rather than art works. While flashes of the man's shadowy personality may reflect projective aspects of some social type in Ghana before or since independence, he has meaning far beyond those reflections.

Allegorists and the Comparatists seem to me to share a common difficulty: to stress the protagonist's anonymity and to point out its similarity to what we find in European and American literature does not help the reader very much unless it is followed by a significant discussion either of the man or of those protagonists he resembles, or of both the man and the parallels. Part of my intention in this chapter is to attempt to resolve this problem.

Claim to Anti-Heroism

Charles Larson specifically uses the word "Anti-Hero" with reference to Armah's protagonist, and indeed, several of the essential traits which are traditionally associated with Anti-Heroism are realized in the man's entire mode of existence in the novel. There is first of all his anonymity which as Glicksberg's citation at the beginning of this chapter indicates, has been declared as a characteristic of Anti-Heroism. Secondly, there is the question of his status: he is a mere functionary in the Civil Service, what one critic has described as "a down-at-heel-Morse operator in the employ of the Ghana Railway Corporation in Takoradi."[12] It is not that being a

Morse operator condemns him to an Anti-Heroic existence. After all, Koomson, the most attractive character and the man usually referred to as hero in the book, began life as "a railway man, then a docker. Pulling ropes."[13] But Koomson's lowly point of departure did not stop him from rising to the enviable position of Minister in the administration of the country. The man's Anti-Heroism springs from the fact, as Davis Dunbar McElroy says of Farrell's Studs Lonigan, that "throughout his entire life which was nasty... he does not do a single thing that could conceivably be regarded as having made the world a better place than he found it."[14]

There is also the question of the man's fate in the story. Wylie Sypher says of Samuel Beckett's *The Unnameable* that he is an Anti-Hero because he is:

> *one to whom things bafflingly happen...[a figure who] by a logic of contradiction exists only as evidence of his own insignificance, and whose experience is a way of raising doubts about the reality of his own being.*[15]

Ayi Kwei Armah's protagonist can be described as an Anti-Hero too because throughout the book he exists at the receiving end of all insults, accusations and reproaches from almost everybody else, to whom he never ceases to apologise.

The first time we meet him, he absorbs with uncanny placidity the bus conductor's "you bloodyfucking sonofabitch! Article of no commercial value" (p. 6). It is not exactly his fault that he drools in his sleep. But when the conductor sees his viscous ooze" (p. 7) and insults him, we are told that "shame dwarfed him inside and he hastened to clean it" (. 7).

No sooner he escaped with a good amount of the conductor's spit on his upper lip than he is almost run over by a taxi whose driver calls him "uncircumcised baboon.... Moron of a frog" (p. 10). These labels, says the narrator, may have "expressed only the most banal of truths" (p. 10). In response to these insults we are told that "the man took a step forward in order to be closer to the taxi driver, and said apologetically: 'I wasn't looking. I'm sorry." This apology, we learn, "only seemed to inflame the taxi driver's temper" (p. 10), and before he departs from the man he dishes out an even more vicious insult: "your mother's rotten cunt" (p. 11).

The rhythm of shame and disgrace continues unabated throughout the rest of the book: when he refuses to take a bribe from the timber merchant, he is blamed not only by his wife but also by his only friend, Teacher. The man apologises to Koomson when he visits them and wants to go to the man's toilet: "It isn't a toilet, you see. Just a latrine" (p. 157).

A fourth qualification for Anti-Heroism is the question of loneliness. (Loneliness is a central element in the portrayal of the protagonist in Armah's writings in general. Baako, the protagonist of *Fragments* is completely alienated from the rest of society. Armah emphasizes the theme of isolation in *Why Are We so Blest* by naming the protagonist "Solo") In the moral darkness that enfolded his entire society, the man "was the only thing had dad no way of answering the call of the night" (p. 55). And while he wanders "alone in the world outside," at home, he is condemned to live or bear" the loneliness of the beloved surrounded by the grieving ones" (p. 57). His is the kind of "loneliness that corrodes the heart with despair" (p. 118).

Henry Wadsworth Longfellow once said in his "A Psalm of Life" that:

> *In the world's great field of battle,*
> *In the bivouac of life,*
> *Be not like dumb, driven cattle!*
> *Be a hero in the strife.*[16]

Not so Armah's protagonist who, like the unnamed hole-in-the-corner man of Barbusse's *L'Enfer* (1908) is content or really or really condemned to a peripheral position of an outsider, a passive spectator in the great field of battle for survival which the Ghanaian society in the novel has degenerated into, before his own eyes. In the very first chapter of the book he is described variously as "the watcher" (p. 6), "the sleeper" (p. 6), and "the walker" (p. 10). All these designations have one thing in common - they imply or suggest only a semi-conscious state, or an absence of active participation in what is going on. As a matter of fact, the man never seems to be completely roused from sleep throughout.

The main cornerstones of his character from which a personality structure can be intuited are his meekness, inertia or abulia, an extreme instance of indolence or lethargy prompted by cerebration, reflection and withdrawal when confronted with a situation that calls for immediate and positive action. I use the word "intuited" quite consciously because as it will be seen later on in a consideration Armah's style, the character is not formally drawn but exists only in flashes and vignettes with a minimum of explicitly descriptive details.

Tied to these essential elements of his personality structure, or growing from them and ultimately governed by them, is an affective disposition that is dominated by a detached amusement, gentle irony toward the world around him, the world of the Koomson's which his wife and everybody else worships. When, upon refusing to accept the timber merchant's bribe the latter ask him "so, my friend what do you drink?" Armah tells us that "The man looked levelly at the visitor and gave his answer. 'Water'" (p. 35).

He is an eccentric, a paradox of a personality who displays an even masochistic relish in provoking incidents that inevitably unsettle his already muddle mind. He, for instance, knows that any mention of Koomson to his wife will always draw scorn and taunts from her, directed at him. He is also more aware than anybody else about how his wife would react when she hears that he has not exploited the opportunity to take bribes. But, returning from the office where he has left the contractor high and dry, he volunteers the information, even going into the details (in Koomson's case) of the perfume on Estella's hand: "I shook hands with his [Koomson's] wife, and I can smell her still. Her hand was wet with the stuff" (p. 49). And there is no indication that he is telling this to mock or tease her, for soon after her caustic raillery, he goes out in total desperation to seek advice from Teacher.

He knows that he would not sign the boat deal that Koomson has offered his family, but rather than remain in his own house, he risks the emotional torture of the trip - the beautiful sights and the luxurious apartments, all of which ceaselessly impinge on his consciousness and assail his manhood- only to go right to Koomson's house and say he would not sign. His feeble refusal does not affect the arrangement at all because he does not stop his wife from signing.

Possible his dubious and incomprehensible character results from another characteristic trait of Anti-Heroism which he embodies - pessimism. Anti-Heroes are by definition pessimistic, and the man belongs to this group because a major element in his personality structure is the fact that he looks on life as "a dark tunnel so long that out in front and above there never could be an end to it" (p. 54). He does not even think he has anything to do with his fate because "all I remember these days is that I have been walking along paths chosen for me before I had really decided, and it makes me feel the way I think impotent men feel" (p. 70). Teacher, his alter-ego, virtually speaks for him when he says "when you can see the end of things even in their beginnings, there's no more hope, unless you want to pretend, or forget, or get drunk or something" (p. 71). An Existential Psychological Interpretation of Character Structure.

The central theme of *The Beautiful Ones Are Not Yet Born* is quite simply the inevitability of corruption in Ghana. The novel posits two moralities, or rather two systems of morality, adherence to which determines the overall character design in the book. On the one level, there is the morality, or more appropriately the immorality which places a premium on wealth, individual success and self-aggrandisement, without due regard to the means of acquisition. This is the morality for which Koomson- he reminds one of Achebe's Chief Nanga of *A Man of the People* (1966) and Ralph Adams Cram's Malcom of *The Decadent: Being the Gospel of Inaction* (1893) - is the very incarnation. But it could also be called the morality of the bust conductor, of the timber merchant, of Oyo and her mother. In fact, it is everybody else's morality, except for the man and his friend, Teacher.

The controlling power of money is established very early in the novel when the bus conductor literary worships a cedi that had been given to him:

The cedi lay there on the seat. Among the coins it looked strange, and for a moment the conductor thought it was ridiculous that the paper should be more important than the shiny metal. In the weak light inside the bus he peered closely at the markings on the note. Then a vague but persistent odour forced itself on him and he rolled the cedi up and deliberately, deeply smelled it. He had to smell it again, this time standing up and away from the public leather of the bus seat. But the smell was not his mistake. Fascinated, he breathed it slowly into his lungs. It was a most unexpected smell for something so new to have: it was a very old smell, very strong, and so very rotten that the stench itself of it came with a curious, satisfying pleasure (pp. 3-4)

Those who do not worship it, know the part it plays or ought to play in the execution of one's duties. The timber merchant tells the man, "Everybody prospers from the work he does" (p. 38). And, talking about Koomson's luxurious life, Oyo tells the man that "everybody is swimming towards what he wants" (p. 52). When he tells Teacher that "people want so much," Teacher answers that "they want what they see others enjoying, that's all. It doesn't matter how they get it" (p. 62).

On the second level, there is the morality of the recluse and the impotent, the idle craving for a sense of honesty in an amoral society. It is the morality of Teacher and the man. Theirs is a morality that can only be upheld by inflicting serious inconvenience on oneself and one's family, a morality that can only be upheld at the cost of one's association with other human beings in the society.

Those critics like O.R. Dathorne and Eustache Palmer who have seen in the man a paragon of virtue and rectitude,[17] and have seen the book as an African version of *The Pilgrim's Progress* may have failed either to give sufficient attention to Bunyan's Christian or to the precise nature of the problems that confront the man. In Bunyan's book, the issues are clearly dichotomised - Good pitted against Evil. We are never in doubt as to the side to which Christian belongs. Nor do we imagine that he may never reach the long-sought-for palace. Christian is like Dante's Pilgrim (though the latter is slightly tainted with sin) - he suffers, but he triumphs because he is inherently virtuous and untainted in the strict sense of destructive sin. With Armah's protagonist, nothing is certain, for, as he tells Teacher, "I do not know whether it is envy that makes me hate what I see. I am not even sure I hate it" (p. 109). It is not a simple question of good versus evil. His essential crisis is presented in the form of an existential problem. Evil is the accepted standard and all the elements of his personality are *organized* around his reaction to that central norm. he himself emphasizes the existential nature of the crisis when he says "it is not a choice between life and death, but what kind of death we can bear, in the end" (p. 65). He tells Teacher that there is no salvation in their Ghana.

Furthermore, Armah goes to great lengths to establish the inevitability of destruction for any dissenting elements. As far as arrest for corruption are concerned, he says:

> *the net had been made in the special Ghanaian way that allowed the really big corrupt people to pass through it. A net to catch only the small, dispensable fellows, trying in their anguished blindness to leap and attain the gleam and the comfort the only way these things could be done. And the big ones float free, like all the slogans. End bribery and corruption. Build Socialism (. 180).*

It is against this reality that the man's feeble idealism must be considered, and it is my intention here to show the extent to which the existential psychological construct of unauthentic will may provide a renewed appreciation of the man's personality throughout the novel. As pointed out by Adrian van Kaam and Kathleen Healy in their existential psychological analysis of Angelo from Shakespeare's *Measure for Measure:*"

> *The existential psychologist is always concerned with the observable behaviour of people. Existential psychological constructs, when tested and interpreted by clinical and theoretical psychologists, provide frames of references for data of human behaviour.*

The authors further states that:

Man discloses his true nature by his participation in reality. From an existential point of view, one may say that man actualises himself only when he participates spontaneously in reality as it reveals itself in his own personality and in his daily situation. If he attempts to take a vantage point outside of himself from which he strives to control all that happens in his life, he becomes a compulsive and withdrawn "outsider" ... The man who refuses to be open to reality is more or less neurotic or, at worst, psychotic.[18]

According to this useful paradigm, Armah's protagonist's whole existence in the novel, his "observable behaviour" is unethical, neurotic and even psychotic. Another apt expression which van Kaam and Healy use in their discussion is "an authentic openness to reality" [my emphasis]. They distinguish three psychological characteristics of the authentic person- the authentic person is spontaneously open to reality, he possesses insight, a term which they define as "a perception of reality evoked by a fundamental openness to what-is, and it includes taking a 'stand' toward the uncovered reality." Psychologically, they say, "such understanding is fostered only by commitment to reality without repression. It can never be achieved through a reasoning process alone."[19] The third psychological characteristic of the authentic person is dialogue. They add that:

On the psychological level, the authentic person is engaged in a never-ending dialogue with the reality which he discovers. By means of this dialogue, he listens to the multifarious manifestations of reality and is able to respond in differentiated judgements, choices, and actions. His functional (or secondary) willing is a natural outgrowth of this dialogue with reality.[20]

Even a mere glance at the events in *The Beautiful Ones Are Not Yet Born* would indicate that the man's response to corruption which is the order of the day, is anything but authentic. He does not participate in the reality, he remains an outsider, not as the result of any well- thought out philosophy of life. He does not engage in any dialogue with the corrupt officials. Instead, his life becomes one continuous monologue. Van Kaam and Healy have provided an even more illuminating comment on such a personality in saying that:

> *For the unauthentic person, on the other hand, the functional will becomes dominant over the primordial will. Such a person is in danger of a schizoid split in his personality. Less and less able to respond spontaneously and intuitively to reality, he becomes more and more blind to whatever collectivity governs his functional will.*[21]

This, as illustrations from the text will indicate, accurately describes the man.

The first indication of his inauthenticity towards the reality of his society is provided by his encounter with the timber merchant. When the merchant gives him money, he refuses. The reason for his refusal, we suspect, is that he knows that to accept would be to condone and encourage corruption, the canker which is eating up the body politic of the state. But when the merchant asks him why he refuses to accept the money, the man does not seize the opportunity to give him an honest view of what he sees as the dangers of giving and taking bribes. He does not engage in the type of dialogue which would have made the world a better place, even if he would not suddenly reform the merchant. He simply answers "I don't know" (p. 36). Anybody anxious to abolish corruption would not only have refused the money, but would have talked to the merchant and then, possibly proceeded to render him the service for which he wanted to give money. That way, he would have made it impossible or unnecessary for the merchant to make a second trip and perpetrate corruption by bribing a less honest person as he actually does. But, in his unauthentic way, he does not help the merchant, does not help himself, and does not help the country. Thus, after the merchant has come again and has succeeded in bribing someone else, Armah vividly, though tongue-in-cheek, describes the extent of the man's folly. The clerk who has just received the bribe reflects:

> *...it is so normal, all this, that the point of holding out against it escapes the unsettled mind. Everyone you ask will say the timber merchant is right, the allocations clerk is right, and you [the man] are a fool, and everyone is right the way things are and the way they will continue to be. The foolish ones are those [like the man] who cannot live life the way it is lived by all around them, those who will stand by the flowing river and disapprove of the current (pp. 126-127).*

When he returns home after having refused the bribe from the merchant, one would have expected that in telling his wife about his refusal to take it, he would carefully explain the full moral implications of giving and taking bribes. He doesn't. The picture of him as he listens to his wife berate him is the very apogee of abulia:

> *There was nothing the man could say to his wife, and the woman herself did not look as if she thought there could be anything said to her about what she knew to be so true. But inside the man the confusion and the impotence had swollen into something asking for a way out of confinement, and in the restlessness he rose and went out very quietly through the door, and his wife sat there not even staring after him, not even asking where he was going or when he would come back in the night, or even whether he wanted to return at all to this home. (p. 54)*

This is no way to solve a problem. His wife, prior to this scene, had called him a chichidodo, the bird that "hates excrement with all its soul. But...feeds only on maggots...[which as we know] grow best inside the lavatory" (p. 52). He has done very little to refute this accusation. Instead he has only become confused because the accusation is not exactly false. His departure to see Teacher is prompted more by his anxiety to have his fears about the accusation confirmed than by any desire for positive action. The clue to his rather controversial reaction to corruption is provided by the very Teacher who is supposed to be the answer to every question that has always bothered him: "It may be," Teacher says, "that you cannot tell a lie very well, and you are afraid to steal". (p. 67)

The man's lack of conviction in the rightness of his moral position is depicted in the story of his compatriot Rama Krishna who had done everything to stay away from any corrupting influences. Yet in the end he had died of consumption, "so very young, but already his inside had undergone far more decay than any living body, however old and near death, can expect to see" (p. 56). He is almost sensitively aware of the fact that, despite his unnecessary abstemiousness with regard to corruption, there is no guarantee that he will not suffer the same fate as Krishna.

It is not that he is unaware of what can be done. Rather, he has allowed disenchantment to crush the *élan vital* of his life, and cerebration to replace positive action. "I feel like a criminal," he tells Teacher. "Often these days I find myself thinking of something sudden I could do to redeem myself in their [his loved ones'] eyes. Then I sit down and ask myself what I have done wrong, and there is really nothing' (p. 63). Instead of getting up and acting, he, as his wife would say, "wants to remain on the beach asking the wind,' How….How…How?'" (p. 52).

His life, as a matter of fact, cannot be said to have resolved the existential problem that society has posed. When the story begins, he is a "watcher," and when it closes, he is still a watcher:

> *The passengers leaned back in their seats and the bus took off. The driver must have seen the silent watcher by the roadside, for, as the bus started up the road and out of the town, he smiled and waved to the man. The man watched the bus go all the way up the road then turn and disappear around the town boundary curve. Behind it, the green paint was brightened with an inscription carefully lettered to form an oval shape:*
>
> *The Beautiful Ones Are Not Yet Born (p. 214).*

Characterization Techniques: An Anatomy of Armah's Style

The man is an extremely complex character, because Armah employs a whole array of complicated characterizing techniques which serve to intensify his complexity. According to Roman Jakobson, every work possesses a "dominant." This he defines as:

> *the element which specifies a given variety of language and dominates the entire structure and thus acts as its mandatory and inalienable constituent dominating all the remaining elements and exerting direct influence upon them.*[22]

In so far as character portrayal is concerned, the "dominant" technique employed by Armah borders on impressionism. This technique, as C. Hugh Holman has pointed out:

> *is a highly personal manner of writing in which the author presents characters or scenes or moods as they appear to his individual temperament at a precise moment and from a particular vantage point rather than as they are in actuality…The literary impressionist holds that…the fleeting impression of a moment is more significant artistically than a photographic presentation of cold fact. The object of the impressionist, then, is not to present his material as it is to the objective observer but as it is seen or felt to be by himself in a single passing moment. He employs highly selective details, the "brush strokes" of sense-data that can suggest the impression made upon him or upon some character in the story.*[23]

In the opinion of the editors of the *Princeton Encyclopaedia of Poetry and Poetics;*

> *the art of the impressionist defies all rational explanation. It scorns logical progression and relies on the unpredictable movement which is effected by mental associations…, outlines are blurred, forms dissolved and images stillborn. Instead of naming the thing he is concerned with, the impressionist describes the effect which it produces. As the observer disappears, the organs of sense perception are confused (synaesthesia).*[24]

Inadvertently, and in a purely negative context, Ben Obumselu has drawn attention to this aspect of Armah's style. In the article already mentioned in the early part of this chapter - "Marx, Politics and the African novel," he judges and dismisses Armah as a poor caricaturist. Talking about one of Armah's most unforgettable characters, the timber merchant, he says:

> *In the pages which follow Armah is involved in an amusing game of denying that there is a man out there to see ad relate to. The ravenous teeth, the corrupt belly, the tasselled feet of the dandified traditional exploiter are there, but no person. The mode is caricature, but caricature in which the artist is determined that the exaggerated strokes will not add up to any kind of identity. Armah's description of persons pays attention to the social trappings, cars, gowns, perfumes, but never to character or to that obscure intuition of it we receive, or think we do, from people's faces.*[25]

What Obumselu sees as a flaw is, in fact, Armah's *forte*, when considered against critical judgments concerning contemporary approaches to the portrayal of character in the Western novel. Although not stressed by Nkosi in that important chapter of his *Tasks and Masks* dedicated to modernism in African fiction, modernism does not stop at the depiction of a human condition. It is most emphatically revealed in the problematic structure of character. If taken in earnest, Virginia Woolf, herself a practitioner of impressionistic techniques, could be said to have faltered by being too accurate when she declared categorically that "In or about December, 1910 human character changed."[26] But she did indicate the essential truth - that characterization as practised by the nineteenth-century masters -George Eliot, Flaubert, Tolstoy and Hardy, (whose techniques Obumselu most probably had in mind in his reading of Armah), became a thing of the past at the turn of the century.

As Alfred Kazin says in his "The Alone Generation: a Comment on the Fiction of the Fifties," "the kind of person who in the nineteenth century novel was a 'character' now regards himself as a 'problem'".[27] This point has been expressed even more forcefully by

Seymour Chatman in his *Story and Discourse: Narrative Structure in Fiction and Film*. There he says about the modern novel to which tradition *The Beautiful Ones* belongs, that in it:

> Not only are the traits more numerous, but they tend not to "add up," or more germanely, "break down," that is, reduce to any single aspect or pattern. They cannot be discovered by ramifying dichotomies; forcing the issue only destroys the uniqueness of characters' identities. What gives the modern fictional character the particular kind of illusion acceptable to modern taste in his personality.[28]

Armah's techniques of characterization in *The Beautiful Ones* largely operate therefore along the lines prescribed by the modern critics. As we watch the development or rather the creation of each of the central characters, Armah presents us with flash shots of somewhat disconnected actions, mannerisms or parts of the body rather than any really steady process of continuous and progressive development. The entire scene in which we meet Koomson or are made aware of his presence for the first time, adumbrates in a small way the larger pattern of characterization employed by Armah in the rest of the novel:

> *The driver steps out and swings the door shut with the satisfied thud of newness. The wire voice within seems to wail something more, and from the back of the limousine a man dressed in a black suit comes out and makes straight for a little covered box with bread in it.......*
>
> *"I have bought some already." The voice of the suited man had something unexpected about it, like a fisherman's voice with the sand and salt hoarsening it forcing itself into unaccustomed English rhythms.....*
>
> *Inside the car the pointed female voice springs an coils around, complaining of fridges too full to contain anything more and too much bread already bought. Outside, the seller sweetens her tones.........*
>
> *The car door opens and the suited man emerges and strides slowly toward the praise-singing seller. The sharp voice inside the car makes one more sound of impatience, then subsides, waiting. The suit stops in front of the seller, and the voice that comes out of it is playful, patronizing.......*

> *The suited man looks around him. Even in the faint light his smile is easy to see. It forms a strange pattern of pale light with the material of his shirt, which in the space between the darkness of his suit seems designed to point down somewhere between the invisible thighs..........*
>
> *"Hell-low," says the smile to the invisible man of the shadows," "what are you doing here" I almost didn't see you."*
>
> *"Going home from work. At first I wasn't sure." A pale cuff flashes, and the suited man looks at his watch and just murmurs something to himself, very low. "By the way," he says, "we'll be over to see you soon, Estie and myself" (pp. 43-44).*

At this juncture, the reader begins to wonder who the suited man might be. But he assumes that the invisible man of the shadows is the protagonist himself. No notion of character is definite under the circumstances because all that is presented is an assemblage of disjointed and almost inconsequential impressions of voice, cuffs, invisible thighs, the suit, smiles, fridges too full to contain anything more, and the like. Armah here is deliberately playing games with the reader's sensibilities, making him not just a passive receiver of sense-data but also a participant in the creative process out of which the semblance of character emerges. Just as we find in the Anti-heroes in Beckett's novels and especially those of Alain Robbe-Grillet, we see no entities, but merely fragmentary impressions of parts of the whole, which the reader is called upon to piece together.

It is no easy task for the reader because the fragments do not, and are not supposed, within such a literary technique, to render the characters fully alive or realistically. Armah is primarily concerned with the associations that a given personality conjures up - wealth, good living, prominence, praise-singing, in the case of the suited man, and obscurity, invisibility, poverty, in the case of the man - rather than with the concrete realization of the realities of individual characters.

On a larger scale, the same approach has been followed in the depiction of the protagonist, and subsumed under this broad spectrum of impressionism are a series of other interrelated devices which serve, together or separately, to emphasize and intensify those factors which have already been isolated as elements of Anti-Heroism in the depiction of the man. These include the effective use of imagery and symbolism, and the manipulation of point of view.

The man's anonymity was cited as a major element in his make-up as an Anti-Hero. Many of the techniques which Armah employs are designed to emphasize that point. In the first place, there is the fact of concealment. In his *Circles Without Centre: Paths to the Discovery and Creation of Self in Modern Literature*, Enrico Garzilli has made a point about names which can throw some light on our appreciation of Armah's technique. He asserts that the use of a person's name calls the person into being and makes him present. He adds:

> *Whatever has been fixed by a name, henceforth is not only real, but is Reality. The potential between "symbol" and "meaning" is resolved; in place of a more or less adequate "expression" we find a relation of identity, if complete congruence between "image" and "object", between the name and the thing.*[29]

In his *Language and Myth*, Ernst Cassirer also stresses the point. He says:

> *The essential identity between the word and what it denotes becomes even more patently evident if we look at it not from the adjective standpoint, but from a subjective angle. For even a person's ego, his very self and personality, is indissolubly linked, in mythic thinking, with his name. Here the name is never a mere symbol, but is part of the personal property of its bearer; property which must be carefully protected, and the use of which is exclusively and jealously reserved to him.*[30]

From these two arguments then, it is obvious that the absence of a name symbolically reflects the man's sense of unreality and his lack of an "essential identity". By labelling his protagonist "the man," "the watcher," "the giver," or "the walker," Armah very effectively defines the character's personality at the same time that he conceals it.

Armah thus withdraws the man from the actions of the scenes which generally constitute the story, making of him a spectator rather than a spectacle, thereby transferring attention to the objects being watched. This partly explains the almost gothic prevalence of darkness and shade in the novel, and the virtually crepuscular life that the man leads: when the book opens it is not yet day; the timber merchant comes to meet him at night; it is twilight when he meets Koomson, and when he decides to take his complaint to Teacher it is already dark outside. Thus, while darkness may symbolize, as many critics have pointed out, the depth of immorality of the society of the novel, it is even more effective as a means of characterization. By a technical *tour de force,* Armah employs it to mask character while at the same time emphasizing passivity, separation, non-recognition or inconspicuity in terms of positive achievement in society. In the scene just quoted above, Armah goes out of his way to actually call the man, "the invisible man of the shadows" (p. 44). The effectiveness of this piece of direct characterization lies in the fact that it reinforces at the literal level what Armah has all along treated and will long afterwards portray mainly at the symbolic level.

Armah also emphasizes the man's anonymity by employing what Chatman calls the "scatter" in the depiction of personality. This is directly related to point of view. Armah does not appear tied to any one angle of vision in the depiction of his protagonist. His point of view is generally omniscient, which permits him to talk about the character directly as in the case just quoted, or indirectly, using the opinions of others, as when his wife tells him that "You are the chichidodo itself" (p. 52). Sometimes he allows the man to characterize himself, as when he confesses that he feels "the way I think impotent men feel" (p. 70).

Under normal or traditional circumstances, the omniscient point of view has the merit of providing the writer with a more comprehensive view of character and situation. But in Armah's case, the shift from direct to indirect characterization does not produce a whole because the character is empty at the centre. What we see - the various impressions of him - is precisely what we get, a scattered and fragmented image. The man's life is narrated in jagged and discontinuous episodes from the past. We are given separate moments of personal history, but they do not give us any sense of continuity in his psychic life, as we have in the case of Ngugi's Mugo in *A Grain of Wheat,* whose story is presented in a far more involved fashion.

Usually, the scenes in which the man appears involve only a few evocative details that in a way suggest the essential quality of the concealed whole. In the opening scene in the bus we are not told the kind of trousers or shoes he is wearing. All we see is spittle crawling out of his mouth, and then the lining of his pocket along with the mass of used bus-tickets. Armah's style in this and other scenes approximates a distortion of actuality in the sense that he focuses only on almost inconsequential and usually nauseating details unduly abstracted from the continuum or totality of the human being and his surroundings. To this extent, it has to be stressed that the flashes of personality which we are shown, or the reminiscences in which the protagonist indulges are designed to reveal his repulsiveness, his weakness, his sense of isolation and frustration.

Symbolism and impressionism go hand-in-hand. In the words of Ruth Moser in her *L'Impressionisme français* (1951), "en literature, le symbolism et l'impressionisme se servent, en partie, des mêmes formes d'expression."[31] This explains why the word symbolism has figured frequently in the description of Armah's style up to now. But it has to be pointed out here that symbolism is one of the central techniques which Armah employs to embody his meaning. This question has been treated by critics so often that one only needs here to point out the extent to which it affects his depiction of the man as an Anti-Hero. In this respect, special mention has to be made of filth, the chichidodo and Rama Krishna.

If, as it has been generally accepted, filth serves symbolically to articulate Armah's revulsion against corruption,[32] then it could also be said to serve to articulate revulsion against the way of life the man leads in the book. From the first chapter, Armah makes his physical state virtually conterminous with the decaying bus. Then, as though the external world is a mere objectification of his own inner rottenness, he is the only one who is obsessively concerned with physical decay. He is the only one who is sensitively aware of the circles of decay and rejuvenation through which the banister immediately outside his office has passed; he is the one who is fascinated by the excrement on the walls in the public latrine. Then, as though this were not enough, he tells us the story of his old friend, Rama Krishna, whose life is relevant to him only in terms of the rottenness it evokes. Then, apparently suggestive of the fact that this is where he truly belongs, Armah makes him follow the fleeing Koomson through a latrine hole without considering any other possibility of following Koomson.

The story of or rather the image of the chichidodo too, apt as it is in describing the man's hypocrisy and self-contradictory attitude towards life, centres around excrement and maggots. What Armah has achieved here is to present us with a double vision for interpreting the same symbol: from the point of view of the reader, filth equals corruption and therefore anybody associated with filth as the man is, should be despised. Then at the second level, the level of the characters within the text, anybody who fails to dance to the tune of national music, is filthy, rotten inside, even if he hides it.

It is necessary in a study of this nature to indicate however briefly, the extent to which Armah's protagonist resembles some more widely known Anti-Heroic protagonists. The character that comes readily to mind is Meursault of Albert Camus's *L'Etranger*. The man never murders anybody like his prototype, but he follows a lifestyle that is similar to Meursault's: they are both office clerks. But even more important than this, both men display a disturbing sense of apathy. Camus says in the *avant-propos* of the text that

> *Je voulais dire seulement que le héros du livre est condamné parce qu'il ne joue pas le jeu. En ce sens, il est étranger à la société où il vit, il erre, en marge, dans les faubourgs de la vie privée, solitaire, sensuelle.*[33]

Although the fictive world of Meursault differs radically from that of the man, and although it has been impossible to get Armah to say a word on his intentions in any of his writings, it is clear that the man's suffering results from a similar rejection of society ad his inability or unwillingness to play the game, to give lip service to those things which his society prizes most. Like Meursault, the man declines almost by instinct, to make any commitment to society's ideals, despite the fact that he sees the direct effects of his ruthless honesty on those who count on him.

It can therefore be briefly summarised that in *The Beautiful Ones Are Not Yet Born* Armah gives us a problematic but nevertheless very fascinating portrait of an Anti-Hero in the modernist tradition; a portrait so rich that it offers rewarding efforts at almost every level of interpretation.

Notes

[1] *Literature and Society* (The Hague: Martinus Nijhoff, 1972), p. 41.

[2] This classification is merely a convenient framework to enable me to isolate the elements in the various critical studies. In actual fact the critics do not divide rigidly into such groups, and several critics will be seen to embody all these characteristics.

[3] *The Twentieth Century Studies* n. 10 (December 1973), pp. 114-115.

[4] Ibid., p. 116.

[5] *ALT* no. 3 (1969), p. 55.

[6] *An Introduction to the African novel*, p. 131.

[7] *The Novel and Contemporary Experience in Africa* (London: Heinemann, 1977), p. 89.

[8] *The Emergence of African Fiction* op. cit., p. 258.

[9] *Tasks and Masks*, op. cit., p. 65. The quotation is taken from Laurenson and Swingewood's *The Sociology of Literature* (London: MacGibbon & Kee, 1971), p. 214.

[10] *Tasks and Masks*, p. 65.

[11] (London: Heinemann 1975).

[12] Robert Fraser, *The Novels of Ayi Kwei Armah: A Study in Polemical Fiction* (London: Heinemann, 1979), p. 16.

[13] Ayi Kwei Armah, *The Beautiful Ones Are Not Yet Born* (London: Heinemann 1968), p. 104. All further quotations are from this edition. The title is shortened for convenience to simply *The*

Beautiful Ones, and page numbers from which references are made are indicated after each quote.

[14]*Existentialism and Modern Literature: An Essay in Existential Criticism* (New York: Greenwood Press, 1968), p. 25

[15]*Loss of the Self in Modern Literature and Art* (New York: Vintage Books, 1962), p. 148.

[16]*Longfellow: Poetical Works* (London: Frederick Warne & Co., 1934), p. 9.

[17]*African Literature in the Twentieth Century* (London: Heinemann, 1974), p. 105. Palmer describes him as "a man of unquestioned integrity," in his *An Introduction to the African Novel,* p. 131.

[18]*The Demon and the Dove: Personality and Growth through Literature* (Louvain: Duquesne Univ. Press, 1967), pp. 147-148. This aspect of the present chapter was greatly inspired by some of the parameters the two authors applied in their study of Angelo.

[19]Ibid., p. 149.

[20]Ibid., pp. 149-150.

[21]"The Dominant," in *Readings in Russian Poetics: Formalist and Structuralist Views,* eds. Ladislav Matejka and Krystyna Pomorska (Cambridge Mass: The MT Press, 1971), p. 82.

[11]*A Handbook to Literature* (Indianapolis: The Odyssey Press, 1975), pp. 268-269.

[24]Alex Preminger et al (Princeton, N.J.: Princeton Univ. Press, 1974), p. 381.

[25]*Twentieth Century Studies,* p. 115.

[26]"Mr. Bennett and Mrs. Brown," in *Collected Essays* vol. I (London: Hogarth Press, 1966), p. 320.

[12]*Contemporaries* (New York: Brown & Co., 1959), p. 115.

[13](Ithaca: Cornell Univ. Press, 1978), p. 112.

[14](Cambridge Mass: Harvard Univ. Press, 1972).

[15](New York: Dover, 1946), pp. 49-50.

[16]In *Encyclopaedia of Poetry and Poetics,* op. cit., p. 381.

[17]Eustace Palmer, *An Introduction to the African Novel,* p. 134.

[33](London: Methuen, 1958), p. 1.

Chapter Four

Ahouna (Olympe Bhêly-Quénum's *Un Piège Sans Fin*, 1960)

Encore plus affaibli, plus passif, l'antihéros apparaît dans la littérature du XXe siècle comme une victime; proie d'une machine sociale au mécanisme étrange, voire incompréhensible..., [l'homme qui] ne connaît que misère et solitude; [chez qui] l'angoisse est le lot..., l'homme de l'absurde et de la dérision errant lamentablement dans le labyrinthe d'un univers hostile ou larvaire. L'un des pauvres chômes aux quelles toute insertion semble refusée, moins à cause des conditions économiques peut-être que parce que dans la grisaille de la vie quotidienne, aucune aventure n'exalte, et que tout y est nivelé.

(Aziza and Oliviéri)[1]

Plot Summary

Un Piège sans fin, the first novel of this Dahomean writer, is the struggle of a single individual, Ahouna, against an endless stretch of snares, family misfortunes and a cruel fate that culminates in his own painful death.

The novel begins with a brief and idyllic picture of pastoral life which is almost immediately shattered by the introduction of a chain of disasters. First a plague of cholera attacks and kills the cattle of Bakari, Ahouna's father. The family has hardly gotten over this calamity when a swarm of locusts arrives and wipes out the family crops. Undaunted, Bakari manages to rebuild his source of livelihood and almost succeeds when fate strikes again: he is suddenly summoned by the French colonial administrator to take part in forced labour. Bakari, always a proud man, refuses on the grounds that he is rich enough to engage somebody else to work in his place, a common practice at the time. The district commandant will not compromise and goes on to subject Bakari to such tortures and degradations that Bakari stabs himself to death in the view of people who include his fifteen year old son, Ahouna.

With Bakari's death, Séitou, Ahouna's run-away sister returns to their home with her second husband, Camara, who soon takes over the responsibilities of the head of the family. Ahouna continues, visibly unperturbed by his father's cruel end, to tend their flock, to the accompaniment of music from his *"Kpété"* or read-flute. On one occasion in the field his melodious music draws from beyond the neighbouring mountains, Anatou, destined to be both his wife and his destroyer.

Ahouna and Anatou eventually get married after all the necessary customary rites have been performed, and for fifteen years as he himself puts it, "la vie était agreeable."[2] Then all of a sudden, when their fourth child is only nine months old we get the first major indication that all has not been well with them: Anatou is seized with a jealousy so intense and followed by a hatred so fierce and uncompromising that the usually cool and unexcitable Ahouna is forced to flee his home.

In the deep southern territories into which he escapes he comes, in a state of mind dithering towards total collapse, across a window, Kinhou; with no apparent provocation or motivation he murders her. From this point he becomes a wanted man, and during his flight from the vengeful anger of the family of his victim, Ahouna encounters M. Houénou, the archaeologist who gives him asylum and to whom he tells the story of the events which comprise the first part of the book.

Ahouna is finally caught ad in a scene loaded with obvious Christological implications he is paraded through the streets of Ganne with a cross on his shoulder before being thrown into jail. His troubles, though, are far from over: while awaiting trial he undergoes more and more tortures, particularly in the quarry where prisoners in his category are sent to work. Meanwhile, a relative of the deceased woman has succeeded as part of a plan of vengeance to get himself imprisoned in Ahouna's camp. There he proceeds to encourage Ahouna to escape: Ahouna falls into his trap and as they escape he is ambushed in the forest and burnt alive.

State of Criticism

One of the most salient characteristics of *Un Piège sans fin* is the deliberateness with which the author seems to have stamped the text with philosophical speculations and mythopoeic echoes. Commencing with the two quotations from Thomas à Kempis and Baudelaire with which he prefaces the story, we are plunged over and over again into a world of existentialist anguish, of absurdity, of being and nothingness.

The pervasiveness of this philosophical content has not gone unnoticed and, for better or for worse, it has been the chief determinant of the direction that criticism of the novel has taken. One of the earliest critics to take Bhêly-Quénum to task on that account was Yves Guermond who said of the author's style that "cela crée l'impression qu'il s'agit de façons de penser européennes, exprimées par des personages africaines."[3]

But far from condemning the author, a majority of the critics have devoted considerable (one might even say, far too much) attention to the discovery and establishment of thematic and mythopoeic correspondences between the novel and those works in other literature with which it invites comparison. Roger Mercier, Monique and Simon Battestini have come up with a study that could very conveniently be regarded as an authoritative interpretation of the novel, and which clearly illustrates the general trend of criticism on the book. A central achievement of their study lies in the extent to which the authors have succeeded in isolating the major themes which Bhêly-Quénum develops in the novel: "le bonheur," "La jalousie," "L'amour," "L'adultére," "L'amitié," "L'amitié," "L'angoisse," "L'horreur," "L'humeur," "Le suicide," "L'antinomie colonisateur-colonisé," "L'univers clos," "Le destin, la mort, le sens du cosmique," "Psychologie de la foule et vengeance."[4]

To Bhêly-Quénum's chagrin - he had declared that his novel was authentically African - this trio of collaborating critics went on to specify what they considered to be the author's obvious indebtedness to Sartre, Camus, Baudelaire and Dostoevsky. They further indicated a definite affinity between the novel and the Orpheus and Orestes myth of Greek literature and also such modern works as Samuel Beckett's *Endgame* and Jean Cau's *La Pitié de Dieu.*

The contributions of these critics to an appreciation of the extent to which the African writer is capable of subjecting local material is immense. But for studies of the nature represented by these critics to be finally rewarding, there needs to be a reduction of emphasis on the philosophical content and its transference to the less adequately handled problem of character analysis. Bhêly-Quénum's injunction that he had written an apolitical novel, was made in earnest and not to divert attention to what critics have come to regard as the main subject of the book. He pointed out that at the centre of the novel lay a "chute perpétuelle inhérente à la condition humaine," and warned that "quiconque lira *Un Piège sans fin* sans tenir compte du pauvre Ahouna et des gens parmi lesquels il vivait à Kiniba, ne me comprendra pas."[7] This firm caution has often been disregarded, perhaps because for some unknown reason, subsequent editions of the book did not carry it. Consequently, the essence of his novelistic intent has been frequently ignored. The human element has been consistently downplayed and Ahouna, the very heart of the novel, has come to be regarded as a mere excuse for the ideas that float and reverberate everywhere in the text.

François Salien, for example, never saw the book as a novel. He says:

> *Ce récit…sans fin - manifestement imprégné de l'influence de Camus et de son angoisse existentielle - n'a sans doute jamais prétendu, sérieusement (malgré l'indication), être un roman. Ce serait plutôt un essai destiné à illustrer la thèse de la "viduité" de l'existence comme, l'écrit malencontreusement Olympe Bhêly-Quénum (p. 114-142) qui veut évidemment dire le vide de l'existence.*[8]

This I think is to push the philosophical content too far. *Un Piège sans fin,* most critics will agree, is a novel in the best sense of the word, and not a dramatized treatise on existentialist terminology. Ahouna is a flesh and blood character, "un homme," Bhêly-Quénum has said, "dont l'image me hantait depuis plus de vingt ans."[9] He possesses an inner life capable of being reconstructed both at the conscious and unconscious levels, and the crux of his personality lies not in the philosophies he mouths but in the problems that beset that inner life. It is here too rather than in any superimposed or underlying philosophical doctrines that is to be found the key to the mysteries surrounding his conduct, his victimization, in short, his Anti-Heroism. Abdoulaye Sadji may have struck the right chord to Ahouna's inner world when he said that:

Avec ce roman, nous entrons véritablement dans le monde noir avec ses terreurs et ses passions, son tragique et sa farce et cette confusion des certaines sur un plan supérieur, de sorte que les préoccupations contemporaines nous semblent bien provisoires.[10]

To enter "veritablement" into the passions and terrors calls for an unearthing of those intra-psychic contingencies which express the passions and terrors. This calls for a psychoanalytic interpretation of Ahouna's character. Such an approach would reveal that he is so much an Anti-Hero because his problems at the physical and conscious level are aggravated by certain unconscious psychic impulses and inhibitions.

Ahouna's Personality Structure and Claim to Anti-Heroism

If, as it stands, victimization is a major characteristic of Anti-Heroism, then Ahouna is an Anti-Hero *par excellence.* The absence of heroism in his make-up was first pointed out by Bhêly-Quénum himself when he remarked in his preface that "je voyais en lui [Ahouna] un paragon de l'effort infini - mais *sans héroisme*" (my emphasis).[11]

In the very first sentence in the novel the narrator confronts us with the soul-destroying picture of a man who appears to have been permanently placed at the receiving end of society's misfortunes and cruelties. He says of the protagonist that:

> *C'était un noir de taille moyenne, à la peau ternie et desséchée par la misère. Chétif, le corps squelettique, la tête osseuse, il avait un visage d'enfant rachitique qu'allongeait une petite barbe sale, poussiéreuse, humide de bave et de sueur (p. 10).*

This is a picture of defeat, of man at his most Anti-Heroic state. If this is how Ahouna looks at the end of the journey, the various stages through which he has passed to arrive at this state of misery place him squarely in the anti-Heroic mould, from the standpoint of Aziza, Oliviéri and Sctrick. As indicated in the citation from their definition of the concept, they hold that "l'antihéros apparaît dans la littérature du XXe siècle comme une victime…; [l'homme qui] ne connait que misère et solitude; [chez qui] l'angoisse est le lot." By making him a prey as well as a victim of misery, solitude and anxiety, Bhêly-Quénum makes Ahouna part of that literary tradition.

Even without going into the nature of his suffering, Ahouna's Anti-Heroism is announced by the occurrence on several occasions of the label of "victim" with reference to him. For example, at the fateful moment of the accusation of infidelity from his wife which triggers off the disintegration both of his marriage and his personality, his wife talks of him as someone who is prone to "poser victime devant tout le monde" (p. 117). He himself admits: "je suis une victime" (p. 177). Other insistences of words related to Anti-Heroism include "Et ce fut la misère dans toute sa puissance" (p. 36), "inutilement armé" (p. 36), "des cris de douleur" (p. 52), "angoissés" (p. 54), "absurdité de ma personnalité" (p. 115), "un rien qui s'anime dans l'espace" (p. 114).

The pattern of his anti-Heroic existence is set very early in the second chapter of the novel where we are given a catalogue of disasters: "un matin du début de la saison des moissons, mon père alla dans l'étable et y vit deux vache mortes" (p. 29); "un mois après le ravage cholérique vint le jour des moissons" (p. 34). But instead of the harvest, the entire village is invaded by locusts: "Des criquets, il y en avait partout, le champ en était couvert, ils rampaient, trottaient, sautaient d'épis en épis" (p. 36). With the cattle dying, and the harvest destroyed by locusts, Ahouna's father's misfortunes (and his by implication) could have been mitigated if his creditors were in a viable position. Ahouana tells us that "mes parents toujours trop sociables, en avaient prêté à des amis qui, eux aussi complètement ruinés, étaient, partant, incapables de rembourser leurs dettes" (p. 36). From this point onward, the path followed by the rest of his life is as ominous as the route he follows to Founkilla after the locust invasion. He says of the route that it was "infinie, déserte et fort malaisée" (p. 37). It is into this pattern of unrelieved misery that his father's death and his marriage problems and eventual death must be placed if we are to appreciate his Anti-Heroic existence in the novel.

The importance of anxiety in Bhêly-Quénum's conception and creation of Ahouna as an Anti-Hero has been stressed by Mme. Monique Battestini. In the section entitled "L'Angoisse" in the work which she co-edited, we are told with respect to the fate of the protagonist that:

> *Le bonheur menace est une source de malaise qui ne tarde pas à s'alimenter partout pour atteindre des proportions terrifiantes. L'angoisse grandira à mesure que la colère des dieux se fera plus implacable. Le problème du Mal, la constation de l'absurdité de l'existence, de même que la conscience de l'irrémédiable, amènent le héros jusqu'aux confines de l'épouvante. De traquenard en traquenard, il se sent condamnés sans qu'il lui soit possible de rien faire contre la condamnation. Sa grande Peur ne peut trouver d'issue que dans la mort qu'il attend non avec l'indifférence du sage, mais avec la souffrance de la victime choisie en raison même de son innocence.*[12]

Then in her article "L'Angoisse chez les romanciers africaine," she elaborates on the main points of the arguments mentioned here. In that article she says "Ahouna souffre de toutes ces vies écrasées pour rien," and goes on to list several kinds of anxiety which Ahouna undergoes. In particular, she says: "Dans le cas 'Ahouna déjà condamné, l'amour d'Anatou n'est qu'un masque sinister, le négatif de la jalousie dévastatrice de son demon."[13]

Self-abasement has often been pointed out as a mark of Anti-Heroism. Ferdinand Oyono's Toundi emphasized his inclusion in the ranks of Anti-Heroes by admitting that he was nothing but "la chose qui obéit," and that he was "le chien du roi" as well as "le roi des chiens."[14] Ahouna also emphasizes his own Anti-Heroic status by looking at himself as:

> *Un rien qui s'anime dans l'espace et le temps des qu'il fait chaud, et qui doit, ridiculement, disparaître dans le néant sans que personne s'en soucie (p. 114)*

In assuming such a defeatist attitude to life's problems, reminds us very strongly of Armah's protagonist, "the man." In existential psychological terms, the principal affective dispositions of his personality are a neurotic and even psychotic refusal to be open to reality. Instead of confronting his destiny openly he chooses to resign himself to it and prefers as he himself boasts, to "balancer dans le vide, de me cogner contre les parois du Kinibaya, pareil à un caillou ricochant à la surface du lac ou il a été jeté, puis de me tomber mort là-bas parmi les bêtes" (p. 115).[15] He therefore fails to lead an authentic existence because, like Armah's protagonist, he does not participate spontaneously in reality as it reveals itself in his own personality and in his daily situation.

Because the book is not a dramatized treatise but a novel, it has to be pointed out that Ahouna's affective dispositions grow out of or are inextricably woven into the texture of the plot and can be shown to be a result of the interplay between three apparently separate but actually interrelated crises that shape and determine his destiny:

a) The death of his father and Ahouna's lack of emotion toward the loss;

b) The carrying over to his married life of the repressed grief and his subsequent inability to respond spontaneously to his wife's passion;

c) His murder of Kinhou which comes as the result of an outburst of frustration and accumulated repressed impulses.

Talking about the application of psychological theories to the interpretation of character in narratives, Uri Margolin said in his very enlightening article "Characterization in Narrative," that "all character inferences are hypothetical or probabilistic in nature and are modalised, to read 'if p then probably/possibly/unlikely q with respect to a given sent of substantive rules of psychological inference."[15] Applying such an analytic model to the interpretation of Ahouna's behaviour in the novel, the argument is as follows: a certain type of relationship calls for grief at the loss of one party, and anybody who represses the emotion makes himself a potential victim of psychotic or psychopathological problems. Such problems could be particularly serious if the individual repressing the emotions is simultaneously predisposed to other inhibitions. They can be much worse if such a man is attached to a woman whose psychological make-up is not designed to help protect the emotions from exploding with disastrous consequences for both that individual and society at large. From the perspective of these facts, we may conjecture that Ahouna is earmarked for eventual destruction from the moment of his father's death.

Bereavement and Personality Development

Of all the social ruptures that could possibly have a serious impact on the psychological development of a child's future personality structure, the death of a parent ranks above desertion, separation and divorce as the most decisive. In their article "Childhood Bereavement and Behaviour Disorders: A Critical Review," Erick Markusen and Robert Fulton have established that "a causal relationship exists between childhood bereavement and later disorders. The bereaved individual," they have said, "must face not only a personal loss, but also a disruptive vacancy in his social system."[17] Thus, whether Arouna admits it or not, and whether critics are aware of it or not, from the moment of his father's death,

Ahouna is going through a crisis situation for which his subsequent actions can be viewed as expressions of defence mechanisms.

In a crucial study, "Symptomatology and the Management of Acute Grief," Erich Lindemann distinguishes two main responses to grief in the life of an individual: the normal and the morbid responses. Normal grief, he says, entails five responses which include somatic distress, preoccupation with the image of the deceased, guilt, hostile reactions and loss of patterns of conduct.[18] One of the big obstacles to what he calls the *grief work* "seems to be the fact that many patients try to avoid the intense distress connected with grief experience and try to avoid the expression of emotion necessary for it."[19] This is what gives rise to what he called "morbid grief reactions" or distortions of normal grief. Central to the abnormal response is the delayed reaction or postponement - where the reaction to the loss is repressed until some future event provokes it to surface.[20]

The idea here is not to test the accuracy of Bhêly-Quénum in depicting psychological states according to the findings of clinical psychology, or to investigate similarities between the art of Bhêly-Quénum and the findings of psychologists. Rather, it is my contention that the plot of the novel and the destiny of Ahouna exhibit a certain construct of repression which in clinical literature as well as in existential psychological thinking, is deemed ineffective in dealing with stress, and invites later problems. That is why even in the very diluted form to which I have reduced Lindermann's theory, that theory still offers some psychological framework for analysing the ways in which Ahouna's personality has been depicted in *Un Piège sans fin*. In so far as normal and abnormal grief reactions go, Mariatou, Ahouna's mother's attitude is the more remarkable. Ahouna's lengthy description of her in her grieving mood needs to be quoted in full because it is in her unpretentiousness or spontaneity of response to her husband's death that we could trace the secret as to why she remains the most integrated and psychologically stable character in the entire narrative. Ahouna says:

> *La mort de mon père l'avait terriblement défigurée. Elle, grande, souple, avec les muscles longs, portant à peine son âge, mais avant tout belle, était devenue une femme décharnée, avec les pommettes saillantes et les yeux fuyants; elle n'était plus droite et fière, mais voûtée et craintive. Des rides profondes commençaient à déformer la peau de son front d'ordinaire tendue et ce front était comète désormais contraint à toujours regarder la terre. Ses cheveux de veuve, dénoués et négligés, lui donnaient un air de vieille folle ou de mendiante. Mariatou ne sourtait, plus, elle ne mangeait guère. Si, de son mieux, elle s'occupait encore du ménage, c'était bien par amour pour moi. Elle eût été seule qu'elle se laissait mourir dans les désordres semé autour d'elle et en elle par la mort de mon père huit mois plus tôt. Elle passait des journées entières, assisse sur un tabouret, les jambes serrées et replies, les coudes sur les cuisses, les bras, croisés sur la poitrine et les mains cramponnées aux épaules, à verser des flots de larmes en fredonnant des mirologues (p. 55-56).*

The effectiveness of this passage lies not so much in the accuracy with which Bhêly-Quénum depicts a grieving African widow, or how closely his depiction of the woman conforms to what Freud and his followers have often described as the normal grief syndrome,[21] but in the way it is made to contrast with Ahouna's attitude toward the same loss.

Some preliminary considerations must be addressed before we decide on the complicated nature of Ahouna's response. Prior to his father's death, the relationship between the two was one of love and mutual respect. In Freudian psychological terms, the Oedipus complex could be said to have dissolved in the best possible manner, leaving the child emotionally attached to the mother and yet respectful of his father whom he acknowledged as his ego-ideal. There is not here the bitterness and desire to kill the father which we encountered in *Une Vie de boy*. He relationship is healthy.

According to Lindemann, the intensity of interaction with the deceased before his death usually provides an index to the severity of the grief reaction.[22] Prior to Bakari's death, Bhêly-Quénum has made of him the type of personality Lindemann considers "a key person," one whose death could be followed by disintegration of the social system, by a profound alteration of the living and social conditions for the bereaved. The loss of such a person is apt to produce intense grief even "in persons who had no former history of a tendency to psychoneurotic reactions."[23] In *Un Piège sans fin*, the peaceful coexistence which is the trademark of the Bakari family is stressed on more than one occasion, and there is every indication that Bakari had made life comfortable for everybody. Ahouna tells us that "la vie était belle, l'existence facile; nous travaillions jusqu'à la tombée de la nuit, puis nous rentrions, mon père et moi, accompagnés de nos travailleurs" (p. 16). Sometime later he sees the joy with which the entire family goes about its farm duties, defying the elements: "Nos vêtements de travail collés à la peau, nous oublions la pluie qui ruisselait sur notre corps et nous aveuglait. Ma mère entonnait de sa douce voix une chanson gaie, entraînante, reprise en choeur par mon père et moi" (p. 19). And finally he tells us that:

> *Tout allait assez bien. Allongs! Il faut l'avouer, tout allait bien, Bakari était riche, Mariatou était riche, et moi, le petit Ahouna, j'étais riche aussi, du moins je me considérais comme tel, pensent que le bien de mes parents était aussi le mien, puisque Séitou n'était pas avec nous. Nous étions heureux* (p. 28).

To all intents and purposes therefore, "a prognostic evaluation" (to borrow Lindemann's expression)[24] of Ahouna's attachment to his father points to an individual to whom the death of the father would come not only as a shock but would provoke a severe if not passionate grief. Even more significantly his father had not just died from a natural cause. He had been driven to commit suicide, a deed which he had performed in the conscious presence of Ahouna himself. To swear vengeance or succumb to intense grief was the only logical step to be taken by a son whom we know loved his father dearly, and of whom he said "mon père, du seul être humain que, outré ma mère, je vénérais vraiment" (p. 48). Nor would such rashness be out of place for a son whom we know had not only once routed an army of monkeys to save Bossu's life, but had courage enough to have stared a viper straight in the eyes before strangling it when he was just ten years old. He seems well on the way to this natural response when his father is first seized from his home, taken away and beaten. He tells us how:

> *Je lançais dans l'espace vide le cri de mon malheur et de ma douleur. gues heures je confiai à tue-tête mes sentiments les plus intimes à la terre, la verdue, aux montagnes, aux bêtes et aux arbres familiers (p. 48).*

But when the man dies, there is a sudden contradiction, an unexpected break in the logic of emotional response. After running about for an hour following the death of Bakari, Ahouna settles down as if nothing had really happened. Then, as if to brag about his composure, and as if to condemn his mother's behaviour he says "je n'aimais guère ces chants plaintiffs, lents, don't la douloureuse monotonie me faisait souffrir" (p. 56).

Mourning or the expression of grief has often been regarded as a safety valve for the emotions, a cathartic device by means of which the human animal purges his system of disturbing emotions. Although Karen Horney has pointed out the fear that the expression of such emotions "would endanger the person's need to like others and by liked by them,"[25] she has also been quick to stress that for the person who does not give the emotions expression his "whole way of life would be endangered" because the artificial unity which he thinks he is creating for himself is bound to explode someday.[26]

Ahouna has therefore not actually given vent to his feelings about the death of his father, which with time would metamorphose into murderous impulses. In Freudian terms, all he has done is to repress them.[27] And since this is an artificial or inauthentic approach to the problem, the emotions would by and by come to the surface as soon as his ego-defence mechanisms slacken. He has merely delayed the grief, and until the suppressed feelings re-emerge when he sees his father's ghost, he can hardly be described as a normal personality. Frantz Fanon, in enquiring "le jeune enfant noir a-t-il vu son père frappe ou lynché par le blanc? Y a-t-il eu traumatisme effectif?"[28] has tried to establish that witnessing the lynching of one's father is bound to produce a neurotic personality, if the consciousness of the deed is repressed.

In an existential psychological study of Marcher, the protagonist of Henry
James's *The Beast in the Jungle* (1903) van Kaam and Healy make observations which can be used to throw more light on the issue of repression and characterization in *Un Piège sans fin*. They say:

> *Psychologically speaking, he [Marcher] is fixated early in life in existential transference to his impregnable ego. His fear of encounter with the beast in the jungle of his own psyche, with the demon of his "other self," has its central source in the transference which diminishes his capacity for openness to reality, encounter with other human beings, and the decision which alone would make him truly different.*[29]

Without stretching the comparison between Marcher and Ahouna too far, it is fitting to say that Ahouna too is fixated after his father's death in existential transference to his ego, and lives constantly in fear of the beast in the jungle of his psyche breaking loose. It is this far too that makes it impossible for him to respond to life authentically. This point is very forcefully brought out by Ahouna himself when, after the murder of Kinhou he enquires from a fantasized image of Anatou:

> *Pourquoi, n'avais-tu naguère cessé de me faire remarquer, à chaque instant, qu'au-delà de la douceur de mon regard, de la tendresse de mon Coeur et de l'envoûtante harmonie de ma musique, il y avait un autre regard et un Coeur: le monstre que chacun de nous porte en soi? Tu as réveillé le mien…(p. 145).*

"Réveillé" here implies a previous state of dormacy, or repression which he soon describes significantly as "un poids énorme qui m'écrasait" (p. 145).

It is in this context of repression of the monster within him that Ahouna's obsession for music must be rightly understood. It is true as François Salien has said, that "Ahouna joue avec dexterité…ou du tôba et parvient à traduire ses sentiments les plus intimes."[30] More will be said about Bhêly-Quénum's organization of symbols to highlight character, but it is important to note here that musique is for Ahouna not just a pastime. It is a palliative, the supreme weapon with which to keep that beast in the jungle of his psyche under control. This is particularly evident when upon the appearance of his father's ghost on the Kinibaya hills, he tells us that "je fus bouleversé et, pour ne pas laisser couler les larmes que ce souvenir précipitait au bord de mes paupières, je pris mon kpété" (p. 108).

Bhêly-Quénum uses the *Kpété* for the same symbolic purpose that Arthur Miller uses the flute in his *The Death of a Salesman*. *Un Piège sans fin* does not open and close with the sound of the flute as Miller's play does. But whenever it is played, the *kpété* conjures up, at least in Ahouna's mind, the same images of a distant, faraway world, a dream world of another existence, as we encounter each time the flute sounds in Miller's play. It serves as a diversion from the harsh realities of Ahouna's world.

Ahouna as a Victim of Repressed Eroticism

Bhêly-Quénum does not permit us to see much of what transpired between Ahouna and Anatou during the thirteen years of their marriage. However, there are enough symptoms or clues from which to infer that the marriage was far from total blissfulness. On the surface, Anatou's jealousy (as many critics have pointed out), would appear to spring from no significant and convincing motivation. The temptation here to compare her's with the jealousy which drives Leontes crazy in Shakespeare's *The Winter's Tale,* is very strong.[31] But a jealousy so corrosive and so pathological in the extent of the hatred it engenders cannot be sufficiently explained outside the dynamics, however hypothetical, of Anatou and Ahouna's married life, or more appropriately, the sexual aspect of their married life.

Ahouna loved and respected his father, but, as we have already seen, it was his love for his mother that occupied pride and place: "Mon Père du seul être humaine que *outré ma mere,* je vénérais" he said (p. 48). And with the death of Bakari it does not take too much imagination to conclude that he would be drawn even closer to his mother. In fact, it is his marriage that pulls them apart. As he himself puts it, "mon union avec Anatou m'éloigna un peu de ma mere" (p. 107). Between mother and son, however, the success with which the Oedipus complex had been dissolved and rendered it impossible or unlikely for Ahouna to develop a really erotic attachment to his mother. Yet he continued to love her and share intimacies with her, a relationship which was amply fed by the fact that he was treated like an only child.

Psychoanalytic research suggests that in such a situation the boy would have to undergo a repression of his sexual excitations, just so that his relationship with his mother remains at a healthy level. A prolonged repression of those urges, however, is invariably bound to have a debilitating effect on his sexual potency, particularly, as Freud said, "when the libido which is prevented from finding a satisfactory discharge is strong and has not been dealt with for the greater part of the sublimation."[32] Even Ahouna himself has mixed feelings about his virility, and it would seem that one major reason why he got married was to prove that he had not actually lost his manhood. For, as he says with a sense of personal achievement and relief, "n'ayant pas l'aiguillette nouée, je ne tardai pas à faire mes épreuves" (p. 101). Why, one may ask, would he be anxious to prove his manhood if it had never been in doubt? The point at issue here is not that he was actually impotent but that he went into marriage with a severe handicap that boded ill for the obligation of reciprocal love that the husband-and-wife relationship naturally demanded.

This handicap is explainable chiefly in terms of the unavoidable mother fixation which his relationship with Marietou had created in him. As Otto Fenichel said with regard to such circumstances, "every sexual attachment has to be inhibited, because every partner represents the mother."[33] Even in cases where the wife is not too enthusiastic about sexual intercourse, a husband with a history of inhibitions behind him can be a bore. In a home where the woman, having never been subjected to any particular inhibiting influences, turns out to be more passionate and more sexually demanding than the man, this could spell disaster. It is this latter context that the

Ahouna-Anatou relationship and subsequent crisis must be understood.

If there has been nothing reprehensible said about Anatou prior to the dream and the jealousy, it is because Ahouna wanted us to believe her to be very likeable. And there is enough evidence to prove that he is not a very perceptive character. When he first falls in love with Anatou and gives her the orange which she takes as a symbolic acceptance of his intentions, there is more than a hint of what may lie in wait for him. She jokingly warns him: "il faudrait se méfier des symbols: un orange peut être très amère ou très douce sans qu'on le sache tant qu'on ne l'a pas pelée; on ne s'en aperçoit qu'en y goûtant" (p. 89). Again, if we are not made to see any direct reference to sexuality here, it is because it is Ahouna who is doing the listening, and it is because it is through his sexually repressed consciousness that we are receiving the information.

The entire scene leading up to the warning which Anatou delivers, carries with it enough seeds for future discord between the two. There, Ahouna displays a total ignorance of those avenues which lead to a lover's heart. He tells us with great excitement how Anatou came to the field to see him regularly. But then he confesses at once that "je m'inquiétais ni de ses retards, ni de ses absences, car il lui arrivait de ne pas venir du tout et cela pendant des jours" (p. 86). Lovers always seem to want each other mores during the very early stages of the relationship. Anybody therefore with a burning desire for the other partner, "the sentiment to consume and be consumed by the loved one" as Phanuel Egejuru puts it,[35] should feel disturbed by Anatou's absence during that crucial period.

What is worse, Ahouna cannot even remember what lovers never forget - the first song he played to Anatou. He tells us: "Un jour, elle me demanda de lui chanter l'air que je modulai le jour de notre première rencontre,...mais je ne m'en souviens pas du tout!" (p. 86). He admits that it was tactless for him to have responded the way he did. On her part, Anatou, like passionate lover that she is, feels a slight sense of mortification. Ahouna tells us that "Anatou me regarda avec étonnement, mais me parla avec plus de familiarité" (p.

86). She tells him that she still remembers it because it was already engraved on her heart, and goes on to remind Ahouna of the tune.

In that scene too it is Anatou who seems to initiate every erotic move: "Anatou se blottit contre moi," "elle pressa mon bras" (p. 91). Anybody whose capacity for love has not been tampered with would respond to these actions in a manner which would excite the female partner all the more. Not so Ahouna. He only seems to be embarrassed by her actions. When, for example, she leans on him and touches him with her breast, he is so naïve as to think it was never premeditated. He says: "volontairement - puisqu'elle ne se retira pas vivement comme si ç'avait été un geste inconscient de sa part - son corps toucha le mien. J'éprouvai la fermeté de son sein" (p. 87).

Instead of excitement he feels perplexed because he had thought that would be the very last thing that she would thrust at him: "je fus interdit, d'autant plus que s'il y avait quelque chose à quoi je m'attendais pas" (p. 87). It is only as an afterthought that he says "c'etait bien de voir Anatou se serer ainsi contre moi" (p. 87). Anatou, however, succeeds, despite his coldness and naiveté, to register an erotic message. But instead of responding with enthusiasm and passion, he confesses that "je cessai de jouer et lui demanda avec émotion: c'est vrai, Anatou, que tu voudrais seulement que nous soyons des camarades? C'est vrai que tu ne m'aimes pas?" (p.87).

Only a man as sexually unawakened and as naïve as Ahouna can continue to doubt whether the girl in his arms is interested in him. It is said that doubt breeds doubt. So when he puts the question so many times to her, a certain strain of hesitation enters her voice: "elle hesitat un peu," Ahouna tells us. The hesitation is foreboding, and we can see the seeds of the future trouble already. At this point, we do not need a day-to-day account of their married life to know that a man who behaves so coldly on the initial encounter may never actually get any warmer towards his wife.

Upon closer examination of the evidence afforded by the text, even those passages which are supposed to tell us how happy they are, only serve to reveal a conscious or an unconscious effort on Ahouna's part to conceal the real truth. What he gives us is Ahouna's part to conceal the real truth. What he gives us is Anatou's relationship with other people, and how they receive her. As to what he himself thinks and does, we are given very little. He tells us, for instance, that his mother "l'aimait beaucoup, Séitou et elles étaient tout le temps ensemble tells deux soeurs inséparables; l'une achetait rien sans penser à l'autre" (p. 101).

Of the relationship between Anatou and himself we are given only one mention - the first month of their marriage, up to three days before the birth of their first child when "Anatou aimait venir me tenir compagnie au pâturage quand ses activites domestiques terminées, rien ne la retenait à la maison auprès de Séitou" (p. 102). But even here too, the initiative has definitely been provided by Anatou and not by any particular desire on the part of her husband that they be together.

Jealousy as Proof of Lack of Satisfaction in Marriage

One of the central questions that critics of this novel have still to answer has to do with Anatou's jealousy and the resultant vision of another woman in her husband's eyes. Although their sex life remains a secret, it would not be out of place for one to hypnothesize that her jealousy was connected with Ahouna's sexual inadequacies.

Angel Garma's expansion of Freud's theory of dreams indicates that the unfulfilled wishes of a sexual nature lay at the bottom of visions of the sort we encounter in Anatou's case.[36] If such an allegation be granted, then Anatou's vision would fit squarely into the context of deprived eroticism which we have established as characteristic of her married life. This point could be made much stronger by consideration of the intensity of the jealousy which ensues. Whether we see it as a reflection of her own actual unfaithfulness (of which there is no evidence), or a reflection of impulses towards unfaithfulness in her which have succumbed to repression[37] (which is more likely), an argument presented by Karen Horney on jealousy should strengthen the conclusions already established. She states that "jealousy and the demands of unconditional love are the main expressions of insatiability concerning affection."[38]

The Murder of Kinhou

Although Ahouna is to blame for the breakdown of his marriage, it would be wrong to side with his wife that the marriage failed because he was unfaithful. To doubt his love for her is to reduce his disappointment of the failure to sheer hypocrisy. It is to underestimate the force of the impact her decisions was likely to have on his life as a human being. He was sincere when he said that "je n'ai jamais menti, je ne mentirai jamais de ma vie" (p. 112). It is against this background of innocence and sincerity that his murder of Kinhou can be adequately appreciated.

In his important book on the psychology of murder, *The Murdering Mind,* David Abrahamsen says:

> *The mind of the murderer is charged with a turbulence of emotions stored from early childhood. When thee often repressed emotions are tantalized, made hot, stirred up or activated, the mind, particularly when aroused or frustrated, becomes violent. And so it is that a person who may appear quite normal and well-adjusted on the surface becomes possessed by a mind that murders.*[39]

To a very great extent, Ahouna's fate in the novel would appear to fit this paradigm. He was not born a criminal, but the potential for the type of violent impulses out of which murderous instincts grow was never absent. Mention has already been made of the attack he single-handedly executed against the team of monkeys and the killing of the viper which earned for him the nick-name of "celui qui a étouffé une vipère" (p. 96). Both of these are hostile emotions which may have been made doubly violent by the bitterness of the traumatizing circumstances surrounding his father's death. But the emotions were repressed and the grief over the death of his father suppressed until the appearance of his father's ghost shattered the aura of invincibility that seemed to surround his heart. For the first time in fifteen years he gives way to tears.

As Abrahamsen said, whenever our ego-protective defences crumble under the impact of a prolonged repression of hostile feelings, "murderous acting-out impulses emerge.[40] Anatou's accusations of infidelity could therefore never have come at a worse time for Ahouna. The worst possible moment for him to be falsely accused was when he had just brought back to mind memories of his father's death. When he finds himself incapable of convincing her of his innocence, his love for her turns instantly to virulent hatred. Thus when she comes up to tease him in the field he tells us that "j'eus envie de la gifler, tellement j'étais exaspéré" (p. 125). For once he confesses to those murderous instincts which he has fought all his life to conceal: "la bouch pleine de rage, l'esprit soudain envahi d'une idée sinistre que j'essayais d'écarter de moi" (p. 125).

In his psychoanalytic interpretation of Raskolnikov's motives for murder in *Crime and Punishment,* Edward Wasiolek comes up with a case akin to the situation of intense hatred that confronts Ahouna. He establishes that in a case of that nature,

> *the hate, by the law of psychic economy, has to go somewhere, it will tend to be displaced on someone else, chosen as a surrogate for the loved one, or, as is also quite frequent, it will be expended against oneself. The more violent the hate, and the closer the loved one, the more hidden and more remote will be the object against which the hate will be expended.*[41]

The relevance of this theory to Ahouna's murder of Kinhou is self-explanatory: rather than take the bull by the horns, he runs away from his home into the remote territories of the south where he singles out a passer-by, Kinhou, on whom he expends the hate. At this juncture it has to stressed that Sunday Anozie's description of the murder as an "acte gratuity" from which Ahouna indirectly achieves "une satisfaction quasi-sexuelle"[42] is inaccurate in that it undermines the carefully worked out psychological structure upon which the character of Ahouna is built.

Kinhou becomes a surrogate for Anatou as well as for Ahouna himself and when he kills her, he has the odd sensation that he is killing himself. But what is significant for the theme of repression which we have been trying to establish is the fact that the murder lifts a heavy load off Ahouna's shoulders. He tells us after the crime:

> *Je me sentais léger comme du duvet, heureux comme un dieu, s'il l'est et s'il en est. Oui, j'étais à jamais débrasé d'un poids énorme qui m'écrasait depuis cette nuit affreuse où, excédé par les folles extravagances d'Anatou, je décrochai le poignard de mon père et le serrai dans ma main. Je m'étais libéré de ce fardeau qui m'étouffait encoure quelques instants plus tôt: j'ai enfin assume mon destin et je me sens libre, extraordinairement libre (pp. 145-46).*

Characterization Devices and Style

What I have tried to establish up to this point is that *Un Piège sans fin* possesses considerable merit as a work of art, and that its Anti-Heroic protagonist is not just an excuse for philosophical discussions but a true creation of human complexity; that he possesses an inner life, thoughts, motives, frailties, fears, fantasies and memories which are very consciously intensified or reflected in both the structure and a skein of images and symbols. But the sophisticated craftsmanship out of which Bhêly-Quénum fashions the type of Anti-Heroic personality that we encounter in Ahouna does not seem to me to have received the credit it actually deserves. Dorothy Blair, who has gone further than any of the author's critics in showing the precise extent to which the structure and style of the novel are indebted to the French literary tradition, has raised a number of issues in her study which should provide a convenient point of departure for an examination of Bhêly-Quénum's characterization techniques. She admits that the first part has more unity both of action and of tone, but remains decidedly unimpressed by the second part because:

> *the interest that should be intensified with the tragedy closing in on Ahouna is dispersed over a number of incidents, with secondary characters taking the centre of the stage. What now occurs, after Ahouna finishes telling his story to Houénou, until the time of his death, is told in a series of*

dramatic or tragic tableaux in which Ahouna is more often an onlooker than the main actor.

Later on she makes the argument even stronger:

The first part proceeds on the stylistic level of romantic lyricism, consistent with the bucolic idyll and with the sensitive exalté nature of the hero. The second part suffers from the lack of synthesis and unity of structure, from the confusion as to the source of the narrative, from a superfluity of trivial descriptive detail, from the cliché-ridden banality and often incongruity of the style. The digressions into ethnic lore, as with the descriptions of different funeral rites and the introduction of the moral fable told by Dâko to his family to warn them not to play with danger, also detract from the desired atmosphere of terror and tension in a world dominated by invisible, inimical powers, determined on the destruction of their victim.[43]

Nobody who has read *Un Piège sans fin* with any degree of attention would find Blair's charges unjustified. There is a distinct difference between the first and second parts of the novel no doubt; but that this differences is a flaw rather than a consciously worked out technique for the presentation of character is highly contestable. The truth about it is that Bhêly-Quénum very deliberately makes structure conterminous with character, with the result that style becomes an almost symbolic reflection of the fortunes of the protagonist, his psychological state or his implied philosophy of life. To this extent, therefore, the strength of the work must not be sought in surface unity, realistic description or Bhêly-Quénum's handling of the principles of probability and causality. The author's intentions appear to be more literary and artistic than realistic or historical. His *forte* lies in the range of imagery he employs at every stage in the novel to highlight one aspect or other of the protagonist's peculiar mode of existence. What we are to look for then is the metaphoric or symbolic elements which hold the episodes together and which are bound by association and/or implication to Ahouna's life.

In the first part of the novel where Ahouna himself admits that "la vie était agréable" (p. 101), the happiness in his heart is reflected in the structure of the imagery. Bhêly-Quénum uses two significant images here - the sun and water, both of which are archetypal symbols of life and vitality. The author describes life at that time as "calme, tranquille, paisible et prèsque sans rides, telle la source du Kiniba coulant dans son canal embelli de verdure" (p. 29). During this time too, all the elements worked in Ahouna's favour: "le soleil,...' sommeillant dans la gueule du Caiman de l'horizon,' ne rougeoyait pas encore le bout du ciel" (p. 18); And during the planting season, there was nothing to complain about because:

> *Le temps était agréablement frais; le soleil, dont nous précédions le lever afin d'abattre le plus de travail possible, ne paraissait pas de la journée. La pluie tombait, fine, serrée et douce; quelques oiseaux, cependant, chantaient dans les arbres tandis que nous plantions avec joie. La souriante verdure de céréales s'étalant à perte de vue ajoutait un agreement sans nom à notre ardeur, et la seule idée que, dans quelques mois, nous retournerions dans notre champ pour la récolte, qui s'annonçait très bonne, nous inondait l'âge de bonheur (p. 19).*

Whenever this peace and happiness in Ahouna's family is threatened or disrupted, however, Bhêly-Quénum makes the structure of the imagery coincide with the disruption. The arrival of locusts to destroy their harvest is preceded and intensified by a sudden and bizarre change in the atmospheric condition:

> *Un mois après le ravage cholérique vint le jour des moissons. Tout était prêt comme d'habitude; nos gens étaient dans la cour de la maison et nous y attendaient; le soleil commençait de monter, mais il s'assombrit brusquement; l'atmosphère devint bizarrement lourde et un malaise planait dans les airs. Nous percevions un grondement lointain, mais sans rapport avec le bruit du tonnerre. D'ailleurs nous étions dans la grande saison sèche, et il eût été assez surprenant qu'un orage se fût préparé de la sorte et crevât soudain (p. 34)*

On the day that he sees the ghost of his father, he has had to climb to the top of mount Kinibaya. Then in a scène reminiscent of Camus' use of the sun in Chapter six of *L'Etranger* to prefigure doom, the elements take on an uncanny nature: "je m'y tenais debout sous le soleil déjà assez haut; la réverbération, pareille à un lac de verre avec sa transparence vraiment étrange, frétillait au ras du sol au-dessous de moi" (p. 107). What Bhêly-Quénum is doing here is ostensibly describing the landscape, but in fact what we have is a heightened perception of it from Ahouna's perspective. Thus the imagery emerges with the character and becomes the very embodiment of his state of mind as well as an essential element of the plot.

The general peace that reigns in this first part of the novel is reflected not only in the structure of the imagery but also in the structure of the work. There is unity, in the sense in which Blair employed the word: one event grows out of the other by logical necessity. We see that Ahouna's father is beaten because he refuses to obey the commandant; because he is beaten and disgraced, he kills himself: because he kills himself, Camara comes to take over the leadership of the family; because Ahouna plays music in the fields, his music charms and invites Anatou; because she comes they fall in love, get married and produce children; because she becomes jealous and accuses him falsely, Ahouna fortuitously.

When the strength of a novel is indissolubly bound to the range of its imagery and symbolism, one does not talk of or ask for unity, one talks mainly of effectiveness. In the second part of the novel, prior to which Ahouna's inner life has been completely shattered by the groundless accusations of his wife, one does not ask for logical progression but for the extent to which the structure of the novel has been used to reflect or amplify the protagonist's mental or psychological status. In this regard, what Eugene H. Falk says about the relationship between character and style should enhance our appreciation of Bhêly-Quénum's artistic ingenuity. In his "Stylistic Forces in the narrative," Falk says:

> *When an author aims to represent man's experience of disparateness and fragmentation, he may do so by intentionally disrupting the probable*

sequential order of incidents or by omitting any causal coherence. Thereby he hopes to set the reader on a course of emotional and intellectual exploration that leads to an apprehension of different interrelationships between phenomena, culminating in an essential vision of correspondence beyond time or cause.[44]

In his study of the novel, Ortega y Gasset puts the point even more vividly when he says:

The form ...contains the same thing that was in the content, but it presents in a clear, articulated, developed way that in the content was only a tendency or a mere intention.[45]

What these arguments amount to is that the apparent incoherence, the unconvincing nature of the episodes and the lack of focus on the main character in the second part of the novel are in actual fact calculated devices for emphasizing the bewildering nature of the ordeals or trials that frame Ahouna's Anti-Heroic existence. Psychoanalytic constructs were seen to provide an explanation for Ahouna's unusual conduct in the second part of the novel. It has to be stressed here that those psychological explanations are satisfying only because they are backed by or occur in the context of an artistic technique that intensifies the structure of his personality in that particular part of the novel.

Reference has already been made to the important imagery of water and the sun. these images recur in the second part of the novel, but they are imbued with an almost human/animal spirit of ferociousness and vengeance, reflecting the tense atmosphere of revenge. As Ahouna flees he says "le soleil me semblait plus brûlant que jamais" (p. 137). When Houénou rises from his dream and opens the door, we learn that "Telle une bête traguée en quête de refuge, le soleil se précipita dans la chambre et l'emplit d'une chaleur" (p. 151). Instead of the fields for cattle to graze on, which we encounter constantly in the first part of the novel, we find swamps and bushes which while depicting the geography of the land through which Ahouna is fleeing, also symbolize the geography of a mind lacerated with guilt, fear and desperation. Structurally we do not see much of him at this time, prior to his capture. But this too is an amplification of the content because at this point he is in flight and actually fears being seen.

Point of view has been employed in this novel as an effective characterizing device. Because the story is being told for the most part by Ahouna himself, we are not given the opportunity to know more than he wants us to know. We are not given the opportunity to know the unpleasant aspect of his married life. This technique of characterization which heightens the hypothetical nature of our deductions concerning the psychological implications of Ahouna's behaviour, is very close to that employed by detective fiction writers. Most of the time we are misled almost in the same way that Agatha Christie misleads us in *The Murder of Roger Ackroyd* (1926) when she makes the criminal the teller of the tale. The use of such a technique should in part explain why there seem to be so many missing links, and why it is necessary to subject a work like *Un Piège sans fin* to psychoanalytic interpretations.

Ahouna and Meursault

Just as Ferdinand Oyono's Anti-Hero compelled comparison with Sartre's Roquentin, Bhêly-Quénum's Ahouna also compels some amount of comparison with Camus's Meursault. Like Meursault, Ahouna looks on existence as absurd, and like Meursault also, Ahouna gets trapped in circumstances which slowly but inexorably lead to his destruction. Both Anti-Heroes inadvertently commit murder, do not show any great sense of guilt or remorse and finally have to face execution for the crime. Finally, both men are poor men of no will, not courageous enough to meet the challenges of life authentically and positively, but who have to let the world decide their fate and the terms upon which they are to live.

In terms of style, then, certain aspects of *Un Piège sans fin* and *L'Étrangere* are comparable: both stories are told in the first person (the only difference being that Bhêly-Quénum breaks off the technique in the last third of the novel); both novels are open-ended in the sense that they offer no coherent systems of thought or offer practical solutions to the problems they raise; both novels show a conscious use of images of the physical world to heighten the tone or reveal depths of emotion in the lives of the protagonists.

In conclusion it can be said with a certain degree of confidence that Bhêly-Quénum has created in Ahouna a protagonist who fits into the Anti-Heroic mould not just because the world is cruel to him but because he fails to create for himself the kind of positive ethos that is necessary to combat the challenges that are thrown at him. And in his creation of this Anti-Hero, Bhêly-Quénum has employed literary devices with such sophistication that the novel loses little in being compared to the works of Western novelists who write in the Anti-Heroic tradition.

Notes

[1] Aziza, Claude et al., *Dictionnaire des types et caractères littéraires,* op. cit., p. 16.

[2] Olympe Bhêly-Quénum, *Un Piège sans fin* (Paris: Stock, 1960), p. 101. All further references is are to this edition, page numbers will follow each quotation.

[3] *Olympe Bhêly-Quénum*: écrivain dahoméen (Paris: Fernand Nathan, 1964), p. 59.

[4] Ibid., p. 6.

[5] In an article in *Présence Africain* of March 1962, Bhêly-Quénum describes what he calls the African regional novel (in which category he includes Bernard Dadie's *Climbié,* Socié's *Karim* and Camara Laye's *L'Enfant noir)* as not sufficiently representative of the African continent and its people. He also calls on Black writers of the second half of the 20th century to purge their literature of false exoticism, stories of primeval forests and their fauna, and primitive tribes in which people who had become tired of inventing too much and who had become slaves to their own machines, think to find the true face to Africa. He sees more of the external Africa and the inner conscience of the African in

Paul Hazoumé's *Doguicimi* than in all the works of Black writers who have merely repeated the formulae of French fiction.

[6]*Africain Literature in French* ..., p. 253. Sunday Anozie has also remarked that "on peut même affirmer qu'au moment de rédiger son premier roman, *Un Piège sans fin*, Bhêly-Quénum s'est montré trop attaché à la thèse de Kafka et de Camus sur le nihilisme absolu et sur la morale de l'absurde;" *Sociologie du roman africaine*, p. 161.

[7]Mercier and Battestini, *Olympe* Bhêly-Quénum, p. 15.

[8]*Dictionnaire des œuvres Négro-africaines de langue française*, ed. Ambroise Kom (Quebec: Editions Naaman, 1983), p. 603.

[9]Mercier and Battestini, *Olympe* Bhêly-Quénum, p. 15.

[10]Ibid., p. 60.

[11]Ibid., p. 15.

[12]*Olympe Bhêly-Quénum: écrivain dahoméen*, p. 12.

[13]*Actes du colloque sur la littérature africaine d'expression française, Dakar, 26-29 mars, 1963* (Dakar: Université de Dakar, 1965), p. 169.

[14]Ferdinand Oyono, *Une Vie de boy*, op. cit., pp. 36,33.

[15]Possibly taking their cue from Ahouna's self-denigration, critics of the novel have been consistently vocal on this particular aspect. Dorothy Blair, seeing him as totally alienated from his environment, calls him "a prisoner of society, subject to man's brutality and stupidity, and at the same time the prisoner of a hard and hostile Nature symbolized by the quary "all these considerations, she argues, render Ahouna "powerless to make a voluntary move for his own liberation....[and he is therefore] condemned to a life which must be a continual death until his final agony is accomplished;" p. 255. Gerard Pigeon describes him as a man who "est depuis la première aurore des temps condamné à souffrir," a man "digne héritier de la fureur céleste, de l'anathème divin," in "Le Thème de la fatalité dans le roman d'Olympe Bhêly-Quénum," *Présence Africaine* no. 7 (Automne 1973), p. 54.

[16] "Characterization in Narrative: Some Theoretical Prolegomena," in *Neophilologus,* 67 (1983), p. 12.

[17]*Omega*, vol. 2 (1971), p. 107.

[18] *American Journal of Psychiatry,* no. 101 (1944), p. 142.

[19] Ibid., p. 144.

[20] This is an absolute simplification for my own convenience, of a rather complicated theory which grows out of Freud's concept of Grief and Mourning.

[21] Freud, "Mourning and Melancholia," *Collected Papers,* vol. 4, pp. 152-170.

[22] Lindermann, "Symptomatology and Management of Grief," p. 146.

[23] Ibid., p. 147.

[24] Ibid., p. 146.

[25] Karen Horney, *Our Inner Conflicts: A Constructive Theory of Neurosis* (New York: Norton, 1945), p. 56.

[26] Ibid., p. 57.

[27] I use the term "repress" here in the sense first stated and expounded upon by Freud (*Collected Papers,* vol. 4, pp. 84-97), implying that Ahouna may or may not be unaware of those murderous impulses, but has so implacable an interest in never becoming aware of them that he keeps keen anxious watch lest they betray him.

[28] *Peau noire, masques blancs,* op. cit., p. 138.

[29] *The Demon and the Dove,* p. 198. The resemblance between Marcher and Ahouna is quite strong: Marcher also leads a life of futility -a kind of death-in-life, is incapable of giving or receiving love, The difference, however, lies in the fact that the beast in the jungle of Marcher's heart which he tries so desperately to conceal is in fact the one thing that would save him. His tragedy lies in the fact that he misunderstood his self.

[30] "Un Piège sans fin," op., cit., p. 604.

[31] The controversy over Leontes's jealousy has been very well treated by Murray M. Scwartz in his article "Leontes' jealousy in *The Winter's Tale,*" *The Practice of Psychoanalytic Criticism,* ed. Leonard Tennenhouse (Detroit: Wayne State Univ. press, 1976), pp. 202-225.

[32] Freud, "Anxiety," *The Complete Introductory Lectures on Psychoanalysis,* trans. James Strachey (New York: Norton, 1966), p. 402.

[33] *The Psychoanalytic Theory of Neurosis* (New York: Norton, 1945), p. 170.

[34] Phanuel A. Egejuru, "The Absence of Passionate Love Theme in African Literature," in *Design and Intent in African Literature,* eds., David F, Dorsey et al (Washington: D.C.: Three Continents Press, 1982), p. 88. To cite from her article is not to suggest that I share the stand she takes. She seems to have completely missed the point of the story when she insists that "the love which triggered off the chain of tragic events in Ahouna's life only served as a mere digression." According to her, "the author's intention is to illustrate a Sartrean existentialist philosophy of man trapped in a world of endless snares." This is inaccurate, not just because it runs counter to what Bhêly-Quénum himself said he set out to do, but because the philosophy only comes into play to describe the failure of love. The love is the thing, and the philosophy the digression. Furthermore, with respect to the entire article, Phanuel Egejuru apparently was not aware of Françoise Fouet's more informed article, "Le thème de l'amour chez les romanciers Negro-africains d'expression francaise" which clearly substantiated the elements of love which she claims are missing. See *Actes du colloque sur la littérature africaine d'expression française, Dakar, 26-29 mars, 1963 (*Dakar: Université de Dakar, Faculté des lettres et science humain, 1965), pp. 139-60.

[35] Dorothy Blair's conclusion that "Ahouna marries Anatou and enjoys thirteen years of unblemished happiness with her" (p. 254, *African Literature in French)*, must be taken with a pinch of salt. There is much more to the relationship than Ahouna is ready to disclose.

[36] *The Psychoanalysis of Dreams* (Chicago: Quadrangle Book, 1966), p. 21.

[37] Freud, *Collected Papers,* vol. 2, p. 233.

[38] *The Neurotic Personality of Our Time* (New York: Norton, 1936), p. 129.

[39] (New York: Harper and Row, 1973), p. 4.

[40] Ibid., p. 10.

[41] "Raskolnikov's Motives: Love and Murder," in *The Practice of Psychoanlytic Criticism,* op. cit., pp. 118-135.

[42] *Sociologie du roman africain,* p. 165.
[43] *African Literature in French,* pp. 254, 255-256.
[44] *Patterns of Literary Criticism,* ed. Joseph Strelka (Univ. Park: The Penn. State University Press, 1971), p. 45.
[45] *Meditations on Quixote,* trans. Evelyn Rugg and Diego Marin (New York: Norton, 1961), pp. 112-113.

Chapter Five

Samba Diallo (Cheikh Hamidou Kane's *L'aventure Ambiguë*, (1961)

> *...the human individual, given a chance, tends to develop his particular human potentialities. He will develop then the unique alive forces of his real self: the clarity and depth of his own feelings, thoughts, wishes, interests; the ability to tap his own resources, the strength of his will power; the special capacities or gifts he may have; the faculty to express himself, and to relate himself to others with spontaneous feeling. All this will in time enable him to find his set of values and his aims in life. In short, he will grow, substantially undiverted, toward self-realization.*
>
> *(Karen Horney: Neurosis and Human Growth)*[1]

Plot Summary

Set in Guinea in West Africa, *L'Aventure ambiguë* is the story of Samba Diallo, a pawn and victim of the clash between two incompatible world views - the traditional African Islamic civilization and that of Europe. It unveils the circumstances leading up to Samba Diallo's loss of self-confidence, his loss of any sense of direction and worth. Above all, it is the record of his systematic depersonalisation (masquerading as education), his total alienation from his God, from his fellow human beings, and finally from himself.

The novel begins with the decision of the principal members of the Diallobé family to guarantee the continuity of the Islamic faith by sending its youngest heir, Samba Daillo to live and study under the tutelage of Thierno, the best koranic teacher in the land. As an indispensable method of Thierno's instructional policy, the young Samba Diallo is not spread any physical torture or humiliation which in the opinion of his teacher would instil a contempt for the flesh and luxury (into which Samba had been born) as a further prerequisite for a profound intuitive understanding of the mysteries of the sacred word of God.

But, despite his keen interest in imbibing the teachings of his master, Samba Diallo is not allowed to follow studies in the koranic school to the logic end. Ostensibly to give Samba Diallo an opportunity to learn how to integrate Islam with European technology as a means of preserving traditional values, but actually to encourage and enable him to learn the white man's art of conquering without being in the right, Samba Diallo's aunt La Grande Royale causes him to be withdrawn from the koranic school and sent to the French school in Senegal. In taking this decision the Diallobé family has been driven by the awareness of the inevitability of change and the desire to counteract it by having his own son educated in the Western tradition.

From the French school where Samba Diallo has already developed a keen interest in Descartes, Pascal and Nietzsche, he proceeds to Paris. There his knowledge and interest in Western philosophy increases, displacing his early education in Islam. He is impressed by the degree of freedom of belief and expression in Paris, but is repulsed by the total absence of any human touch, the artificiality of life, the inhuman dedication to intellectuality. In the correspondence that goes on between him and his father, the latter detects an alarming decline in his faith and accordingly arranges for his return to Senegal.

Samba Diallo returns to his homeland, but is not the same person who left. He discovers that his boyhood teacher has died, having chosen as his successor, Demba, a peasant youth who pays less attention to the traditional ways of life than Samba Diallo would ever have, and who is more open to change than the now disillusioned Samba. Samba Diallo feels, not unjustifiably, that he has failed both his people and himself. He finds at least one person, Le Fou or the madam, who is disturbed that Demba rather than Samba has been chosen to succeed Thierno. Le Fou, the deceased Thierno's good friend, tries to convince Samba to worship at the traditional prayer house, but Samba has already lost too much faith in the traditional ways to accept. This refusal so inflames the mad man that he stabs Samba Diallo to death.

State of Criticism

L'Aventure ambiguë deals with a subject that has been the stock-in-trade of the African novelist for decades -the confrontation between African and Europe, and between tradition and modernity. The choice of such a theme can be either a blessing or a curse to any assessment of the achievement of the writer. To the extent that it deals with an issue with which every critic can identify and on which he can always find something to talk about, it could be regarded as a blessing. But the very blessing can become a curse when the message of the work is so familiar, rich and tempting that critics tend to lose sight of the medium - character - through which it is effectively conveyed. John D. Erickson, for example, begins his article on the book by saying that:

> The title of Cheikh Hamidou Kane's novel, *L'Aventure ambiguë*, refers to the ambiguous adventure on which the young Senegalese protagonist sets forth, as he makes his way from the heart of things in his traditional society to the peripheral society of western man, estranged from God, others, and himself.[2]

In this opening sentence there is enough emphasis placed on the role of the protagonist to suggest that his depiction would play a major role in the study. However, three quarters of the article is dedicated to the examination of "the differences existing between Western and African civilizations" which provide "the background of Samba Diallo's ambiguous adventure."[3]

In the chapter of her *Black Writers, White Audience* where she discusses Hamidou Kane, Phanuel Egeruru admits that his novel "is structured in the form of a debate in which the cultural conflict between Europe and Africa is presented and later dramatized by the hero."[4] But in the text that follows, the personality of Samba Diallo is given very slight treatment, while the bulk of her emphasis is placed on "the distinction between the two parties" involved in the debate.[5] Thus, even though these two references and over a dozen others in the same vein offer valuable insights into the study of many general aspects of the novel, the character of Samba Diallo whose fate *is* the story receives only occasional glimpses. It is as though his existence in the novel is incidental to the debates that are carried out, which is not true.

A second issue raised by criticism of the novel has to do with the source of Samba Diallo's tragedy, or Anti-Heroism. Makouta-Mboukou's argument is very misleading in this respect. He cites the Directeur's declaration that "je n'ai mis mon fils à l'école que parce que je ne pouvais faire autrement,"[6] and indicates that the foreign schools exercised an irresistible attraction for the whole of Africa, adding that 'il y à incertitude quant à la nature de cette école, ce mirage, qui deviendra un objet de curiosité, qui capture." But he seems to ignore a major aspect in Hamidou Kane's craft when he goes on to argue that it is the uncertainty surrounding the foreign schools alone "qui affaiblit la resistance et accélère la chute, la défaite [de Samba Diallo]."[7]

That Africa is the victim of European Imperialism is a fact that has been stated *ad nauseam* by African novelists, poets and dramatists. Cheikh Hamidou Kane is no exception, and it has been customary to regard *L'Aventure ambiguë* in that light.[8] But when examined more closely, Samba Diallo's ultimate failure will be seen to result not because, but in spite of the tyranny of the West on colonial Africa.

It has to be understood that apart from the stories narrated by the old men about the sudden arrival of foreigners on their land and the subsequent defeat of the Dialobé some one hundred years ago, there is very little to suggest in an obvious sense that the African is being victimized, scorned or exploited.[9]

At least three studies exist, however, which have tried to focus attention on Samba Diallo's portrayal in the novel - Mme Jeanne Lydie Gore's "Le Theme de la solitude dans *L'Aventure ambiguë* de Cheickh Hamidou Kane,"[10] the rejoinder it provoked in W.S. Shiver's "Hamidou Kane's Hero,"[11] and A.C. Brench's chapter on the book in his *The Novelists' Inheritance in French Africa*[12]. In both Mme Gore's and

Shiver's articles, Samba Diallo's solitude, a central element in his depiction in the novel, is the focus of attention. But unfortunately, in either case the reader is denied the opportunity to benefit fully from the critic's potential for character analysis. Had Mme Gorë not allowed her immense knowledge of Islamic mysticism (which seems to be the main point of her discussion) to get in the way of her interpretation we would have had in her article a very powerful study of solitude and death in the novel. Shiver also dedicates far too much space to the pointing out of Mme Goré's shortcomings to examine the character of Samba Diallo in depth. A study which combines the strengths of these two without their weaknesses, and which suffers only by being too brief, is A.C. Brench's chapter.

In this chapter, beginning with the hypothesis that the cause of Samba Diallo's Anti-Heroism is traceable to his total submission to the will of Thierno, I will apply Third Force psychological constructs to explain why he behaves the way he does in the novel.

Personality Structure and Claims to Anti-heroism

One of the central paradoxes or ironies in the interpretation of Samba Diallo's depiction in *L'Aventure ambiguë* is that he has every reason to be a hero, and to act out a heroic part in the drama which centres around his person. Freud saw the weakling (or in my view, the Anti-Hero) as one who comes of poor stock. Samba Diallo is not of poor stock like Toundi, with parents of little or no means of livelihood in the village. He is not like Ahouna who loses his father when he is just fifteen, and has to struggle through life with that vacuum unfilled. Samba Diallo is the son of the Chevalier, who unlike Ahouna's father is very much respected by the French administrators and is himself the deputy administrator for his area. The Diallobé to which he belongs is a family distinguished not only by a long history of nobility and leadership but also marked by a physique that seems larger than life. As though the epithets "Grande" and "Royale" in her name were not sufficient indication of her authority, his aunt "La Grande Royale" is described almost like an Amazon: "Les traits étaient tout en longuer, dans l'axe d'un nez légèrement busqué. La bouche était grande et forte sans exagération. Un regard extraordinairement lumineux répandait sur cette figure un éclat impérieux" (pp. 34-35). She was only the sister of the Chief but we are told that "c'est elle que le pays craignait," and later that "elle avait pacifié le Nord par sa fermeté [ou] son prestige avait maintenu dans l'obéissance les tribus subjuguées par sa personnalité extraordinaire. C'est le Nord qui l'avait surnommée la Grande Royale" (p. 32).

The potential for heroic action in this family therefore unmistakable, and if consanguinity means anything at all, we have no reason for doubting that any son of that line will ultimately acquit himself with distinction in everything that he attempts. But Samba Diallo does not seem to be cast in the same heroic mould. Along with his playmate, Demba, as Professor A.C. Brench has said, Demba and Samba Diallo "are ordinary beings."[13] Ordinariness is the mark of an Anti-Hero rather than a hero. Samba Diallo's very proximity to the legendary heroes and heroines of the Dialobe race, as will be illustrated later, proves his undoing.

In the Preface to the novel Vincent Monteil describes the central crisis in a manner which strongly emphasizes Samba Diallo's Anti-Heroic qualities. The novel, he says, "C'est le récit d'un déchirement, de la crise de conscience qui accompagne, pour l'africaine 'européanisé' sa propre prise de conscience." He adds that a good number of Africans manage to escape this predicament by interrupting their studies. Such people would include those who are destined to be national heroes. Quite rightly so, Vincent Monteil does not see Samba Diallo as belonging to this group. He says "Le héros de Cheikh [Hamidou] Kane est désarticule; et sa mort ressemble à un suicide" (p. 10).

Again, disarticulation is a mark of Anti-Heroism, and Samba Diallo's death, which the author has described in an interview as the warning which the whole book works up to,[14] is devoid of either dignity or tragic loss. Had he died before the death of his teacher Thierno, the death would have carried much weight because there would always be the regret that he died before he as given the opportunity to assume responsibilities as the new teacher. But the old teacher dies and a new one is chosen, who is not Samba, and he loses his life at the hands of a mad man.

Bernard M.W. Knox was quoted as saying that it is a distinguishing characteristic of the hero that he is "immovable once his decision is taken, deaf to appeals and persuasion to reproof and threat, unterrified by physical violence."[15] Against this concept of heroic resolve must be set the inability of the typical Anti-Hero in general, and Samba Diallo in particular, to meet the obligation to make a decision or to give his undivided attention to any worthy cause. Irving Howe in *Decline of the New* describes his modern hero (synonym for Anti-Hero), in terms which could also apply to Samba Diallo's fortunes in the novel. He says such a protagonist:

> *is a man who believes in the necessity of action; he wishes, in the words of Malraux, to put a "scar on the map." Yet the moral impulsions that lead him to the map." Yet the moral impulsions that lead him to believe in action, also render him unfit for action. He becomes dubious about the value of inflicting scars and is not sure he can even locate the map.... [He] often continues to believe in the quest, and sometimes in the grail, too; only he no guest, and sometimes in the grail, too; only he no longer is persuaded that quest is necessarily undertaken through action and he is unsure as to where the grail can be found ... [He] discovers that he cannot be a hero. Yet only through his readiness to face the consequences of this discovery can he salvage a portion of the heroic.*[16]

Samba Diallo fits into this paradigm excellently. At the beginning of the novel his belief in the necessity for union with the deity is unmistakable. Not only does he mouth his teacher's doctrines, but he has to abandon his rich background and go from door to door, praying and begging: "La paix de Dieu soix sur cette maison. Le pauvre disciple es en quête de sa pittance journalière" (p. 26). He would compose edifying litanies every morning: Sous le vent du matin, Samba Diallo improvisait des litanies édifiantes, reprises par ses compagnons, à la porte close de son cousin, le chef des Diallobé" (p. 27). At this time he is not just an echo but a voice, talking to the people.

By the end of the mission, he has lost all trust in God, all enthusiasm in his sense of dedication. Thus he muses that "Dieu pouvait être un obstacle au bonheur des homes" (p. 147). In his prayer to God at this critical moment he feels that something very serious has happened to him, that fate is toying with him. He begs God: "Je t'en supplie, ne fais pas que je devienne l'utensile que je sens qui s'évide déjà" (p. 148). As Howe suggests in the citation above, Samba Diallo realizes to his heart's bitterness that victory is impossible, that "le monde est silencieux, et je ne résonne plus," and that he has instead become "comme un balafong crevé, comme un instrument de musique mort" (p. 174). This feeling of anguish, of defeat and the futility of any further effort is distinctly Anti-Heroic. Esther Jackson's declaration that "the anti-hero is evidence of a growing fear among men, a fear of self-annihilation,"[17] is quite well demonstrated here.

Esther Jackson also declared that the anti-hero is a divided man. She said "man in the twentieth century is a divided creature, anti-heroic in his lack of conflict."[18] Such self-division, a mark of Anti-Heroism, is a major structural element in the make-up of Samba Diallo's personality. This quality is very effectively depicted in the relationship that exists between Samba Diallo and the other important characters. It also emerges when one attempts to analyse Samba Diallo's role in the story in terms of the structure of the novel, in terms of the interlocking system of contending ideologies out of which crystallizes the structure of his suffering, his alienation, his Anti-Heroism.

As far as the art of the novel is concerned, Samba Diallo is strategically situated in such a way that either by blood relation or social obligation, he is associated with characters like the Chevalier, Grande Royale, Thierno and the chief, all of whom, for better or for worse, have a claim to his affection and well-being. Thus, the structure that his life in the book takes is determined by the combination and permutation of the various spiritual, cultural and political convictions of these personalities.

In this sense, Samba Diallo does not actually exist as an independent individual whose destiny lies exclusively in his own hands. Vincent Monteil saw the characters in this novel as pieces in the chess game: "Les personnages sont des 'types' - ou des pièces de jeu d'échec: le maître, le chef, le chevalier, le fou (et cette femme de Coeur et de tête: la Grande Royale - incarnation de l'Africaine)" (p. 12). He merely needed to add one more piece - the pawn, to make his argument complete. In that case, Samba Diallo would be the pawn, which is actually what he is in the ideological game which his parents, relatives and Teacher play above his head.

It is part of the essential ambiguity of his adventure that Samba Diallo's position in the novel is not clearly defined. At one level he is the point of intersection of the various ideologies. And to that extent his mode of existence is not much different from what Jonathan Culler calls "the ethos of structuralist conception of character portrayal," according to which character is seen as a configuration of "the interpersonal and conventional systems which traverse the individual and which make him a space in which forces and events meet rather than an individuated essence."[19] Monique Battestini's observation in this respect is very pertinent. She says:

> *Samba Diallo n' était pas un personnage, mais un symbole de la lutte des contraires, venue de la rencontre des deux mondes... Samba Diallo est aussi bien l'abstraction du personnage, que l'incarnation authentique du symbole, en ce sens qu'il est de toutes ses forces celui qui a vécu intensément ce drame intérieur de l'homme engagé dans une aventure qui pousse dans les deux sens.*[20]

A major factor in his claim to Anti-Heroism lies in Samba Diallo's inability to reconcile these conflicting issues. This in turn is inevitably reflected, at a wider structural and even thematic level, in the irreconcilability of the standpoints raised and deliberated upon and finally left unresolved at the end of the book. He confesses to this element in his existence in the novel when he tells Pierre-Louis towards the end of the story that "Je ne suis pas d'un pays Diallobé distance, face à Occident distinct, et appréciant d'une tête froide ce que je puis lui prendre et ce qu'il faut que je lui laisse en contrepartie. *Je suis devenu les deux*" (p. 174; my emphasis).

Out of this self-division grows what has become a central distinguishing characteristic of Anti-Heroism - loneliness. In his *The Divided Self* R.D. Laing describes the character exhibiting the type of split we find in Samba Diallo as "schizoid." This term, he says, "refers to an individual the totality of whose experience is split in two main ways: in the first place there is a rent in his relation with his world and, in the second, there is a disruption of his relation with himself." Such a person, he adds, "is not able to experience himself 'together with' others or 'at home in' the world but, on the contrary, he experiences himself in despairing aloneness and isolation."[21] Samba Diallo is an intensely lonely figure, both by choice and by circumstances: by virtue of his noble birth, he is alienated from youth, from his age group even while still a disciple of Thierno's. this separation is further sharpened by the nature of his education which called for ceaseless meditation on the human condition. As he grows up, therefore, introspection becomes a central affective disposition in his personality structure. This becomes most evident in Paris where he finds it impossible to establish any lasting bonds of friendship with anybody. He sees people only from a purely intellectual or philosophical standpoint, and not from any really human stance. He describes the people in the street as "des objets de chair" (p. 150). All he sees is himself: "Il y a rien ... que moi ... que mon corps" (p.151).

The Psychological Dimensions of Samba Diallo's Victimization

Samba Diallo's tragedy is a result not of the tyranny of the West but of "the tyranny of the 'shoulds.' In assuming this standpoint which runs directly counter to what has traditionally been taken as the cause of his suffering, I have shifted the emphasis from his encounter with European society to his training under Thierno as the main cause of all his woes.

In his study, *Character and Conflict in Jane Austen's Novels,* Bernard Paris describes himself *Mansfield Park* as "the story of a girl whose selfhood and spontaneity have been crushed by a pathogenic environment and who develops, in response, a set of socially sanctioned but personally crippling defensive stategies."[22] With only a slight modification, Samba Diallo's fate can be ascribed to the same factors. Against the backdrop of Third Force psychology, we can perceive that what predisposes Samba Diallo to defeat is the nature of the philosophies of those set in authority over him prior to his entering the French Primary School in Senegal. He will be shown to be a victim of what Karen Horney called "the tyranny of the shoulds," in her *Neurosis and Human Growth*.[23]

Third Force psychologists see healthy human development as a process of self-actualization, and unhealthy development as a process of self-alienation. They contend that man is not just a tension-reducing or a conditioned animal, but that there is in him a third force, an evolutionary, constructive force which urges him to realize his given potentialities. Each man, they argue, possesses an essential biologically based inner nature which, if permitted to guide the individual's life, would enable him to grow healthy, live fruitfully and happy. But if that inner nature is suppressed or denied, the possessor falls sick. This inner nature, they say, is weak, delicate and subtle and is very easily overcome by habit, cultural pressure and wrong attitudes toward it.

There are ever so many attitudes towards inner nature which can be considered destructive. Karen Horney has labelled one set of such attitudes, "shoulds." These, she says are those inner dictates which demand of the individual that:

> *He should be the utmost of honesty, generosity, considerateness, justice, dignity, courage, unselfishness ... He should be able to endure everything, should like everybody, should love his parents, his wife, his country; or he should never feel hurt, and he should always be serene and unruffled... He should be above pleasure and enjoyment. He should spontaneous; he should always control his feelings. He should know, understand and foresee everything. He should be able to solve every problem of his own, or of others, in no time. He should be able to overcome every difficulty of his own as soon as he sees it. (NHG, p. 65).*

Although Horney herself confesses that this is only a brief survey which does not pretend to cover all inner dictates, she points out that "this survey, roughly indicating the scope of inner dictates, leaves us with the impression of demands on self which, though understandable, are altogether too difficult and too rigid" (NHG, p. 65). It is a major characteristic of *shoulds,* she says, that they exhibit *"disregard for feasibility* ...[and] are of a kind which no human being could fulfil" (NHG, p. 66), they "show a complete *disregard for the conditions* under which they could be fulfilled" (NHG, p. 66); they are "exactly like political tyranny in a police state, [and] operate with supreme *disregard for the person's own psychic conditions* - for what he can feel or do as he is at present" (NHG, p. 68; all emphases are Horney's).

A closer examination of the first three chapters of *L'Adventure ambiguë* reveals that Samba Diallo is a victim of the shoulds more than anything else. The *shoulds* which he imbibes and makes a philosophy of life are not self-created, but are drilled into him in the most brutal way possible. He is given "corps et âme" (p. 25) into the care of the ascetic master of the Koranic school at the age of seven. The first line and the first page of the story set the tone for the crudity of the methods of education employed by Thierno, his teacher:

Ce jour-là, Thierno l'avait battu. Cependant, Samba Diallo savait son verset. Simplement sa langue lui avait fourche. Thierno avait sursaute comme s'il eut marche sur une des dalles incandescentes de la genhenne promise aux mécréants. Il avait saisi Samba Diallo au gras de la cuisse, l'avait pince du pouce et de l'index, longuement. Le petit enfant avait halite sous la douleur, et s'était mis à trembler de tout son corps. Au bord du sanglot qui lui nouait la poitrine et la gorge, il avait eu assez de force pour maîtriser, sa douleur; il avait répété d'une pauvre voix brisée et chuchotante, mais correctement, la phrase du saint verset qu'il avait mal prononcée. La rage du maître monta d'un degré (p. 15).

It is a cardinal principle in Thierno's philosophy of education that the pupil *should not make a mistake.* He warns:

Sois précis en repentant la Parole de ton Seigneur ... Il t'a fait la grâce de descendre Son Verbe jusqu'à toi. Ces paroles, le Maître du Monde les a véritablement prononcées. Et toi, misérable moisissure de la terre, quand tu as l'honneur de les répéter après lui, tu négliges au point de les profaner. Tu mérites qu'on te coupe mille fois la langue (p. 16).

"La Parole qui vient de Dieu," he says, "doit être dite exactement" (p. 17). Dorothy Blair has summed up Thierno's intentions rather neatly when she says "by the inhumanity of his treatment the Master deliberately aims at instilling a contempt for the flesh, an absolute exaltation, a sole passion for the mystery and the beauty of the Word of God, of which he feels his young disciple is capable."[24] Every possible method of inflicting pain is devised and employed on the poor pupil just so that he should conform to the master's conception of a good pupil. Thierno is not above holding him by the ear and, cutting through the cartilage of the lobes until his nails meet. Thierno sees nobility as synonymous with pride, both which were a complete contradiction to an attainment of spirituality, and so in their place he injects a feeling of humility or, more aptly, humiliation. The narrator tells us that

Le maître croyait profondément que l'adoration de Dieu n'était compatible avec aucune exaltation de l'homme. Or, au fond de toute noblesse, il est un fond de paganisme. La noblesse est l'exaltation de l'homme, la foi est avant tout humilité, sinon humiliation (p. 37).

If, as Sunday Anozie has observed in his *Sociologie du roman africain*, "L'appréhension intuitive de l'Externel constitue donc une condition préalable à l'apprentissage du rôle de successeur du Maître au quelle Samba Diallo est destiné,"[25] it must be understood that the exercise renders him psychically incapable of tackling life's other problems once he is taken out of Thierno's control.

One way of understanding Samba Diallo's problem and the reasons for his inevitable failure and Anti-Heroism is to analyse his relationship with Thierno in terms of the dialectics between self-actualization and self-alienation. Although most of the time an author's comments on his book are not necessarily the most illuminating things to be said about it, Cheikh Hamidou Kane seems to me to be more tacitly aware of the root cause of Samba Diallo's tragedy than most critics. When asked about the end of the book in an interview with Phanuel Egejuru, he said among other things that:

> *The difference between Samba in Europe and Samba back in Africa is that while in Europe he learnt something about religion, he knows now that when one has the faith, one also must have the liberty of thought and expression. The society should not impose religious belief on you. You can have faith in God, and nobody has the right to impose this faith on you. However, in our society we have not reached that level of thinking. Our society controls the religious practice of individuals.*[26]

Before turning back to Karen Horney whose writings among the Third Force Psychologists are the most illuminating in this respect, it has to be ascertained that Samba Diallo's environment is pathogenic, that it is unhealthy for any really positive development. The most significant point is the fact that nobody seems to care about his personal feelings. People look on him as an object for the gratification of their separate desires. When Thierno, prior to taking over the control of Samba, tells his father that "votre fils, je le crois, est de la graine dont le pays des Diallobé faisant ses maîtres" (p. 25), it is no oracular pronouncement, because if they had taken advantage of his royal blood and brought him up according to his desire and potentiality for noble endeavours, he would have become a leader. But as soon as Thierno says that, he wins Samba's father's heart and he is given away. Thierno himself, as we have seen, works on him not like a psychologist or a teacher with compassion but like a bull-dozer.

There is no indication that Thierno is being hypocritical about his teaching methods, and when he tells Grande Royale with undistinguished optimism that "après cette blessure profonde pratiquée d'une main paternelle, je vous promets que plus jamais cet enfant ne se blessera" (p. 42), he is sincere about it. But this does not imply that the beating and wounding is best for the child. Yet the parents accept Thierno's logic and it is only as a political or rather military ploy that Samba is taken from Thierno and sent into the French Primary School. Even the idea of sending him to the French school has very little to do with his personal interests or potentials - the fact that Samba does well should not invalidate the force of my argument - but is designed to serve the interests of the politically-minded Grande Royale. Her ambition is for Samba Diallo to "aller apprendre chez eux l'art de vaincre sans avoir raison" (p. 52).

To Thierno himself the education of Samba Diallo had more to do with his own ego than that of the pupil. Ferdinand Oyono's Toundi had stressed his Anti-Heroism by boasting how he had become the lucky object for the gratification of others' wishes. Of Father Gilbert he said "il me présente à tous les blancs qui viennent à la Mission comme son chef-d'oeuvre."[27] Samba Diallo finds himself in virtually the same position, for Thierno's intentions were "de faire de lui le chef-d'œuvre de sa longue carrière" (p. 37).

According to Karen Horney, people respond to a pathogenic environment by developing three basic strategies of defence: they move toward people and adopt a self-effacing or compliant solution; they move against people and adopt the aggressive or expansive solution; or they move away from people and become detached or resigned. Each of these solutions, she says, carries with it "certain needs, qualities, sensitivities, inhibitions, anxieties, and last but not least, a particular set of values."[28] Each of these solutions involves also a view of human nature, a sense of the world order and a bargain with fate. Samba Diallo belongs to the complaint personality type, in whom compliant trends are dominant needs "to be liked, wanted, desired, loved; to feel .. approved of, appreciated; ... to be protected, taken care of, guided" (OIC, p. 51). His values "lie in the direction of goodness, sympathy, love, generosity, unselfishness, humility; while egotism, ambition, callousness, unscrupulousness, wielding of power are abhorred" (OIC, pp. 54-55).

Although Samba Diallo definitely exhibits all or most of these qualities, they appear to me to have been super-imposed on a personality whose natural line of development lies in a different or even in the reverse direction. The natural disposition for anybody from a royal family, a family that has bred a 'La Grande Royale' would be to wield power, give instructions, eat well and dress well. That Thierno succeeds in exacting from him undying humility, abstinence and total self-denial can only be described as an act of repression of Samba Diallo's potentialities for self-actualization. The natural concomitant to this is self-alienation and neurosis, and the assumption of what R.D.Laing has described as a "false-self system."[29]

The false self of the schizoid personality, says Laing, "is compulsively compliant to the will of others, it is partially autonomous and out of control, it is felt as alien; the unrealness, meaninglessness, purposelessness which permeate its perceptions, thoughts, feelings, and actions, and its overall deadness, are not simply productions of secondary defences but are direct consequences of the basic dynamic structure of the individual's being.[30] Samba Diallo can only pretend that he is doing fine, for the loss of his true self continues to haunt him. The narrator tells us that "la noblesse de son origine lui pesait non point comme un fardeau dont il eût peur, mais à la manière d'un diadème trop encombrant et trop visible. A la manière d'une injustice aussi. Il désirait la noblesse …" (p. 30).

It is in the nature of the depiction of the Anti-Hero that either by design or fortuitously, nothing ever happens that is answerable to his dreams. Samba Diallo's futility in trying to hide his real self is well expressed:

> *Il s'était humilié et mortifié, par manière d'exercise et aussi pour manifester hautement qu'il revendiquait d'être aligné au niveau de tous ses condisciples. Mais rien n'y avait fait. Il semblait au contraire que ses camarade lui en voulussent de ce que, par devers eux, ils n'étaient pas loin de considérer comme le comble de l'orgueil. Il ne passait pas de jour que quelqu'un ne fît de remarque sur la noblesse de son port ou sur l'élégance racée de son maintien, en dépit des haillons sordides dont il se couvrait. Il arrivait même qu'on lui fît grief de ses mouvements naturels de générosité et jusqu'à franchise. Plus il se surveillait, plus on le dénonçait. Il en était exaspéré (pp. 30-31).*

Psychoanalysts describe the circumstances under which Samba Diallo found himself as anxiety neurosis. The fact that he no longer feels either safe or loved and accepted generates a feeling of self-alienation within him. Neurosis, Karen Horney has said, begins as a defence against basic anxiety, which is "a profound insecurity and vague apprehensiveness" (NHG, p. 18), which as we have seen, surrounds Samba Diallo. This, she says springs from feelings of isolation, helplessness, fear, and hostility, which again, has been well depicted by the author in his description of Samba Diallo's predicament above. In *New Ways in Psychoanalysis* she indicates that it involves the dread of the environment as a whole, which is "felt to be unreliable, mendacious, unappreciative, unfair, ... begrudging ... merciless."[31] As a result of this dread, Horney says, the child develops self-protective strategies, which in time become compulsive. His "attempts to relate himself to others are determined not by his real feelings but by strategic necessities. He cannot simply like or dislike, trust or distrust, express his wishes or protest against those of others, but has automatically to devise ways to cope with people" (OIC, p. 219).

Kane's depiction of Samba Diallo seems to follow this paradigm rather closely. When la Grande Royale decides that Samba Diallo should be sent to the French School, he does not remonstrate, despite the fact that it was impossible for him to dissociate himself emotionally from his involvement with the teachings of his teacher Thierno. We are told that "Samba Diallo se laissait gâter avec apparemment la même profonde égalité d'âme que lorsqu'il subissait les mauvais traitements du foyer" (pp. 54-55).

Before he enters the French School therefore, the pattern of his future personality is almost irrevocably formed. Henceforth life will become an ambiguous adventure. He will behave in a manner not different in any way from what Horney calls the detached, self-effacing personality, determined to shut others out of his inner life. He will wander into the cemetery along and lie down to pray for a friend, and for all his stay in Paris we will not be given access to his mind. Only on one occasion does he talk directly about his feelings towards Europeans: "Je les ai aimés trop tôt, imprudement, sans les connaître assez" (. 184). And we are not surprised that he accepts from childhood to obey without question, without reasoning because he has been conditioned. His depiction as Anti-Hero becomes complete.

Style and Characterization Techniques

One of the most significant features of *L'Aventure ambigue* is the versatility of Cheikh Hamidou Kane's techniques of characterization. He defies any specific categorization like point of view or any single characterizing device. He employs with relatively equal sense and effectiveness, at least six different techniques of depicting character, ranging from description, dialogue, action, and interior monologue, to setting and manipulation of point of view.

Une Vie de boy and (to a very large extent) *Un Piège sans fin* were written from a strictly first person narrative point of view. In *L'Aventure* ambiguë Hamidou Kane employs the omniscient point of view, but in a manner which differs from what was seen in the case of Armah in *The Beautiful Ones:* as if viewing the characters from behind a pair of bifocal lenses, he presents each individual to us first through a wide-angle lens and then through a close-up lens, or vice versa. Generally he follows or watches his characters from a distance, focusing on one or the other, depending on the circumstance, or the issue at stake. Very rarely does he actually look through the eyes of any one of them, the way Armah used "the Man's" perspective, or the way Oyono used Toundi's. the technique which he uses here approximates what we find in popular films: Hamidou Kane's personalities are not presented impressionistically like Armah's. They are described as realistically as possible. But as in films where directors decide on particular scenes because they produce particular effects, without paying too much attention to what has transpired between the scenes, Hamidou Kane also presents us with a series of very vivid scenes, strongly revealing of character.

The appropriateness of the device of multiple perspectives to a novel like *L'Aventure ambiguë* whose central theme is ambiguity has been fairly well expressed by Majorie Boulton in her *The Anatomy of the Novel* where she says: "telling a story from several points of view has obvious possibilities for representing characters in depth, or the ambiguities of life."[32]

Description

Description seems to be Hamidou Kane's most effective technique. Generally, description implies the detailed presentation (though not exclusively) of the physical aspects of a personage which suggest that individual's character traits. Hamidou Kane's technique in this context is almost the same as what Geoffrey Chaucer employs in his *The Canterbury Tales:* he first gives us a thumb-nail sketch of the character, and then proceeds to show us the character in action. In every instance, the character we find in action does not contradict what we already know of him in the summary description. For example, before Grand Royale makes any monumental decisions on the life and destiny of Samba Diallo, Hamidou Kane gives us both a wide-angle as well as a close-up view of her:

> *Lorsqu'il [Samba Diallo] leva la tête, son regard rencontra un grand visage altier, une tête de femme qu'emmitouflait une légère voilette de gaze blanche.*
>
> *On la nommait la Grande Royale. Elle avait soixante ans et on lui en eut donne quarante a peine. On ne voyait d'elle que le visage. Le grand boubou bleu qu'elle portrait traînait jusqu'à terre et ne laissait rien apparaître d'elle que le bout pointu de ses babouches jaunes d'or, lorsqu'elle marchait. La voilette de gaze entourait le cou, couvrait la tête, repassait sous le menton et pendait derrière, sur l'épaule gauche. La Grande Royale, qui pouvait bien avoir un mètre quatre-vingt, n'avait rien perdu de sa prestance malgré son âge (p. 34).*

Hamidou Kane achieves practically the same effect when he describes Thierno for the first time (pp. 18-19), and the Chevalier (p. 106). He describes Grande Royale in terms which exude authority and imperiousness, and when it comes to deciding Samba Diallo's future, it is this personality that reigns supreme. Thierno too is portrayed as moody and fanatically devoted to the responsibilities of his religion. This is the personality that emerges to assume control of Samba Diallo's spirit.

In this connection it must be mentioned that Hamidou Kane's description of his major personalities is calculated to pander to foreign tastes. Although in an answer to a question on audience posed by Phanuel Egejuru in an interview Hamidou Kane confessed that he had no particular audience in mind when he wrote the novel, the interviewer was right in insisting that the author had consciously employed in his creations a combination of images that would appeal both to European and African readers.[33] The very titles La Grande Royale, and Le Chevalier, are out of character with traditional African society, and were deliberately put there along with their medieval background, to appeal to the European's sense of greatness and of history. In this sense, Hamidou Kane confirms (though he would not admit it), Clayton Hamilton's observation that "our judgment of characters in a novel should be conditioned always by our sense of the sort of readers to whom the novel is addressed."[34]

Dialogue and Action

Because of the philosophical nature of the text, all action is reduced to intellectual debates centred around the cultural conflict between Europe and Africa in which dialogue is an essential stylistic contour. Most of the time, the characters reveal their various personalities through verbal exchange. Here I am thinking particularly of the various arguments they propose and insist on, rather than of Hamidou Kane's use of the idiom of particular speakers. Unlike what we would find in Achebe's use of language, but quite similar to what Ngugi does in *A Grain of Wheat*, peculiarities of language are not crucial elements in distinguishing between one character and the other. The speeches of the mad man differ from those of Samba Diallo or any other character only in the forcefulness with which they are presented. Thus, the entire work reads like the minutes of a debate in which the secretary has been concerned more with the topics and opinions than the tone of rendition.

Interior Monologue

It has already been established that Samba Diallo is given to much introspection. As such, the greater part of his conflict, suffering and final defeat tend to be interiorized. This cannot be described as a stream-of-consciousness novel by any standard, although the interior monologue is often associated with such writing. But by recording the internal emotional experience of the character - which is one of the main qualities of interior monologue - Hamidou Kane is able, says Shiver, to make Samba Diallo's consciousness "a synthesis of the Word and knowledge." This device, says Shiver, is used as the means by which "the hero's consciousness is detached from necessarily limiting experiences in the uncertain and conditional world that now apprehends its own nature."[35] This fact is fairly well expressed in any of Samba Diallo's numerous reflections while in Paris. For example he says:

> *Il me semble encore qu'en venant ici, j'ai perdu un monde de connaissance privilégié. Jadis, le monde m'était comme la demeure de mon père: toute chose me portrait au plus essential d'elle-même comme si rien ne pouvait être que par moi. Le monde n'était pas silencieux et neutre. Il vivait. Il était agressif. Il diluait autour de lui. Aucun savant jamais n'a eu de rien la connaissance que j'avais alors de l'être (p. 174).*

Setting and Imagery

Setting or the use of background, accentuated by a wide range of imagery constitutes the last important device Hamidou Kane employs to give meaning to the type of characters that he creates. The major characters are of noble stature, and the subject of debate is serious. But the nobility is undercut by a fusion in the narrative of an atmosphere of tension and a sense of doom. Although the stories of the wars in the past are designed to place the present events in true historical perspective, and to give a sense of urgency to Samba Diallo's mission, they prepare us for disaster. This point is very effectively brought out by Samba Diallo's father in the first chapter of the novel:

> *Il est certain que rien n'est aussi bruyamment envahissant que les besoins auxquels leur école permet de satisfaire. Nous n'avons plus rien ... grâce à eux, et c'est par là qu'ils nous tiennent. Qui veux vivre, qui veut demeurer soi-même doit se compromettre. Les forgerons et les bûcherons sont partout victorieux dans le monde et leur fer nous maintient sous leur loi (p. 23).*

Thus even though we know that Grande Royale wants Samba Diallo to learn the tricks by which to beat the white man at his own game, we also know that the mission is futile.

Images of disease, death or violent destruction abound: the scene of Samba Diallo's lessons with Thierno is a hearth, and Thierno is said to be holding "une bûche ardente tirée du foyer tout proche [pendant qu'il] regardait et écoutait l'enfant" (p. 17); the hut itself in which the teaching takes place is described as "la case silencieuse" where the disciples sit "envolé avec le crepuscule" (p. 43); the new school to which Samba Diallo is sent is equated with gunboat, cannons and magnets: "l'école nouvelle participait de la nature du cannon et de l'aimant à la fois" (p. 65).

In his defence of Shakespeare, Samuel Johnson said "he that tries to recommend him by selecting quotations will succeed like the pedant in *Hierocles,* who, when he offered his house to sale, carried a brick in his pocket as a specimen."[36] What this means here is that no amount of selections can do justice to the range of versatility of the styles and images which Hamidou Kane employs in this novel. All I have tried to do is indicate directions in which *some* of them occur.

L'Aventure ambiguë is an extremely complex novel in which the issues are so interrelated that it is almost impossible to attempt to isolate any one characteristic of the novel and discuss it intelligently. It has, however, been possible and necessary for us to deviate from the tradition of balancing one of the philosophical issues discussed in the novel against the other in order to talk about the philosophies as though the protagonist is indefinable. This has been done mainly by focusing attention on the often neglected or generally misunderstood psychological cause of his victimization, failure ore Anti-Heroism.

This in turn has been vitality connected with a series of technical devices which Hamidou Kane has employed in his portrayal of character in the novel as a whole. Focus on character type and characterization, in fact, allows us to discuss complexities in the novel which rescue it from the aesthetic misapprehensions and misjudgements of the majority of its critics to date. Whereas character may not be the focus of the novelist's intent, it is more than a vehicle for ideological argumentation, and when we scrutinize the novel's architecture closely, Africa becomes less of a set of ideas, and more a place of people who suffer because of them. Scrutiny of Kane's skill as a literary creator rather than as a political commentator, then, brings us to a deeper understanding of politics as something human, as a scene with living actors, than it is a set of clothed abstractions.

Notes

[1] *Neurosis and Human Growth: The Struggle Toward Self-Realization* (New York: Norton, 1950), p. 17. In this chapter references will be made to this edition only. The title will be represented by NHG following each reference.

[2] "Cheikh Hamidou Kane's *L'Aventure ambiguë,*" *Yale French Studies,* no. 53 (1976), p. 92.

[3] Ibid., p. 95.

[4] *Black Writers, White Audience: A Critical Approach to African Literature,* New York: Exposition Press, 1978), p. 149.

[5] Ibid., p. 150.

[6] Cheikh Hamidou Kane, *L'Aventure ambiguë: Récit* (Paris: Rene Julliard, 1961), p. 22. All further references to the novel are from the present edition. Page numbers are indicated after each citation.

[7] *Introduction a la Litterature noire,* op. cit., p. 67.

[8] This seems to be the central argument in much of the criticism that exists now on the book. A.C. Brench is one of the very few critics to indicate that "the political and social implications are relegated to a position of secondary importance while the emphasis is

placed on the philosophical conflict between Islam and European rationalist materialism"; "Cheikh Hamidou Kane: *L'aventure ambiguë,*" in The Novelists' *Inheritance in French Africa* (London: Oxford Univ. Press, 1967), pp. 99-100. Brench, however, does not establish the cause of his failure clearly.

[9] In this novel we have come a very long way from the world depicted by Mongo Beti and Ferdinand Oyono which virtually dramatizes Fanon's affective erethism affective ankylosis, or Mannoni's Prospero/Caliban cult. The Africans here do not carry everywhere with them scars or wounds, indicative of the oppression of the white man. They do not grovel. They approach the Europeans not as a mortal approaching a deity but as equals. Samba Diallo is well respected by the European students with whom he studies. The Europeans are generally unprejudiced and there is mutual respect between Laroix and Samba's father. To this extent, therefore, one has to look elsewhere for the cause of Samba Diallo's failure.

[10] *Actes du colloque sur la littérature africaine d'expression française* (Dakar: Faculté des lettres, 1965), pp. 177-188.

[11] *ALT,* no. 12 (1982), pp. 49-69.

[12] op. cit., pp. 99-109.

[13] *The Novelist's Inheritance in French Africa,* p. 105.

[14] *Towards African Literary Independence: A Dialogue with Contemporary African Writers,* ed. Phanuel A. Egejuru (Westport Conn.: Greenwood Press, 1980), p. 147.

[15] *The Heroic Temper,* op. cit., p. 44.

[16] (New York: Jarcourt, Brace, 1970), pp. 29-30.

[17] "The Emergence of the Anti-Hero in the Contemporary Drama," op. cit., p. 95.

[18] Ibid., p. 96.

[19] *STructuralist Poetics: Structuralism, Linguistics and the Study of Literature,* op. cit., p. 230.

[20] *Actes du collogue sur la littérature africaine,* p. 164.

[21] *The Divided Self: An Existential Study in Insanity and Madness* (London: Tavistock Publications, 1960), p. 15.

[22] (Detroit: Wayne State Univ., 1978), p. 23

[23] Op. cit.,
[24] *AFricaine Literature in French,* p. 263.
[25] (Paris: Aubier-Montagne, 1970), p. 149
[26] *Towards African Literary Independence* ..., p. 26.
[27] *Une Vie de boy,* p. 26.
[28] *Our Inner Conflicts: A Constructive Theory of Neurosis* (New York: Norton, 1945), p. 49.
[29] *The Divided Self,* p. 100.
[30] Ibid., p. 102.
[31] (New York: Norton, 1939), p. 75.
[32] (London: Routledge & Kegan Paul, 1975), p. 40.
[33] This is the view taken by Egejuru on the subject of style and audience in the novel. She describes Hamidou Kane's technique here as "reversed anthropology, that is, using European cultural images to describe African characters," *Black Writers, White Audience,* op., cit., p. 150.
[34] *Methods of Fiction* (London: Grant Richards, 1909), p. 76.
[35] "Hamidou Kane's Hero," pp. 55-56.
[36] "Preface to Shakespeare," *The Great Critics,* op. cit., p. 446.

Chapter Six

Obi Okonkwo (Chinua Achebe's *No Longer At Ease*, 1960)

> *"The anti-hero ... is the hero of 'what might have been,' but who never in fact achieves heroic proportions."*
>
> *(G.R. Ridge: "The Anti-Hero").*[1]

> *It is evident almost from the beginning of No Longer at Ease that Obi is not of heroic nature and that his tragedy will not be a falling in full battle but rather it will result from an inability to face up to that battle. He never rises to greatness; he only sinks further and further and further from it, succumbing to what he has labelled the sin of the "old African."*
>
> *(Steven Gale: Chinua Achebe's No Longer at Ease).*[2]

Plot Summary

No Longer at Ease tells the story of Obi Okonkwo, a young Nigerian who has just returned from London with a B.A. Honours degree in English. Along with this rare accomplishment Obi is bringing with him a burning determination to rid his country of corruption and to play a major role in the moulding of the country into a respectable state according to the pledges he and his compatriots had always made at student conferences while still in England. His intentions, no doubt, are excellent. But he seems doomed from the moment he resolves to carry out those pledges because he does not make any allowance for extenuating circumstances, or the natural disposition of the average Nigerian civil servant.

On the boat that is bringing him back to Nigeria, Obi meets (though not for the first time) and falls in love with Clara, an Ibo nurse whose family background he does not find it necessary to know. (They will meet again while she is working at a Lagos hospital, and Obi will decide against all odds to marry her. This relationship proves a prime factor in Obi's final undoing.)

Obi had been sent to study in England, thanks to an eight hundred pounds scholarship/loan awarded to him by the Lagos Branch of the Umuofia Progressive Union (henceforth simply, 'the Union'). Upon his return, and because they are convinced that he is being paid what appears to the Union to be an enormous amount of money, the Union expects Obi to pay back the debt as soon as possible. The Union also assumes, and therefore expects that the payment will be made without compromising the pride of the tribe. Obi has come to stand for the very embodiment of the aspirations and pride of the tribe which will not be satisfied if he lives a life-style that does not measure up to and/or surpass that of his fellow officials in the government departments. The Union's prayers are answered and its expectations made all the more valid when Obi is appointed the Scholarship Secretary at the Federal Ministry of Education.

But though the Union expects Obi to pay back the money while living a most enviable life, it also insists that this should be achieved without sacrificing his identity as an Ibo man with a distinct tradition to uphold. Consequently, Obi's decision to marry Clara does not sit well with the Ibo culture because, although Obi does not care about it, Clara is an *Osu,* a descendant of a caste of slaves, and he is the son of a proud family of free-borns.

On his own part, Obi considers his decision a purely personal affair and so will not change it. Upon the confident assumption that it is his indebtedness to the Union that is encouraging it to interfere in his private life, Obi decides against his better judgment to tell the Union's President off at a meeting which is summoned to discuss his commitments, and during which the issue of his relationship with Clara is raised. He decides there and then to start paying back the debt at the end of the month, a pledge which does not leave him with much to take care of his other problems which the mad tempo of Lagos city life imposes on him. He has already bought a car and acquired a chauffeur to go with it; he has also bought a fridge, while still being deeply committed to sending money every month to cater for his brother's education back home.

Meanwhile, the possibilities of his marriage to Clara grow worse: he does not succeed in winning over to his side the one person whose decision matters to him, his mother. Then Clara gets pregnant and he decides to shoulder the responsibilities of aborting the pregnancy, thereby aggravating his extremely precarious financial position. And no sooner has Clara survived the ordeal of the abortion than she flees Lagos for good.

The noose begins to tighten around Obi's neck: his bills and debts mount by the hour and frustration becomes his only bedfellow. His idealism and flimsy moral rectitude, once the bulwarks of his personality, begin to crumble against the repeated requests of ambitious but unqualified Nigerians. He finds it impossible to resist the temptations to which his office has always exposed him. Men continue to offer him money, and young girls their bodies, in order that their names might be included in the very short list of scholarship winners. Obi becomes the unfortunate target of police investigation, is set up and caught with marked notes, tried and jailed.

State of Criticism of Character

A valid appreciation of the character of Obi has been substantially thwarted by the fact that *No Longer at Ease* was consciously conceived and written as a sequel to *Thing Fall Apart*. The text itself emphasizes the element of continuity between the two novels in a scene in the village of Umuofia where Obi has come to visit while awaiting the results of his job interview. There, the old man Odogwu tickles Obi's vanity by saying very proudly of him that "he is the grandson of Ogbuefi Okonkwo who faced the white man single-handed and died in the fight .... He is Ogbuefi Okonkwo come back. He is Okonkwo *Kpom-kpwem,* exact, perfect."[3]

For some reason several critics seem to have seized on these words as though they were Achebe's declaration of his intentions in the book. Such critics have subsequently gone on to use Okonkwo as the yardstick by which his grandson, Obi is to be measured. Not surprisingly, Obi has been found greatly wanting, and his inadequacy beside his legendary grandfather has generally been taken as an indication of a failure of artistic intent on the part of Achebe. This, very briefly, is the thesis underlying the efforts of Abiola Irele, Eustace Palmer and others in examining Achebe's handling of Obi Okonkwo's character in the novel.

In his "The tragic Conflict in Achebe's Novels," Abiola Irele says:

> *Obi's dilemma is contained in the conflict between his developed intellectual insight and his lack of moral strength.... His weakness of character is reflected in his inept handling of his human relationships and of his material problems. He is an individual with no sense of order .... Obi is never really prepared to engage in any sort of sustained effort, with the result that he flounders through life.*[4]

He argues quite forcefully and legitimately that the theme of the novel has all the outward trappings of a tragedy, but regrets that "it is not given an adequately tragic treatment."[5] He sees as the foremost shortcoming of the novel, "the inadequate stature of the hero," and concludes by pointing out that:

> *Obi as he is portrayed is simply not the stuff of which a tragic character is made. He is a pathetic figure without any grain of nobility. Unlike his grandfather, he is a passive sufferer of his fate and the emotion that he inspires is not pity but antipathy.*[6]

In his *An Introduction to the African Novel*, Eustace Palmer has also condemned the protagonist as "weak and insufficiently realized, ... too uninteresting and vaguely portrayed." The crux of his charge is the fact that:

> Rather than determining the course of events, Obi allows events to overtake him, and is merely borne along by the force of circumstance. A tragic hero should possess impressive qualities. Since Obi Okonkwo merely succumbs to the forces against him, he falls short of tragic stature; nor is he a martyr, since he is crushed for betraying his principles, not for championing them.[7]

The truth can hardly be disputed that the characterization of Obi is far less profound than that of his grandfather. And in that case it is possible to speculate that Achebe's creative talents may have diminished somewhat between the writing of *Things Fall Apart* and *No Longer at Ease*. But the weakness of the arguments presented against Obi lies in the failure of Irele, Palmer and other critics who fall within this category to take cognizance of the fact that in *No Longer at Ease* Chinua Achebe is dealing with an entirely different type of protagonist. The mere reason that Obi is a blood relation of Okonkwo of *Things Fall Apart* should not disguise the fact. Ogbuefi Okonkwo was a hero in the best senses of the concept. On the other hand, Michael Obiajulu Okonkwo, to give him his full name, is an Anti-Hero in more ways than one. To this extent he is therefore not to be looked upon as an unsuccessful attempt to produce a replica of his grandfather. This distinction is critical for an understanding of the depiction of the protagonist as well as for an appropriate valuation of Achebe's accomplishment as a creative artist.

Gerald Moore does not mention the term "Anti-Hero," but his observations in his *Seven African Writers* prove particularly illuminating in this discussion:

> If *No longer at Ease* is something less than a tragedy, it is because Achebe does not see Obi as a tragic hero. The pressures that pull and mould him are all pressures making for compromise and accommodation; these are not the stuff of tragedy but of failure and decline.

It was asserted early in this study that heroism loses its emphasis as we move away from literature that depicts traditional society. The relationship between Okonkwo and Obi illustrates the point very clearly. *Things Fall Apart* was set very closer to traditional life than *No Longer at Ease* in Sean O'Faolin describes. Very easily, the one abiding element in the construction or reconstruction of the structures of Obi's personality as an Anti-Hero is his utter lack of perspicacity, a kind of moral myopia that grows from, and is in turn fed by an idealistic conception of society. Blindness constitutes the nodal point about which Achebe weaves the manifest structures of his being.

The nadir of Obi's failures, and the event which places him irrevocably in the Anti-Heroic mould, is his imprisonment. This incident, which Achebe deftly works out and presents as a direct outcome of his incompetence at management of his finances and the clash between Obi's Western education and traditional Ibo values, is ultimately reducible to, and explicable mainly in terms of a dismal "lack of perspicacity." His is a definite case of ignorance masquerading as philosophy, of naiveté masquerading as sophistication.

Obi's end is very clearly foreshadowed in his very first appearance before his tribesmen as a group when a meeting is held on Moloney Street to welcome him back from England. On that occasion Achebe himself singles out two major mistakes: "Everybody was properly dressed in *agbada* or European suit except the guest of honour, who appeared in his shirt-sleeves" (p. 13). This, says Achebe, "was Obi's mistake Number One" (p. 31). It is true that he dressed that way to circumvent the heat rather than out of any deliberate attempt to infuriate his people. But, having lived among the Umuofians, he did not require anybody else to tell him, as Achebe says that on such an occasion "everybody expected a young man from England to be impressively turned out" (p. 31). To be ignorant of this, or even to take it lightly, indicates an obvious lack of judgment on his part. The second mistake, the less culpable charge of speaking unimpressively, is again a failure on his part to discern the likes of his people and to place this above his own ideals.

The break with the Union on the fateful day when he is summoned to discuss plans for paying back his loan, could very easily have been avoided with only a little more sagacity on his part. If he had chosen not to discuss the relationship with Clara, he would still have been allowed to work out a more convenient way of paying back the debt. That decision to start paying back the money at the end of the month completely failed to take in to consideration the fact that he still had to pay for the car and its insurance, that he had to pay his chauffeur, and that he had to send money home to pay his brother's education. It was rash in all senses of the word and his ruin may very well have stemmed from this moment. The same rashness which leads him to tell the Union off governs his attitude towards Clara. He is outraged that anybody should allow himself to be bound by an unnecessary tradition taboo:

> *It is scandalous that in the middle of the twentieth century a man could be barred from marrying a girl simply because her great-great-great grandfather had been dedicated to serve a god, thereby setting himself apart and turning his descendants into a forbidden caste to the end of Time (p. 72).*

Although he would like to think so, his decision to marry Clara is no personal matter. It cannot be justified by mere cerebration or logical hair-splitting. It completely violates community imperatives, and it is in the nature of his personality as an Anti-Hero that he remains the only person who fails to see it the way it ought to be seen - the traditional way. When he first mentions marriage, Clara tells him: "I can't marry you .... I am an *osu*" (pp. 70-71). When he brings up the question during conversation with Joseph, he is asked whether he knows the implications of the term. Mistaking his own blindness for insight Obi claims: "I know more about it than yourself.... I'm going to marry the girl" (p. 72).

From the manner in which *osu* is presented in the book - Obi's father describes it as a kind of leprosy - nobody in his right frame of mind would risk marrying Clara unless such an individual belonged to the same caste with her. Yet, "accentuated by a foolhardy ....personal courage," as O'Faolin would have said, Obi refuses to take advice from anybody on the issue.

His actual handling of money proves to be even more disastrous than his judgment of societal norms. He decides to buy a car not upon receipt of his first salary but "one week after he received his letter of appointment" (p. 66). And not only this, he acquires a chauffeur, an act which clearly demonstrates his immaturity in handling money.

A more clear-headed lover would have hesitated indulging in any unnecessary expenditures in Clara's behalf until he had successfully overcome all impediments to their marriage. Not so Obi. Despite the fact that his mother has threatened to kill herself if he went ahead to marry Clara, as soon as Obi gets his first salary, he goes to Kingsway and buys "a twenty-pound ring" (p. 72).

Characterization in the rest of the novel appears to have been deliberately designed to demonstrate how these forces connive to bring about his failure and disgrace. Achebe has consciously deprived the other characters of any independent existences. They seem to exist more or less to test the validity or to expose the hollowness of Obi's principles, and to dramatize the tragic consequences of his unthinking intransigence.[10]

Joseph Okeke exists to show up the completeness of Obi's pride in the rightness of his actions. He belongs to Obi's age-group and as a former class-mate he is uniquely placed to talk to Obi without fear. He is proud of Obi's intellectual achievement, and talks freely about it to her people. But he does not live in awe of Obi. And since they share a common past makes it clear that any judgment he passes on a situation cannot be dismissed as unenlightened. When Obi rejects his advice on the Clara issue, it becomes clear to us that he has alienated himself completely from his society, for it deprives him of the whole-hearted support of the one individual with whom he could have identified without too much inconvenience to himself.

There is also the messenger, Charles Ibe, a seemingly insignificant character who borrows thirty shillings and fails to pay back when due. His inability to pay back the debt as promised elicits from Obi a lecture which reverts ironically on himself because he is also in debt and cannot manage his affairs the way he expects others to do. Charles therefore serves the structural purpose of adding another dimension to Obi's lack of self-knowledge. When the latter says "I shall find it difficult to trust you in future" (p. 96), the implication is that he is very aware of the dangers to one's reputation in taking on debts one is incapable of paying back. But his own continuous sinking into debts contradicts the very foundation of his advice.

The entire Umuofia Progressive Union, generous in its commitment to the service of the group, inordinate in its demands for adherence to the ideals of the clan and even naïve in its expectations, constitutes the most powerful single force that Obi has to confront as he fights his way unheroically from one crisis to another. It is the group to which he owes his education, and the fat that Obi has no second thoughts about quarrelling with the Union is a very significant indication of his lack of respect and gratitude.

There is a further purpose the Union serves in the book. While Obi could be blamed for ingratitude, it has to be admitted that the very contradictions and even naiveté which frame their demands on Obi, are among the decisive elements in the disintegration of his personality. The Union, for instance, wants him to pay back the debt at the same time that it expects him to remain a loyal member of the "exclusive club whose members greet one another with 'How's the car behaving?'" It wants him to find jobs for every member of the tribe that is jobless. The very fact that it fails to consider his own private commitments to himself prepares the ground for the conflict out of which he emerges completely disadvantaged.

There is Clara, too, who though not making any particular demands on Obi directly, constitutes the test that he has to pass to remain respectable in the eyes of his Umuofia community. She is the excuse as well as the touchstone for all the irrational behaviour which is the prelude to Obi's eventual fall from grace.

Finally there is the city of Lagos itself which, though an inhuman character, plays a crucial role in the formation of Obi's Anti-Heroic tendencies as any human personality. Obi has always been awed by the glamour of that city ever since he was a child listening to tales told by soldiers returning with stories about a place in which "there was no darkness ....because at night the electric shines like the sun" (p. 14). He has always been fascinated by tales of the city where "people are always walking about," and in which "if you don't want to walk you only have to wave your hand and a pleasure car stops for you" (p. 14). In terms of his personality structure, this enchantment with the image of the city life is a strong manifestation that he does not belong to the class of individuals who would be prone to face realities. This is particularly evident when, upon returning from England, he is standing "beside his car at night in one of the less formidable of Lagos slum areas waiting for Clara to take yards of material to her seamstress" (p. 16). The filth rises before him in the form of the rotting remains of a dog lying in the open gutter. Quite uncharacteristically – for he is never given to deep thought – he reflects on the incompatibility of filth and glamour. Achebe says "he had not thought places like this stood side by side with cars, electric lights and brightly dressed girls". (p. 16).

This moment which should have been a turning point in his life departs without leaving any deep impressions. Being the poet that he seems to be, he should not have missed the clear warning the scene implies - that Lagos life is not all sweet, and that the dividing line between beauty and rottenness is extremely thin. In fact, Achebe makes this point even more emphatic by symbolically introducing Obi to the filth only on this particular occasion when he is travelling with Clara who, in his own life plays the ambivalent role of an object of intense desire and also of final destruction. The lightness with which Obi treats the stark incompatibility between childhood fantasies and adult realities is a symbolic foretaste of his eventual lightness in the handling of the *osu* element in Clara's life, as well as other realities which confront him. To him, he would say, *osu* is sheer nonsense (p. 75).

It is not just as a repository of filth that Achebe uses Lagos to emphasize Obi's Anti-Heroism effectively. Although the city is presented as a physical place which makes a distinctive impression upon the mind of the characters, it seems to have been imbued with certain anthropomorphic qualities. It is made to appear like a distinct individual personality placed in omnipotent authority over everybody else, and whom everybody in his own way is determined to impress. An excellent example of this is given in the episode of the boat bringing Obi and Stephen Udom back home. As it approaches the harbour we are told that "As soon as Lagos had been sighted he [Mr. Stephen Udom] returned to his cabin to emerge half an hour later in a black suit, bowler hat and rolled umbrella, even though it was a hot October day" (p. 30). Lagos therefore seems to carry with it its own values and manners as well as a frame of mind which moulds character and destiny. In the meeting in which Obi's tantrums drive him to tell off the Umuofia Union, the President emphasizes this shaping influence of the city on character in a warning that could very conveniently have been directed to any young man against the snares of a *femme fatale*. The man tells Obi: "…you are one of us, so we must bare our minds to you. I have lived in this Lagos for fifteen years,… Lagos is a bad place for a young man. If you follow its sweetness, you will perish" (p. 82). Obi's essential tragedy results partly if not mainly from his failure to take this warning seriously. Because he lacks that sharpness of mind that can see through surface appearance into the underlying realities he makes himself into a slave of all the materialistic desires of Lagos.

What Achebe does here is to make the city into a principal actor, an antagonist even, in the drama that culminates in the disintegration of Obi's personality, his alienation and aloneness. Lagos is an obstacle to the fulfilment of his dreams. And it does not take too much imagination to believe that had Obi lived in, say, Omuofia village, things would have been much different. But Achebe places him in Lagos and makes him believe in it, without caring to understand it. A kinsman would say after his trial that "Obi tried to do what everyone does without finding out how it was done" (p. 6). Because of this weakness he fails at every critical moment to integrate his motives and actions so organize his life toward the proper choice and fulfilment of his goals and moral alternatives.

Psychological Dimension of Obi's Characterization

It has been possible to discuss Obi's personality without reference to any psychological theories mainly because unlike Samba Diallo or Ahouna his problems are not obviously psychological. What strikes us first about him is not the depth of his mind but its shallowness, not his thoughtfulness but his lack of it. In fact, a major aspect of his depiction in the story is the fact that he never seems to truly puzzle over anything, to weigh the pros and cons of an act before carrying it out. Mugo will perish for being too self-conscious of the implications of his actions. Obi, on the other hand, perishes because he fails to give his actions thought.

But despite this absence of psychological penetration in his characterization, Achebe's handling of certain relationships in the story suggests appeal to psychological theories for satisfactory answers. The first problem arises from our efforts to understand Obi's relationship with Clara. It is not exactly clear why Obi should be so indissolubly attached to Clara. Her physical attractiveness is certainly not in doubt, nor is her mental life, for she is widely travelled and has attained a sound education.

These, however, are nowhere shown to be factors in their relationship. For one thing, she does not possess that seriousness of personality which Obi displays from time to time. For example, when they go shopping, Obi seems visibly upset that "she would reject an aluminium pot in one shop and walk the whole length of Broad Street to another to buy the very same thing at the very same price" (p. 73). She is not mad about him, and there is no indication anywhere that Obi too is passionately in love with her. He does express some erotic desire for her back home in Umuofia when he says "how heavenly it would be on such a night to feel her cool body against his - the shapely thighs and the succulent breast" (p. 61). But soon occasions are rare. She is not as the cliché goes, the girl of his dreams, or, as Samuel Johnson might have said, she was not "fatal Cleopatra for whom he lost the world and was content to lose it."[11] At no point is he actually concerned with Clara as a person with emotional needs that have to be considered deeply. It is even said of Obi that he is incapable of love. We are told that when he watched people kissing and embracing:

> *There was always a part of him, the thinking part, which seemed to stand outside it all watching the passionate embrace with cynical disdain. The result was that one half of Obi might kiss a girl and murmur: 'I love you,' but the other half would say: 'Don't be silly.' And it was always the second*

half that triumphed in the end when the glamour had evaporated with the heat, leaving a ridiculous anti-climax (p. 70).

Yet he declared that "it was either Clara or nobody" (p. 75). Family tries, we are told, "were all very well as long as they did not interfere with Clara" (p. 75).

This irrationality with which he plunges into the relationship leaves open the possibility that he may be using her to compensate for some inner inadequacy or loss. This in turn suggests that there may be a pathological dimension to his unheroic behaviour. The crucial clue to this line of interpretation seems to lie in the extreme maternal control, the overpowering influence which his mother is said to exercise over him. "If only I could convince my mother ... all would be well" (pp. 75-76) seems to be the constant refrain every time the question arises as to whether he would be able to marry Clara or not.

In Reichian psychology Obi's character structure corresponds to the "phallic-narcissistic character" type. According to William Reich, the typical phallic-narcissistic character is:

> *Self-assured, sometimes arrogant ..., either coldly reserved or contemptuously aggressive. In everyday behaviour toward the object, the love object included, the narcissistic element always dominates over the object-libidinal, and there is always a mixture of more or less disguised sadistic traits.*[12]

Obi exhibits many of these traits. As for arrogance, there is no doubt. Until his world begins to crumble beneath his feet, Obi maintains a decidedly self-confident and contemptuous attitude towards the rest of society. When he describes the society as an augean stable, it is his arrogant self-righteousness that is talking. Sadistic tendencies are also not missing in his conduct. His determination to drag Clara into a relationship that outrages the entire Ibo community is tinged with a measure of sadism, for he seems to overlook Clara's own discomfort completely concerning the marriage; he seems to enjoy what is happening. When, for instance, he first mentions the idea of marriage to her, she tells him: "I can't marry you" (p. 70), "I am an *osu*" (p. 71). She is therefore very sensitively aware of the implications of the relationship and the controversies that are bound to arise. But Obi has no regard for such feelings. In fact, the more she explains why they cannot get married, the more anxious Obi is that they should marry.

Reich further says of the phallic-narcissistic types that:

> *If their vanity is hurt, they react …with lively aggression; …in contrast to other characters, that narcissism expresses itself not in infantile manner but in the exaggerated display of self-confidence, dignity and superiority, in spite of the fact that the basis of their character is no less infantile than that of others.*[13]

In his arguments with Joseph and Christopher and then at the meeting where he flares up against the Union, all these narcissistic elements in Obi come to the force.

Reich finally says of such characters that: "in spite of their narcissistic preoccupation with their selves, they often show strong attachments to people outside their selves."[14] Apart from his unthinking attachment to Clara, he is no longer like Ahouna or Samba Diallo. He maintains a very healthy relationship with Joseph and Christopher. He has no guilt feelings or any of the complexes which make friendship impossible. He is the most outgoing, outspoken and sociable of all the Anti-Heroes examined.

His relationship with his mother is fairly complex, and can be best grasped also mainly in the context of narcissism. In his study of the "Oral-Narcissistic Dilemma," Philip E. Slater depicts a relationship between ancient Greek mothers and their sons in a manner which can illuminate our understanding of the relationship between Obi and his mother. In the Greek context, he says "The male child was at one and the same time a scapegoat for and an antidote to the penis envy of the mother."[15] The social circumstances always isolated the mother from the father. He says:

> *Imprisoned and isolated by her indifferent and largely absented husband, some of the mother's sexual longing was turned upon her son. Along with, and in direct contradiction to, her need to belittle and discourage his masculine striving, she attempted to build him into an idealized replacement of her husband, fantasying [sic] that 'her little man' would grow up to be the perfect hero and take care of his mother all of her days. Such fantasies would also gratify her own masculine strivings - though she might be confined and restricted, her son, an extension of herself, was free and mobile, and she could live her life through him.[16]*

The situation in *No Longer at Ease* is not exactly the same, but the relationship between Obi and Hannah can be viewed as a classic instance of what Slater says elsewhere, is a "deeply narcissistic ambivalence in which the mother does not respond to the child as a separate person, but as both an expression of and a cure for her narcissistic wounds."[17] Like Volumnia in Shakespeare's *Coriolanus*[18] Hannah is depicted as having completely usurped Obi's father's masculine role. This usurpation usually grows out of the woman's "need for self-expansion." Such a mother usually has the tendency "both to exalt and to belittle her son, to feed on and to destroy him."[19] Thus, while Clara provides for Obi the opportunity to exercise the manhood which perennial dependency on his mother has kept in total subjection, Hannah sees in her a threat. As soon as he is married to her, Hannah would lose control over him. The situation is only complicated and aggravated by the fact that Clara is an *osu*. The psychological grounds for refusal had long been laid. Discerning a psychological implausibility in the situation, Eustace Palmer has asked: "would the tender-hearted Mrs. Okonkwo, on her deathbed really threaten to commit suicide if Obi were to marry Clara?"[20] The answer at this point seems positive because her attachment to Obi is life sustaining, at least at the emotional level.

Achebe's Style as Foundation of Character

a) Language

In *No Longer at Ease*, Achebe's use of language both in the technical sense of metaphor, imagery, simile or proverb and in his utilization of varieties of dialects of English, compels examination because these devices enhance our appreciation of the different characters he creates. Achebe himself has spoken on several occasions about the need for employing language with the purpose of influencing judgment and strengthening the value of a work. In his article "The English Language and the African Writer," he said:

> *The African writer should aim to use English in a way that brings out his message best without altering the language to the extent that its value as a medium of international exchange will be lost. He should aim at fashioning out an English which is at once universal and able to carry his peculiar experience.*[21]

He does not exactly fashion an English in *No Longer at Ease*, but he does employ three different dialects in a way which many impressively brings out the individuality of the speakers. Standard English is used by the narrator almost exclusively, although Mr. Green and Obi sometimes use it too. Next to this comes the English of the "been-to," a highly affected variety of standard English which is generally associated with people who have been abroad. The speech of "the officers and members of the Umuofia Progressive Union on the occasion of obi's return from the United Kingdom in quest of the Golden Fleece" (p. 31) is a good example of an extreme form of "been-to" English, particularly when they go on to say "we the officers and members of the above-named union present with humility and gratitude this token of our appreciation of your unprecedented academic brilliance" (p. 31). When Obi talks to Clara, or when the educated African characters converse, they use a language that is between standard English and the pompous style of the speaker for the Union.

One of the earliest grievances against Obi stems from the fact that he refuses at the welcome party to speak a language that would reflect his level of education, by which the Union members mean the "been-to" English.

There is thirdly, pidgin English, the language spoken by the illiterate characters in the novel. It is a combination of English and African dialects out of which emerges something which is at the same time neither and both, as we see in the driver's reactions when Obi ventures to interfere with his bringing of the policeman:

> *Na him make I no de want carry book people,... Too much book na him de worry una. Why you put your nose for matter way no concern you? Now that policeman go charge me like ten shillings (p. 43).*

All these three varieties distinguish one group from another, and the ability of an individual to use all three forms without any inhibitions is used in the book to indicate that particular individual's level of adaptability. Obi, for example, never speaks pidgin English. This reluctance to speak the language of the common man is meant to suggest his sense of superiority over those who use it.

We soon discover that this superiority is founded on Obi's distorted impression of himself, for he does not even know his own mother tongue. During the prayer in his father's house he stumbles unnecessarily. We are told that:

> *Obi remembered with shame how he had stumbled through his portions as a child. In the first verse he had pronounced ugwu as mountain when it should be circumcision. Four or five voices had promptly corrected him, the first to register being his youngest sister, Eunice, who was eleven and in Standard Four (p. 57).*

When he addresses the Umuofia Union during his second meeting with them, we hear that "the speech which had started off one hundred per cent in Ibo was now fifty-fifty" (p. 81).

What Achebe has done in this case is to make lack of proficiency in the use of the mother-tongue a symbolic reflection of Obi's inability to identify effectively with the interests and values of the community. His alienation is therefore complete: he cannot identify with the intellectuals in Lagos because they find his idealism too much for their taste; he cannot identify with the masses because they are too lowly for his liking, a fact which makes him unwilling to speak in pidgin English; and he cannot be completely assimilated into the tribe because his knowledge of its own language is unreliable.

b) Proverbs and Imagery

If as Bernth Lindfors has said, proverbs constitute some of the "palm-oil with which Achebe's words are eaten,"[22] they can also be said to serve as a very effective method for emphasizing Obi's Anti-Heroism. They are used to draw attention to the undignified nature of his actions as well as to reinforce our sympathies or condemnation, depending on the circumstances. In this regard they appear to have been more or less arranged or rather employed in a manner that correspond with the seriousness of the occasion, and become harsher and repulsive as Obi sinks lower and lower into depravity.

Chronologically, the proverbs and similes are mild and even very funny at the start of the story. At the farewell party prior to obi's departure for England, for example, the Reverend Ikedi tells him not to go after "the sweet things of the flesh" (p. 11). He then elaborates on this by using a proverb which no doubt would have drawn a chuckle from the crowd: "Do not hurry to rush into the pleasures of the world like the young antelope who danced herself lame when the main dance was yet to come" (p. 11). The warning is served, that Obi must exercise patience and concentrate on his studies until he has attained what he went for. But the image of the young antelope limping with exhaustion when the main event is still to come is more comical than pathetic.

When he returns and gets involved with Clara, a proverb is used to describe the situation. But at this time the element of humour has evaporated because to *marry* an *Osu* is no laughing matter. It amounts to total defilement of a clan. Accordingly, his friend Joseph Okeke tells him: "What you are going to do concerns not only yourself but your family and future generations. If one finger brings oil it soils the others" (p. 99).

The accumulation of his debts also finds expression in a proverb is repulsive, reflecting the unhealthy effect of debts on Obi's honour. The author does not say it is bad to take on a fresh debt without paying the old one. He says "it is not right to ask a man with elephantiasis of the scrotum to take on smallpox as well, when thousands of other people have not had even their share of small diseases" (p.99).

As Obi's relationship with Clara moves towards its bitter climax, the effect on Obi's mind is reflected in the precision of the images with which he is compared. This is most poignantly expressed in the scene where Obi has just paid the doctor his fee and has allowed him to take Clara away to commit the abortion. His mind is in a quandary as he enters his car and sits down. When he decides to pursue the doctor's car, Achebe says: "he backed, went forward, turned right and left like a panicky fly trapped behind the windscreen" (p. 149).

What Achebe is describing literally is Obi as he gets caught in the midst of traffic. But the simile is dead accurate because on the symbolic level he is a fly trapped behind smokescreen of his own delusions. Achebe has very carefully prepared us for this apt metaphor by telling us how "he sat in the driver's seat, paralyzed by his own thoughts ....he wanted to rush out of his car and shout ... but he couldn't and didn't" (p.149).

Finally, after his court trial, a proverb is used that appropriately signifies not so much the immorality of his act as the stupidity of it. Although bribe-taking is viewed in the book as a way of life, the people, or at least the more objective amongst them, know that it is not a respectable activity. And as Obi's kinsmen return from the court one of them likens it to the eating of toads. 'We have a saying," says the man, "that if you want to eat a toad you should look for a fat and juicy one" (p.6). To eat a toad is quite undignifying. But not only has Obi gone so low as to eat one, he has also characteristically not taken his time to look for a well-nourished one that might justify his indulgence.

In *No Longer at Ease*, therefore it is evident that Achebe never meant Obi to be considered as a hero because his entanglements and the style in which his fate is depicted are unmistakably ingredients for Anti-Heroic literature.

c) Point of View, Action and Description

Although his use of language particularly in the form of proverbs and similes has been singled out as a central device for revealing character, Achebe shares with Hamidou Kane the tendency to approach his material from an omniscient author point of view. Very often he allows the characters to discuss their problems in dialogue- there are far more lines of dialogue here than in *L'Aventure ambiguë* - but he seems forever incapable of resisting the temptation to take over from his characters, to describe and to explain the actions to us in his own voice. The story, unlike in Kane's novel, does not read like the minutes of a philosophical debate, but like a chronicle. Achebe, as it were, takes us on a journey through time and space, telling us what he thinks is happening, what the characters are saying, how and when they are saying it and even what they are afraid to say.

The story, for instance, opens with what is undeniably Achebe's voice: "For three or four weeks Obi Okonkwo had been steeling himself against this moment." He then very briefly tells what Obi thinks: "And when he walked into the dock that morning he thought he was fully prepared." He tells us how Obi is dressed, what is happening in the court room, and then hands over the narration to the judge: "This court begins nine o'clock. Why are you late?" The answer to this question does not come at once because Achebe has to delay for six lines to give us the judge's background. When Obi finally answers "I am sorry, Your honour .... My car broke down on the way," Achebe steps in again to describe what is going on: "The judge continued to look at him for a long time. Then he said abruptly ..."

Authorial intrusion has definite disadvantages, especially when it makes it impossible for the reader to appreciate the idiom of the speaker, and even though Achebe is guilty of that weakness in this particular novel, it enables him to give us a more complete picture of what exactly is happening in the story. It was pointed out in our study of Oyono's protagonist that we are not allowed to know more than is said because the point of view is so terribly restricted. Achebe, I think, was not aiming at making ironic commentary on is protagonist in terms of interpreting phenomena. Our judgment of Obi is thus built on sound evidence both from our own deductions and the guides provided by the author. Consequently, when he falls, we know precisely why he has fallen and have no reservations about condemning him.

Point of view, action and description all come together to lend a predominantly scenic flavour to the novel. Thus, although one talks of the book as a chronicle rather than a debate, the story unfolds in scenes of high drama in which the protagonist is almost invariably the victim.

In summary, it can be said that in Obi Okonkwo Achebe has created for us a protagonist that fits into the category of Anti-Heroes by virtue of his inability to lead the type of life that would make him an acceptable member of his society. This has been achieved not just by chronicling Obi's failures, but also spicing the narrative with proverbs and similes carefully structured to reflect the disintegration of his personality.

Notes

[1] George Ross Ridge, *The Hero in French Romantic Literature* (Athens: Univ. of Georgia Press, 1959), p. 115.

[2] Steven H. Gale, *Chinua Achebe's No Longer at Ease: A Critical Commentary* (New York: Simon Schuster, Inc., 1975), p. 38.

[3] Chinua Achebe, *No Longer at Ease* (London: Heinemann, 1960), p. 53. All further references are to this edition, page numbers follow each quotation from the text.

[4] In *Introduction to African Literature,* Ulli Beier ed. (London: Longman, 1967), pp. 182-83.

[5] Ibid., pp. 183-84.

⁶Ibid., p. 184. Taken in isolation Irele's comments may seem a little displaced. But it must be understood that his charges against Achebe are contained in a study that is devoted principally to the search for classical tragic heroes in the novels of Chinua Achebe.

⁷Op. cit. p. 68. A further compliant which he raises is that Achebe's point of view is responsible for the haziness which surrounds or seems to surround Obi's personality in the novel. The omniscient convention, he argues, does not imply that the hero's activities and though should be presented at second hand. He sees the technique as an impediment in that it fails "to take us close enough to Obi's consciousness: and as result we are left in "ignorance of the mainspring of the hero's actions and this in turn results in a number of psychological implausibilities" (p. 69). This type of characterization is again a peculiarity of Anti-Heroic literature. We are usually not given all the evidence which can be used to condemn the Anti-Hero. We are always left in doubt as to why he would take such a such a line of action when the circumstances demand something else. In fact, thinness of characterization is an aspect of such works.

⁸(London: Oxford University Press, 1962), p. 70.

⁹*The Vanishing Hero,* op. cit., p. 17.

¹⁰Speculating that "Obi Okonkwo was probably conceived as a Jamesian 'central consciousness,' around whom all the events of the novel revolve," Eustace Palmer confirmed this point (An Introduction to the African Novel p. 68) when he said that "the other characters matter only in so far as they throw light on his predicament."

¹¹Speaking of what he termed some of Shakespeare's weakness, Samuel Johnson said of Shakespeare's obsession with quibbles that "a quibble, poor and barren as it is, gave him such delight, that he was content to purchase it, by the sacrifice of reason, propriety and truth. A quibble was to him the fatal *Cleopatra* for which he lost the world, and was content to lose it;" "Preface to Shakespeare," in *The Great Critics: An Anthology of Literary Criticism* (New York: W.W. Norton, 1967), p. 454.

¹²*Character-Analysis,* trans. Theodore P. Wolfe (New York: The Noonday Press, 1949), p. 201.

¹³Ibid., p. 200.

¹⁴Ibid.

¹⁵*The Gl0ry of Hera: Mythology and the Greek Family* (Boston: Beacon Press, 1968), pp. 32-33.

¹⁶Ibid., p. 33.

¹⁷Ibid.

¹⁸Even more relevant to the comparison is the fact that Volumnia had the habit of forcing Coriolanus to bend to her will by threatening him with her own death. Hannah also does some to Obi when he insists on marrying Clara, and it is her refusal more than anything else that makes it impossible for them to get married. However, *Coriolanus* is a tragedy in which Volumnia and her son are very forcefully delineated tragic protagonists, whereas *No Longer at Ease* is a comparatively thin novel in which Obi and his mother never reach any heroic status. In fact, it is the measure of Obi's Anti-Heroism that he retains Coriolanu's weakness-his pride, stubbornness and obsession with his mother's welfare without any of his strengths- the admiration of the public and his readiness to please them all, so long as that did not offend his mother.

¹⁹*The Glory of Hera* ...., p. 33.

²⁰*An Introduction to the African Novel,* p. 69.

²¹*Transition,* no. 18 (1965), p. 21. This article was also reprinted in *Insight,* (October/December 1966), pp. 19-20. His other opinions concerning the subject of language in African literature are contained in his other article, "The Role of the Writer in a New Nation," in *Nigeria Magazine,* no. 81 (June 1964), pp. 158-60. Discussions on Achebe's use language include Gerald Moore's *The Chosen Tongue* (London: Longmans, 1969), and Eldred Jones's "Jungle Drums and Wailing Piano," in *African Forum,* vol. 1, no. 4 (1966), pp. 93-106.

²²In *Critical Perspectives on Chinua Achebe,* eds. C. L. Innes and Bernth Lindfors (Washington D.C.: Three Continents Press, 1978), pp. 47-65.

Chapter Seven

Mugo (Ngugi Wa Thiong'o's *A Grain Of Wheat*, 1967)

> *The anti-hero .... Is the protagonist whose self-consciousness results in a critical, ironic, debilitating self-analysis.... Self-consciousness is his motor force ....This fact is a touchstone for understanding the anti-hero.*
>
> *(G.R. Ridge: The Hero in French Romantic Literature)*[1]

Plot Summary

In spite of the disconcerting shuttlecock structure of the narrative, the facts of the lives of the main characters which constitute the substance of *A Grain of Wheat* can be carefully reassembled to provide a straightforward story line. The plot centres on the personal fortunes of John Thompson (the expatriate District Officer), Mumbi, Gikonyo, Karanja, Kihika and Mugo. Mumbi is the wife of Gikonyo, and the sister of Kihika; Karanja, the clerk turned-informant, is the long-time arch-rival of Gikonyo for the love of Mumbi. Kihika is one of the principal leaders of the underground movement during the Mau Mau emergency, and Mugo whose fate provides the nucleus around which the destinies of the other characters revolve, is a petty landholder who has risen against his wish to the rank of a popular public figure.

With Mugo as the central consciousness, his childhood is the chronological beginning of the story. Orphaned at a very early age, Mugo is condemned to pass several years in the care of a perpetually drunk, filthy and often obscene aunt. This woman eventually dies without ever giving him the education that would prepare him for the rigorous trials that the future life of an orphan is bound to offer. Now entirely alone, but undaunted by the string of misfortunes that have befallen him, Mugo resolves to turn adversity into success: he decides to till the soil and plant seeds and live his life the way he thinks is conducive to such an endeavour - completely alone.

Perhaps he might have been able to succeed in isolation, but inevitably he gets mixed up in the historical changes that have been sweeping his country for decades: the natives of the land, or at least the more revolutionary amongst them who had never approved of the presence of the British, decide that it is time to join hands in an all-out assault through the instrument of the Mau Mau.

The most articulate spokesman for the revolutionary movement is Kihika. Unlike Mugo he is a man of very respectable parentage, has had a happy childhood and has grown into an accomplished orator whose fiery speeches drive his people to a frenzied desire for vengeance against the imperialists. Possibly as a result of his uninspiring upbringing, Mugo does not think the presence of the white man poses a threat to the kind of spirit of economic individualism which he has cultivated for himself. He therefore looks on Kihika's call for total sacrifice to protect their native land as vaunting ambition, a direct intrusion into his private life. As he is vividly reminded by the example of the crippled Githua, there can be nothing but further misery in store for him, should he go out of his way to confront an adversary as omnipotent as the white man. Consequently, he does not hesitate to betray Kihika when the latter plays into his hands: fleeing from the white man, Kihika takes refuge in Mugo's house, but Mugo releases the secret of his whereabouts to the British. Kihika is seized and later hanged.

Meanwhile, Karanja who has never gotten over the pique of his loss of Mumbi to Gikonyo, wins himself a favour from the British by confessing to his involvement in the emergency and betraying Gikonyo. With Gikonyo in jail the way seems open for Karanja to win back Mumbi's love. Accordingly, he wages a relentless struggle which bears fruits and Gikonyo returns from his imprisonment to find his wife with Karanja's child.

On Mugo's part, nothing is going as anticipated. The elimination of Kihika from his life had been expected to free him from the outside interference that made full-hearted devotion to his farm impossible. The reality is different.

First, the betrayal and death turns Kihika into a martyr whose name becomes a household word among the Kikuyu. Second, having never had the opportunity to develop the kind of personality that is capable of shutting out of the mind moral compunctions engendered by a deed like the betrayal of Kihika, Mugo succumbs to guilt feelings so severe that they take on pathological dimensions.

Ignorant of both his crime and his state of mind, the natives continue to hail Mugo as a hero, an honour which he cannot enjoy because he is persistently haunted by the thoughts of his betrayal of Kihika. The sense of remorse rises to a climax when he is unanimously chosen to speak on Uhuru day, a responsibility which includes his denunciation of Karanja for the betrayal of Kihika. Mugo shocks the public when he rises and instead of accusing Karanja, confesses the deed himself. He is not immediately believed, but is gradually denounced.

The State of Criticism and Characterization

All the important elements for an elaborate study of characterization in *A Grain of Wheat* have often been touched on in one way or another by almost every critic of the novel. Lewis Nkosi, in his Tasks and Masks, hints at the relationship between theme and character when he says "the novel is built around a series of ever-widening concentric circles of guilt and betrayal: from the most obvious case of Karanja ....to Gikonyo."[2] In his *Stylistic Criticism and the African Novel*, Emmanuel Ngara talks of the relationship between point of view and characterization when he describes Ngugi as the psychologist who "by using the omniscient narrator technique ....gives himself the power to enter the minds of his characters and probe their deepest thoughts."[3] In his *Manichean Aesthetics: the Politics of Literature in Colonial Africa*, Abdul R. JanMohamed stresses the inner relatedness of the characters and patterns of their depiction when he says:

> *Ngugi uses five characters...to contrast different kinds of personal isolation, love, and sympathy for others, and then orchestrates a complex*

pattern wherein some characters move from isolation into community, some move in the opposite direction, while others remain relatively static.[4]

In spite of the critics' awareness of these important aspects of characterization in the novel, studies which coordinates them into a reasoned character study are very rare indeed. There are two obvious reasons for this scarcity: the first is the direct result of the emphasis placed on historical elements which have been incorporated in the novel. This has led critics away from other aspects of the novel such as character and even structure into concentration on the socio-historical elements. David Cook, one of the most perceptive critics of African literature says in his recent study, *Ngugi wa Thiong'o: An Exploration of His Writings* that "*A Grain of Wheat* concerns the Mau Mau campaign, placed in its lengthy historical setting and the relationship of this movement to independence."[5] Shatto Arthur Gakwandi says "*A Grain of Wheat* comes close to being a historical novel. Its plot owes everything to the violent events of the Mau Mau movement."[6]

Out of these arguments grows a second reason for the absence of serious studies of characterization - the assumption that the novel has no central character. Charles Larson, for example, indicates that "unlike Ngugi's two earlier books which mirrored the turmoil through one or two characters, *A Grain of Wheat* has no central character."[7] Peter Nazareth, too, argues that "there is no central character, just as in *Nostromo*. The novelist wants to show us a whole cross-section of society."[8] This last claim, quite justifiable in terms of the substance of the text, has led several critics to argue that it is a socialist novel.[9]

I am inclined to argue that there is a central character, and to argue that the reason he is not as obvious as the protagonists of Ngugi's previous novels is that the style here is much more sophisticated. Mugo is, in fact the central character, the Anti-Hero in relation to which the other characters exist as touchstones, projections or symbolic amplifications of those qualities which mark him out as an Anti-Hero. In this novel Ngugi has transferred the centre of gravity from overt action to the exploration of the consciousness of the protagonist where Anti-Heroism is revealed through a careful analysis of his verbal behaviour.

Character Structure and Claim to Anti-Heroism

A Grain of Wheat is quite appropriately the last novel in this study because it brings together and even adds to many of the key elements which we have in the previous chapters associated with literature cast in the Anti-Heroic mould. The atmosphere and the language of the narrative are permeated with images of suffering, depression, loneliness, defeat and even death. Ngara's comments corroborate this assumption, for he says that in the novel Ngugi "penetrates the minds of the suffering, the mentally tortured and those on the verge of mental derangement."10 The first page of the novel conveys to the reader a feeling of nervous apprehension, of impending doom and almost Kafkasque, nightmarish helplessness which sets the tone of what is to come:

> *Mugo felt nervous. He was lying on his back and looking at the roof. Sooty locks hung from the fern and grass thatch and all pointed at his heart. A clear drop of water was delicately suspended above him. The drop fattened and grew dirtier as it absorbed grains of soot. Then it started drawing towards him. He tried to shut his eyes. They would not close. He tried to move his head: it was firmly chained to the bedframe. The drop grew larger and larger as it drew closer and closer to his eyes. He wanted to cover his eyes with his palms; but his hands, his feet, everything refused to obey his will. In despair, Mugo gathered himself for a final heave and woke up. Now he lay under the blanket and remained unsettled fearing, as in the dream, that the drop of water would suddenly pierce his eyes.*[11]

The man is alone, confused, frightened by an almost inexplicable danger, and loneliness, confusion, fright and a sense of doom are elements associated with Anti-Heroism.

In an observation that gives a new twist to our already established concept of the Anti-Hero, David Cook has asserted that:

> *Mugo is an anti-hero in two senses. First because he himself is taken by surprise by his own defiant bravery in the face of inhumanity - most obviously when he futiley [sic] leaps to the defence of Wambuku against the trench guards. And secondly through his being miscast by Rung'ei in the role of hero, an irony which forms one of the main structural features of the novel.*[12]

Mugo's precise claim to Anti-Heroism, however, is founded on a peculiar personality structure that has its origin in the unfortunate circumstances of his childhood. Ngugi tells us that "Mugo's father and mother had died poor, leaving him, an only child in the hands of a distant aunt Waitherero ….a widow with six married daughters [who] when drunk, ……would come home and remind Mugo of this fact" (p. 8). Ngugi gets more specific:

> *'Female slime,' she would her toothless gums; she would fix Mugo with a fierce glance, as if he and God had conspired against her. They don't even come to see me - Do you laugh, you - what's your penis worth? Oh God, see what an ungrateful wretch is left on my hands. You would have followed your father to the grave, but for me. Remember that and stop laughing (p. 8).*

The stench of the atmosphere of obscenities is very vividly depicted:

> *She was a small woman who always complained that people were after her life; they had put broken bottles and frogs into her stomach; they wanted to put poison in her food and drink.*
>
> *And yet she always went out to look for more beer. She would pester men from her husband's rika till they gave her a drink. One day she came back very drunk.*
>
> *"That man Warui - he hates to see me eat and breathe - that sly - smile - he - creeps - coughs - like you - you - go and join him-"*
>
> *And she tried to imitate Warui's cough; but in the attempt lurched forward and fell; all her beer and filth lay on the floor. Mugo cowered among the goats hoping and fearing she had died. In the morning she forced Mugo to pour soil on the filth. The acrid smell hit him. Disgust choked him so that he could not speak or cry. The world had conspired against him, first to deprive*

him of his father and mother, and then to make him dependent on an ageing harridan (p. 8).

This type of childhood does not automatically mean that the character will end up as an Anti-Hero, if we remember that Okonkwo had to rise above his childhood disabilities to be the most talked-about individual in his village. And Koomson, the hero of *The Beautiful Ones* rose from a dockyard boy to a Minister. But Koomson and all those who rise from obscurity to eminence, represent not the rule but the exception. Mugo's life follows the tradition of the Anti-Hero in which childhood experiences main the person for ever.

Several African critics would subscribe to the conclusion that his childhood made him what he turned out to be. Abdul JanMohamed, for instance, has observed that "the genesis of Mugo's isolation lies in his childhood."[13] And in the words of David Cook, "certainly Mugo is mentally sick, and we are given detailed insight into his childhood as the origin of his neurosis."[14] It is not enough for a serious study of the character of Mugo to simply gloss over these references to childhood. A more profitable approach is to examine Mugo's situation and his fate in the novel in the context of the psychology of child development.

Parental care and influence have been established by modern psychologists as decisive factors in the building up of ego-strength which in turn is the foundation of a strong adult personality. Specifically, maternal influence constitutes, in the words of David Holbrook, "the basis of our discovery of the reality of ourselves and the world - and it takes place through an I-Thou relationship."[15] In the event of a disruption of this mother-child relationship, or in the case where the parents are just not there, Holbrook says "the individual cannot feel the *I AM* sense, and cannot live in touch with a True Self."[16] In his *The Maturational Processes and the Facilitating Environment,* D.W. Winnicott has said:

> *Only if there is a good-enough mother does the infant start on a process of development that is personal and real. If the mothering is not good enough, then the infant becomes a collection of reactions to impingement, and the true*

> *self of the infant fails to form or becomes hidden behind a false self which complies with and generally wards off the world's knocks .... All depends upon the capacity of the mother to give ego-support ..., it is well-cared-for babies who quickly establish themselves as persons.*[17]

From this premise it is plain that there has been nothing positive in Mugo's childhood to prepare him for heroic action.

As H. Guntrip says in his *Schizoid Phenomena, Object-Relations and the Self*:

> *The feeling of I AM, of being in a real world, is closely bound with the initial experience of the mother's [or mother-figure's] handling and it is in the experience of this handling that he creates his sense of being a whole continuous object, in his body, in relation to a whole continuous object, in a secure world.*[18]

There is therefore a deficiency in the personality structure of Mugo which, despite his determination, will render all aspirations ineffectual. There is in him what Holbrook calls the feeling of "a lack of proper centre and no coherent ground."[19] The rest of his life seems to confirm one of Holbrook's basic assumptions that:"

> *Those individuals who have not been given any sense of being human are also in need of using cultural artefacts for their own desperate ends to feel real - and can use these in "false" ways, in desperate "strategies of survival." .... Thus arises the problem of hate in culture and the possibility of the abuse of cultural trust.*[20]

Herein lies the root and explanation of Mugo's withdrawal from the rest of the world, his hatred for Kihika. A study which is very useful in this context is Leon Mugesera's "Guilt and Redemption in Ngugi wa Thiong'o's *A Grain of Wheat.*"[21] In this article, one of very few I know which approaches characterization in the novel from a Freudian perspective, Mugesera rightly points out that Mugo is dominated by the Id, the selfish irrational part of man, since he is not anxious to get involved in matters concerning others or the common good. He describes Mugo as a misanthrope, whose internal world longs for its own pleasure through anti-social tendencies of loneliness and isolation which have been developed to a degree where he no longer wants to meet people.

Out of his childhood experiences develops a further complication which is needed to explain his future conduct -" the female element" of personality. Guntrip says "the female element may be defined as the need to be emotionally susceptible, the capacity for sensitiveness to what others are feeling .... Or the emotionally sensitive self that can be more easily hurt, and can then be felt as a weakness."[22] A character who betrays an overabundance of the female element like Mugo, Holbrook has pointed out, "can therefore hate *being*, and so come to abuse culture out of fear of it."[23] Mugo's violation of the oath in betraying Kihika is as much an abuse of culture as the fear of it.

His hatred for Kihika and his subsequent betrayal of the man can therefore be seen as a direct outcome of the nature of childhood experiences. In the previous novels we have examined, loneliness and isolation were often shown to be the unconscious results of the peculiar lifestyles adopted by each Anti-Heroic protagonist. In Mugo's case, his isolation is not tinged with any sense of regret because it is a carefully worked out philosophy. We learn that while still at school, he always avoided getting involved in fights for fear that this might ruin his chances for the future. We see the fruits of his determination when he becomes one of the first men "to finish their huts within the given time. He had done the work," Ngugi tells us, "erecting the hut, thatching the roof, mudding the walls, without help from anybody" (p. 163). He tells us that his greatest wish has always been to be left alone: "I wanted to live my life. I never wanted to be involved in anything" (p. 161).

If the desire to be left alone succeeds in the case of constructing his hut, it fails or is doomed to failure when it comes to constructing his life. No man is an island, it has often been said. And having gone through such a disastrous childhood, perhaps a little more companionship might have turned things around for him. Living and mixing with other people and feeling their need for each other might have made it impossible or unnecessary for him to want Kihika more dead than alive. But, like the typical Anti-Hero that he, is he chooses an approach that can only lead to more misery. A person is formed, according to Martin Buber, not by opposition but by relationship: "a person makes his appearance by entering into relations with other persons."[24] And in the words of Sartre too,

> *Pour obtenir une vérité quelconque sur moi, il faut que je passé par l'autre. L'autre est indispensable à mon existence, aussi bien d'ailleurs qu'à la connaissance que j'ai de moi.*[25]

Even if the others were not indispensable to Mugo's existence, he certainly did not possess the capacity to live alone. In Freud's theory, the ego of the hero is always in unquestioned command of the situation. "The hero," as David Riesman has said, "has a certain Spartan, uncomplaining attitude towards life, a sportsmanlike adherence to rules of good breeding."[26] Anti-Heroes, however, are notoriously incapable of psychic greatness. Their ego-strength is usually very weak. Mugo is no exception. The intrusion of Kihika into his life compels him to resort to endless monologues through which he expresses his bitterness and frustration. This self-examination confronts his ego with an almost insolvable dilemma:

> *What shall I do? (...) If I don't serve Kihika, he'll kill me. They killed Rev. Jackson and Muniu. If I work for him, the Government will catch me. The white man has long arms. And they'll hang me. My God, I don't want to die, I am not ready for death, I have not even lived.*
> *... have I stolen anything from anybody? No! have I ever shat aside a neighbour's courtyard? No. have I killed anybody? No. how then can Kihika, to whom I have done no harm, do this to me? (p. 169).*

This incapacity to live alone and to be single-mindedly devoted to a line of action, irrespective of the consequences, can be ultimately traced back to childhood experiences. In his article, "The Capacity to Live Alone," D.W. Walcott asserts that for the individual to be able to live alone, for the adult to possess that ability, he requires a certain inter-relatedness with an ego-supportive mother in an ego-supportive environment.²⁷

The third major element in Mugo's personality structure is his susceptibility to guilt feelings. He possesses what psychologists like J. Frosch and S.B. Wortis have labelled "a punishing superego." The possession of such an affective disposition inevitably causes the individual "to reproach and berate himself for his behaviour, and be frequently depressed by his actions, at times to the point of attempted self-destruction."²⁸ But in this novel, guilt serves as a structural device in the framing of the characters. Apart of Mugo's betrayal of Kihika, there is Karanja who was once involved in the freedom movement but who had sold the secrets of the organisation in exchange for the office of administrative chief, responsible for rounding up suspects of the outlawed Mau Mau movement. Gikonyo too had been one of the henchmen of the freedom fighters, but had to confess the oath to gain his release after the mass arrest. There is also Mumbi, Gikonyo's wife who, in the absence of her husband, submits to Karanja's sexual advances and actually bears his child when her husband is released from detention. The list could be stretched to include the entire white community, each member of which has some major scandal to hide. But the central guilt is Mugo's.

The centrality of his guilt lies in the fact that it is made to touch on or grow out of the lives of the two major characters whose fortunes span the novel. It had its origin in the fact already mentioned, that Mugo gave away the secrets of Kihika's whereabouts and he was captured and killed. The people who know nothing about Mgo's involvement in the treachery, convert him into an object of veneration, an honour which would in turn be converted back to scorn and repulsion upon discovery of the real truth. Ngugi has thus very deftly laid the trap for Mugo. First he arms Mugo with a personality which is defective from childhood in the sense that it is devoid of any real ego-defences. Then having established the grounds of hatred between the two men, he drives kihika into the hands of his bitterest enemies.

That Mugo will betray kihika as kihika hides in Mugo's house becomes highly predictable. But that he will be able to bear the consequences of the act of betrayal is doubtful. For one thing, the services kihika has rendered to the people are such that they will never stop talking about him. The stage is thus set for intensive Anti-Heroic action: Mugo who by birth and upbringing had been forced to take a rather defensive attitude towards life will now make it a policy to cut himself away from the rest of the world, just so that he hears no more about the greatness of the man he has betrayed. Then, behind the walls of this castle of isolation which he strives to build, we know that he will never find peace of mind because he has never been physically prepared to master his emotions. Mugo is thus caught in a vicious circle of torture and futility in which he continues to "wrestle with demons, alone in an endless nightmare" (p. 25).

His tragedy then results from an excessive self-consciousness or self-awareness. In the section entitled "Self-Consciousness" in his *The Divided Self*, R.D. Laing has provided a classic paradigm of self-awareness against which Mugo's behaviour in the novel can be adequately examined. Laing defines Self-Consciousness as the awareness of oneself as an object of someone else's observation. In the schizoid individual (like Mugo who is torn the between reputation he commands and what he knows he really deserves), Laing says there is "a heightened sense of being always seen, or at any rate of being always potentially seeable."[29] The self-conscious person he says:

> *feels he is more the object of other people's interest than, in fact, he is. Such a person walking along the street approaches a cinema queue. He will have to "steel himself" to walk past it: preferably, he will cross to the other side of the street. It is an ordeal to go into a restaurant and sit down at a table by himself. At a dance he will wait until two or three couples are already dancing before he can face taking the floor himself....*[30]

In *A Grain of Wheat* Ngugi does not give us the opportunity to see Mugo's reaction towards cinema queues, dancing or sitting in a restaurant. But the little that we are given of him places him directly in the tradition of the Self-Conscious individual. This almost pathological self-consciousness is poignantly expressed in the scene of the confession where Mugo ruminates:

> *Imagine all your life you cannot sleep -- so many figures touching your flesh --eyes always watching you -- in dark places -- in corners -- in the streets -- in the fields -- sleeping, waking, no rest -- ah! Those eyes -- cannot you for a minute, one minute, leave a man alone -- I mean -- let a man eat, drink, work -- all of you here tonight? Those eyes again ... (p. 161).*

Although Laing says "to suggest ... that the individual is self-conscious 'because' he has guilt secrets ... does not take us far,"[31] I insist that as far as this study goes, it has got to take us very far, because guilt constitutes not only the polemical theme but also the very substance on which character is built.

Mugo, Guilt and the Anti-Heroic Tradition

The importance of the element of guilt in the character design of the novel and the character structure of Mugo make it necessary for us to speculate on precisely where to place Mugo in the tradition of guilt-ridden Anti-Heroes. The first point to note here has to do with his confession in which several critics have seen a true act of heroism.[32] What needs to be stressed is that his confession is an inevitable and virtually indistinguishable from a suicidal impulse. When he confesses, he is merely responding to the cruel devastating logic of events without any really conscious control of himself anymore. He yields not because he thinks is more honourable and dignified but because all his impulses have ruled out the possibility of any other alternative.

In this case Mugo is like Rashkolnikov in Dostoevsky's *Crime and Punishment* who confesses to the murder of the old pawnbroker, knowing that the consequences for him are grave; he is like Dimmesdale in Nathaniel Hathorne's *The Scarlet Letter* who on his own confesses his adultery with Hester Prynne, knowing that the consequences are death; he is like Joseph K. in Kafka's *Der Prozess* who attends the court hearing, knowing that to attend is to admit guilt, and knowing that he is at liberty not to attend; he is like Philip in Somerset Maugham's *Of Human Bondage* who is driven by the oppressive feeling of guilt to display his clubfoot, the worst thing that could ever be known about him. The line could be stretched interminably through all Anti-Heroic literature, but the point to be made here is that it is not in the nature of the Anti-Hero to ignore the guilt that comes with some hidden scandal about his life, or to choose an alternative that brings anything but shame and disgrace or even death upon himself. This is the brief summary of the Anti-Heroic code to which Mugo responds appropriately.

The Peculiarity of Anti-Heroic Guilt

Because Mugo has sometimes been compared to Macbeth - Ngara says he "is like Macbeth who is constantly haunted by the ghost of Banquo whom he has murdered"[38] - a note has to be made in distinguishing his typically Anti-Heroic guilt from that of heroes. Such a distinction has been made in a different context, by Donald V. Morano in his book *Existentialist Guilt: A Phenomenological Study*. In that book, particularly in the two sections, "Paradigms of Guilt: Oedipus Rex ad Macbeth," and "Paradigms of Guilt: Raskolnikov and Joseph K.," Morano establishes a fundamental similarity between the type of guilt suffered by Sophocles' Oedipus Rex and Shakespeare's Macbeth. The basis of his argument is "the social dimensions of guilt [in which] the deficiencies of the protagonist produce a serious flaw in the fabric of the state, that the state is an organism which is particularly sensitive to the disease of its head member."[34]

In *Oedipus Rex* and *Macbeth,* he argues, "because of the faults of Oedipus and Macbeth, Thebes and Scotland respectively, are spiritually and even physically polluted."[35] Oedipus and Macbeth, we must remember were rulers who had attained their positions because they had killed - whether wittingly or unwittingly - the previous rulers. Because of their sacrilegious acts of killing the rightful ruler, Morano shows that not only Oedipus and Macbeth suffer but all society suffers. All Thebes travails under the plague, while the evil brewed up by the murder of Duncan wreaks havoc and violent discord throughout Scotland. This is heroic guilt, in contrast to Anti-Heroic guilt of the nature we encounter in Raskolnikov and Joseph K. the relevance of Morano's judgment to this study is underscored by the fact that I find a remarkable similarity between Raskolnikov's guilt feelings and those of Mugo.

In contrasting the heroes, Oedipus and Macbeth, with the Anti-Heroes Raskolnikov and Joseph K., Morano says something which could be taken as a description of Mugo's fate in *A Grain of Wheat*:

> *Raskolnikov and Joseph K. are loners. They are not important public personages and have no pre-eminent official status; their guilt does not doom or even detract from the general weal. Their guilt is the guilt of the outsider living in spiritual solitude living for the most part incommunicado, alienated from contemporaries. Whatever they suffer will make little or no difference to society; they really have no one with whom to share their problems*[35]

Style and Characterization Techniques

More than any of the novels examined here, and more than any other African novel, Ngugi's *A Grain of Wheat* confirms Mark Schorer's now famous dictum that "technique is the only means he [the writer'] has of discovering, exploring, developing his subject, of conveying its meaning, and finally, of evaluating it."[37] The first thing that strikes the reader in the novel is not so much the mass of historical detail but the range of styles to which Ngugi subjects his material, and through which alone the lives of his characters can be thoroughly apprehended.

I intend here to focus on only two methods Ngugi employs in the depiction of his characters - the application of "Antithesis and Apposition," and *Erlebte Rede* or what the French stylists term "*style indirect libre*". In his depiction of Mugo, Ngugi employs what Mary Doyle Springer describes in her *A Rhetoric of Literary Character*, as Antithesis and Apposition. A characteristic of this technique is that the lines of character "are drawn very sharply according to the opposing qualities for which they stand," and according to the light one character throws on the other " by means of their character differences, having been set up on careful apposition to each other."[38] This device is discernible in *A Grain of Wheat* particularly in the characterization of Kihika and Mugo. In her study of *Lady Barbarina*, Springer says we never grasp the hopelessness of the Lady's type of marriage "until the Anglicism of her character is set up in interaction with the Americanism of the characters in New York."[39] The same thing applies to the portrayal of Mugo. The seriousness of his predicament and his neurotic determination to live alone is not fully appreciated until "Kihika comes into [his] life" (p. 161). Thereafter, his determination to live his life his own way is pitted against the total recklessness of Kihika. The antithetical dispositions of the two characters are revealed in the flash-back early in the book in the scene in which Mugo is listening to Kihika's speech calling for sacrifice, suffering, and the shedding of blood in order that their land may be liberated:

> *"This is not 1920. What we want now is action, a blow which will tell," he said as women from Thabai pulled at their clothes and hair, and screamed with delight. Kihika, a son of the land, was marked out as one the heroes of deliverance. Mugo, who had seen Kihika on the ridge a number of times, had never suspected that the man had such power and knowledge. Kihika unrolled the history of the tribe, the coming of the white man and the birth of the Party...*
>
> *Speaking slowly with emphasis on the important words, he once or twice pointed at earth and heaven as if calling them to witness that what he spoke was the truth. He talked of the great sacrifice.*
>
> *"A day comes when brother shall give up brother, a mother her son, when you and I have heard the call of a nation in turmoil (pp. 14-15).*

This is heroism by any standards, and it is against this that Mugo's Anti-Heroism is reinforced. While Kihika "Received a big ovation from the crowd" (p. 14), Mugo responded with cold indifference and even rebellion, a response which brings into sharp focus the differences that underlie not only the two men but also heroism and Anti-Heroism:

> *Mugo felt a constriction in his throat. He could not clap for words that did not touch him. What right had such a boy, probably younger than Mugo, to talk like that? What arrogance? Kihika had spoken of blood as easily as if he was talking of drawing water in a river, Mugo reflected, a revulsion starting in his stomach at the sight and smell of blood. I hate him, he heard himself say and frightened, he looked at Mumbi, wondering what she was thinking (p. 15).*

Furthermore, Mugo's reluctance to speak at the Uhuru convention at the end of the book, a direct result of what Leon Mugesera had called "the weight of a devastating guilt conscience,"[40] and not of humility and modesty as the people thought, is set by hindsight in direct contrast to the enthusiasm with which Kihika had spoken. The end met by both men is also presented in a manner that emphasizes the differences between the two principles by which they had lived.

Kihika was hanged in public, one Sunday, at Rung'ei Market, not far from where he had once stood calling for blood to rain on and water the tree of freedom. A combined force of Home guards and Police whipped and drove people from Thabai and other ridges to see the body of the rebel dangling on the tree, and learn.

The party, however, remained alive and grew, as people put it, on the wounds of those Kihika left behind (p. 17).

Talking about the execution of Kihika, Emmanuel Ngara has stressed the heroism implied in it which stands in bold contrast to the same fate suffered by Mugo. Ngara says:

> *Kihika here comes a suffering saviour. He is hanged in public like Christ and sheds his blood that all may be free. He becomes the seed that is sown and dies. The grain that comes out is seen in the growth of the Party which continues to flourish after Kihika's death.*[41]

When Mugo confesses, the people who had assembled feel scandalized. Some refuse to believe. As a consequence his fall from grace shocks rather than inspires the people.

At this juncture it needs to be pointed out that what is at stake in the world of the novel is not salvation of the individual soul but the welfare of the Mau Mau movement. It is against the involvement in the movement that the success or failure of any individual must be judged. In this case, the preponderance of religious symbolism in the book may be a bit misleading because of the undertones of redemption which it suggests. Léon Mugesera, judging from a purely religious point of view says "by confessing, Mugo recovers his inner peace ... (and that) Mugo's courageous act redeems his soul but not his body because he is killed."[42] In terms of the ideals to which the community in the book is supposed to be committed , Mugo has failed, even if he may have secured for himself a spot in heaven.

In *The Fabric of Fiction*, Douglas Bement and Rose M. Taylor have this to say about self-revelation as a literary technique:

> *Thoughts are one of the most reliable clues to character. To the outward world, to our friends and acquaintances, we may be able to "put up a front," to act a part. But what we think, deep within the secret privacy of our minds, where no one can observe us or spy on us, is perhaps the truest of what we really are. The Bible says, "As a man thinketh in his heart, so is he," and the statement, echoed by modern psychologists, is almost literally true. In our thinking we reveal our true selves.*[43]

Ngugi would appear to have been very consciously aware of this particular aspect of characterisation when he drew Mugo, for in no other novel in this selection have we been brought into such intimate relations with the consciousness of the protagonist. The method which Ngugi uses here is, in the widest sense, basically identical with what Bement and Taylor call "Characterisation by Thought," one of the techniques which they regard indispensable "in x-raying a character's mind."[44]

It has been taken for granted that what Ngugi does with the thoughts of his characters in this novel is synonymous with stream of consciousness techniques in depicting Mugo. He says:

> *The presentation of internal character in A Grain of Wheat is rendering in a variety of ways: authorial commentary, extended sections of dialogue where the character tells to another the story of his involvement in the Emergency, or stream-of- consciousness technique. The latter is especially effective for depicting Mugo's thoughts to the reader, since he is not the kind of person who can articulate his feelings to someone else.*[45]

Some critics like Ngara take a very safe route out of the problems posed by Ngugi's style in describing it simply as "the omniscient narrator technique" in which the author uses flashbacks extensively.[46] we cannot dispute the fact that Ngugi uses the omniscient narrator point of view. But most readers will agree that the kind of omniscient narrator point of view which we find here is not the same kind that we met I say *L'Aventure ambiguë*, *No Longer at Ease* and *The Beautiful Ones*. There is something remarkably different in Ngugi's case, and we evade our critical responsibility in not investigating that difference more closely because that is what constitutes Ngugi's peculiar style.

In Larson's case, the use of the term stream-of-consciousness takes for granted that we all know what it means. But upon closer examination of the literature of the term we discover that outside the detailed analyses of critics like Cohen, we have never actually known enough about it, and that it is itself a general term for several techniques involving thought processes. Because of the growing importance of the term in the study of the novel in this century, it is necessary for us to grasp, however concisely, the most significant implications of the term. In his article "What is the Stream of Consciousness Technique? Lawrence E. Bowling says:

> *... The stream of consciousness technique may be defined as the narrative method by which the author attempts to give a direct quotation of the mind -- not merely of the language area but of the whole consciousness .... The only criterion is that it introduce us directly into the interior life of the character, without any intervention by way of comment or explanation on the part of the author.*[47]

According to Robert Humphrey in his Stream of Consciousness in the modern Novel,

> *We may define stream-of-consciousness fiction as a type of fiction in which the basic emphasis is placed on exploration of the prespeech levels of consciousness for the purpose, primarily, of revealing the psychic being of the characters.*[48]

And in his very valuable book, *The Stream of Consciousness and Beyond in Ulysses*, Erwin R. Steinberg says:

> *The stream of consciousness writer tries to stimulate reality; to give the impression to the reader that he is receiving the raw data of consciousness as they arrive in the mind of the character.*[49]

Very few critics aware of these definitions of the term would insist that Ngugi uses stream of consciousness technique in the novel. Talking about the practicability and effectiveness of stream of consciousness technique in fiction, Steinberg says "pure stream of consciousness would be difficult, if not impossible to read: for it would be a mass of psychological images, sensations and perceptions which would provide little or no orientation or method of organisation.[50] Nowhere in the novel do we find any true direct quotation of the thoughts of the characters. Most of the time we are presented with the ruminations of the characters who have already organized their thoughts into language or patterns, or formal sentence structures. A typical passage illustrative of the technique Ngugi employs could be the section embodying the dilemma leading up to Mugo's betrayal of Kihika:

> *Mugo stood, still, in the middle of his new hut for a few minutes. The ground below his feet was not firm. Then he ran to the door, flung it open, half-hoping to shout for help. He gazed into the night. For the third time he bolted the door. But why bolt the door? Why should he? It was better to be without a door rather than that it should be there and yet bring cold and danger. He unbolted the door and slowly walked to bed, where he sat and*

held his face in his hands. He took out a dirty handkerchief to wipe his face and neck; but half-way in the act, he forgot about the cold sweat; the handkerchief slumped back to his knees. He had once heard noises in the wind, long ago, and had been unable to pick one consistent note; now the noises were in his head.

A few minutes ago, lying on the bed, in this room, the future held promise. Everything in the hut was in the same place as before, but the future was blank. He expected police or home guards to come, arrest him or shoot him dead. He saw only prison and death. Kihika was a man desperately wanted by the government especially after the destruction of Mahee. To be caught harbouring a terrorist meant death. Why should Kihika drag me into a struggle and problems I have not created? Why? He is not satisfied with butchering men and women and children. He must call on me to bathe in the blood. I am not his brother. I am not his sister. I have not done harm to anybody. I only looked after my little Shamba and crops. And now I must spend my life in prison because of the folly of one man .... My God, I don't want to die, I am not ready for death, I have not even lived .... Have I stolen anything from anybody? No! have I ever shat inside a neighbour's courtyard? No. Have I killed anybody? No (pp. 168-169).

There is no stream of consciousness here. The consciousness of the narrative is certainly Mugo's, but the reflecting mind is rendered in the third person. The syntactical structure of "But why bolt the door? Why should he? It was better to be without a door rather than it should be there and yet bring cold and danger" is that of direct discourse, with rhythms not much different from those of spoken language but the idioms is Mugo's. What Ngugi achieves here is virtually indistinguishable from what Flaubert does in his novels. The original term for such a style is the German *Erlebte Rede*, to which French stylists give the name "style indirect libre," and Bernhard Fehr gives English critics its equivalent," substitutionary speech."[51] Later on Dorrit Cohn called it "narrated monologue," in her well-documented study, "Narrated Monologue: Definition of a Fictional Style." In that article, Cohn said of the technique that:

> *It can be most succinctly described as the rendering of a character's thoughts in his own idiom, maintaining the third-person and the tense narration ..., it enables the author to recount the character's silent thoughts without a break in the narrative thread.*[52]

Closely related to this technique is the interior monologue which we find in the second half of the passage beginning "Why should Kihika drag me into a struggle and problems I have not created? ... I am not his brother. I am not his sister ...." The difference between *Erlbte Rede* and "interior monologue" has been pointed out by Cohn as simply as a question of "grammatical details," a transposition of *Erlbte Rede* "into present tense, and first person."[53]

The advantages of these two interrelated techniques in an assessment of Ngugi's art is tremendous. By maintaining the person and tense of authorial narration, it enables him (as Mrs. Cohn says it enables all users of that technique)" to recount [Mugo's] silent thoughts without a break in the narrative thread."[54] Later on she states that

> *Through its use of Erlebte Rede, the text can weave in and out of the protagonist's mind, can glide from narrator to character and back again without perceptible transitions. By allowing the same tense to describe the individual's view of reality and that reality itself, inner and outer world become one, eliminating explicit distance between the narrator and the creature. Two linguistic levels, inner speech with its idiosyncrasy and author's report with its quasi-objectivity, become fused into one, so that the same current seems to pass through narrating the figural consciousness. Eelebte Rede thus captures the spirits and style of interior monologue within the texture of a third person story, and at the same time casts the immediacy of the present experience into a past narrative.*[55]

Having established the definite advantages of this device, our efforts are wasted unless we show how Ngugi uses it to bring out at least one particular aspect of Mugo's Anti-Heroism. In this case, it will be necessary to take a closer look at the content of the language of Mugo's thoughts. According to Harry Stack Sullivan in *Conceptions of Modern Psychiatry*, consciousness – the central realm on which a story like Mugo's is narrated -- contains among other things, language that is purposively oriented.[56] We have already seen how isolation has been chosen by Mugo, or woven by Ngugi into his being, as a philosophy of life. It is worth our while therefore to show the extent to which the language which Ngugi has assigned to Mugo is purposively oriented towards emphasizing his sense of isolation.

For any such investigation to be easy and meaningful, one has to examine Mugo's language in the context of research in verbal behaviour. In their very important article "Verbal Behaviour Analysis," Louis Gottschalk, Goldine Glesser, and Gove Hambridge Jr. searched for and tested that they called "content and form variables in speech that may be particularly relevant to personality adjustment."[57] Among the categories which they found significant were:

1. Words indicating a sense of belonging to a group (first person plural pronouns, such as "we," "our," and "us."
2. Words belonging to the self;
3. Words indicating negation.

In the second half of the second paragraph of the extended quotation from the novel where we almost hear Mugo speaking in his own idioms, or thinking aloud, the three categories indicated by these authors are forcefully expressed. In the first place, there is a complete absence of the first category - words indicating a sense of belonging. There are no "we's," or "our's," or "us's." On the other hand, there is an alarming number of pronouns belonging or referring to the self: the pronoun "I" is used twelve times, "me" is used twice, and "my" is also used twice. Thirdly, there is a persistent use of the words indicating negations: "have not," "no," "don't," and "not are used eleven times. From this analysis, we are better placed to join Gottschalk and the others in concluding that:

> *While to a great extent man's pattern of speech is determined by the grammar and rhetoric of the language he speaks, it is reasonable to assume that within this framework the individual's choice of words, themes, style of*

speech may reveal something of his personality dynamics and his current emotional state.[58]

If it is possible to summarize what has been achieved in this chapter very briefly, it can be pointed out that an attempt has been made within the scope of the project, to show that Mugo is the protagonist of the novel, that he had been earmarked from childhood as an Anti-Hero, and that Ngugi has emphasized his Anti-Heroism not only at the level of his withdrawal from the world but also at the level of linguistic behaviour, a kind of behaviour which is rooted in individual psycho-history as much as in non-literary, sociological factors, which normally preoccupy critics of the African novel.

Notes

[1](Athens: The Univ. of Georgia Press, 1959), p. 115.

[2]Op. cit., p. 40.

[3](London: Heinemann, 1982, p. 87.

[4](Amherst: The Univ. of Mass. Press, 1983), p. 210.

[5]eds. David Cook and Michael Okenimkpe (London: Heinemann, 1983), p. 69.

[6]*The Novel and Contemporary Experience* (London: Heinemann, 1977), p. 109.

[7]*The Emergence of African Fiction,* p. 139.

[8]*An African View of Literature* (Evanston: Northwestern Univ, Press, 1974), p. 133.

[9]Among the critics who hold this view are Nkosi, in the chapter "History as the 'hero' of the African Novel," *Tasks and Masks:* Ben Obumselu, in "Marx, Politics and the African Novel"; and Peter Nazareth in *An African View of Literature,* pp. 128-129.

[10]*Stylistic Criticism and the African Novel,* p. 87.

[11]*A Grain of Wheat* (London: Heinemann, 1968), p. 1. All further references are to this edition. Page numbers follow each citation.

[12]*African Literature: A Critical View* (London: Longman, 1977), pp. 104-105. Cook does not make clear what he means exactly by an Anti-Hero, but we guess that he equates Anti-Heroism with

unconscious bravery or foolhardiness. He uses the term Anti-Hero again in a more recent work co-edited by Michael Okenimke, *Ngu wa Thiong'o: An Exploration of His Writings,* p. 72. There he is not only briefer but clearer. He says "it is Mugo, ...[who is] the anti-hero of *A Grain of Wheat* [and] in whom Ngugi most clearly portrays complete failure to accept social responsibility [and a man whose] resultant alienate entails grave consequences," p. 72.

[13] *Manichean Aesthetics,* p. 27.

[14] David Cook and Michael Okenimke, *Ngugi wa Thiong'o* ..., p. 73.

[15] *The Masks of Hate: The Problem of False Solutions in the Culture of An Acquisitive Society* (Oxford: Pergamon Press, 1972), p. 16.

[16] Ibid.

[17] (London: Hogarth Press, 1968), p. 263.

[18] (Hogarth Press, 1965), p. 56.

[19] *The Masks of Hate,* p. 20.

[20] Ibid,

[21] *Presence Africaine,* no. 125 (1983), pp. 214-232.

[22] *The Masks of Hate,* p.

[23] Ibid., p. 20.

[24] *I and Thou,* trans. Ronald Gregor Smith (New York: Scribner's 1958), p. 62.

[25] L'Existentialisme est un humanisme. Paris: Editions Nagel (1970), pp. 66-67.

[26] *Individualism Reconsidered,* op. cit., p. 252.

[27] *The Maturational Process* ...., p. 36.

[28] "A Contribution to the Nosology of Impulsive Disorders," *American Journal of Psychiatry* no. 111 (1954), p. 81.

[29] Op. cit., p. 113.

[30] Ibid., p. 114.

[31] Ibid.

[32] See Cook, African Literature: A Critical View, p. 105; and P. Ochola-Ojero's "Of Tares and Broken Handles Ngugi Preaches: Themes of Betrayal in *A Grain of Wheat,*" in *Standpoints on African Literature,* op. cit., p. 78.

[33] *STylisitc Criticism...,* pp. 87-88.

[34] (Assen, Netherlands:

www.ingramcontent.com/pod-product-compliance
Lightning Source LLC
Chambersburg PA
CBHW012041290426
44111CB00021BA/2935